# THE ASSASSINATION OF NEW YORK

Doug **V**an Valkenburgh
97

# THE ASSASSINATION
# OF NEW YORK

## ROBERT FITCH

**VERSO**

London · New York

First published by Verso 1993
© Robert Fitch 1993
All rights reserved

**Verso**
UK: 6 Meard Street, London W1V 3HR
USA: 29 West 35th Street, New York, NY 10001-2291

Verso is the imprint of New Left Books

ISBN 0-86091-390-2

**British Library Cataloguing in Publication Data**
A catalogue record for this book is available from the British Library

**Library of Congress Cataloging-in-Publication Data**
A catalog record for this book is available from the Library of Congress

Printed and bound in the United States of America

# CONTENTS

# PREFACE

The personal origins of this book reach back to the days of New York City's mid-seventies "fiscal crisis." Living on a dairy farm just outside Ithaca New York, where I was teaching in Cornell University's Human Affairs Program, I got a call from a former *Ramparts* magazine colleague in Berkeley. "Could you find out what's wrong with New York in about 3,000 words and have it ready in a month?" asked Adam Hochschild, the Editor of *Mother Jones*?

Somewhat reluctantly, I accepted the assignment. A month to figure out New York? This was a city as famous for its complexity as for its size. Besides, I was a Chicagoan, an outsider, and knew far less about Abe Beame's New York than about Kwame Nkrumah's Ghana – the subject of my first book. Dutifully, though, I began carrying out interviews in New York.

One of the first took place over the 'phone, with a public relations official from the Municipal Assistance Corporation, the state-backed corporation, that had been formed to help restore New York City's finances. "Can you explain what the MAC thinks are some of the underlying reasons for New York's fiscal problems," I asked.

"It's the fucking blacks and Puerto Ricans," the spokesman shot back. "They use too many city services and they don't pay any taxes. New York's in trouble because it's got too many fucking blacks and Puerto Ricans."

Was my interlocutor drunk? Had the 'phone lines gotten crossed with the George Wallace for President Campaign Office? As I continued interviewing other establishment sources, though, I discovered that their analyses, while adding qualifications and explanatory dimensions, and avoiding bad participles, didn't differ all that much. George

Roniger, former Chase Manhattan Bank economist, working for the Economic Development Council, for example, told me that city had an oversupply of blacks and Puerto Ricans too. They suffered from a then newly identified malady: "jobs–skills mismatch." The city was undergoing an inexorable shift to white collar industries and the blacks and Puerto Ricans had only blue collar skills. There was no basis to maintain the city at the old industrial population levels. Blacks and Puerto Ricans would be better off, Roniger explained, in the suburbs or in the sunbelt "where the jobs are."

These were the rough intellectual foundations of the city's famous "planned shrinkage" policies of the mid-seventies. The strategy, articulated by the city's Housing and Development Administration chief, Roger Starr, aimed to cut back transit, sanitation, police and fire protection in poor neighborhoods to the levels which the tax base could support. "We should not encourage people to stay where their job possibilities are daily becoming more remote," observed Starr. "Stop the Puerto Ricans and the rural blacks from living in the city . . . reverse the role of the city . . . it can no longer be the place of opportunity. . . . Our urban system is based on the theory of taking the peasant and turning him into an industrial worker. Now there are no industrial jobs. Why not keep him a peasant.?"[1]

The remarks caused a furore. Starr, the former Executive Director of the Citizens' Housing and Planning Council, the main real estate developers' planning and lobbying group in the city, had to resign. (And was immediately hired to write urban editorials for the *New York Times*.) But city-wide awareness of the dimensions of planned shrinkage really only dawned on a late summer evening in 1976 when Howard Cosell, broadcasting a Yankee game on national TV, scanned the skyline, and noticed that vast areas of the south Bronx were aflame. No one, it seemed, was too concerned with putting out the fires.

The whole debate about who caused the fiscal crisis dissolved ultimately into a cynical exercise in blame-shifting. Starr, and the city's developers knew full well what caused it.[2] The size of New York's welfare population, the share of minorities in its population, the wages and pensions paid to its municipal workers were nothing special in urban America – and yet among American cities, only New York was broke.

What *was* sui generis and ultimately fatal to the city's solvency was the harebrained strategy devised by Nelson Rockefeller at the state level and (Mayor John) Lindsay at the city level, to borrow billions in the short-term money market to enable local housing companies to get long-term mortgages. The greatest office building boom in the city's history – 30 million square feet were built in 1969 – equal to seven of the original Rockefeller Centers – had raised land prices prohibitively and dried up mortgage money even for luxury housing.

A powerful coalition formed. Residential developers who were screaming for billions in subsidies so they could keep on "developing." Investment bankers who made good commissions selling bad debt. And the tax shelter industry that syndicated the equity in these money-losing projects.

New York City had 3 percent of the U.S. population. Still, it was able to borrow nearly half of all the money borrowed for short-term purposes by all the cities in the country. But New York borrowed not just to pay expenses, until revenues arrived, but to make *mortgages*. No other city borrowed even a dollar for this purpose. New York borrowed more than $3 billion.

Starr's solution, which he proposed at an Albany hearing, was to create what he called "a fairy godmother" to buy up all the bad paper. But New York really needed two fairy godmothers. One for the city and one for the state. The state and the city were in a kind of competition to see who could manufacture more mortgages to please their number one political constituency – the city's finance, insurance and real estate (FIRE) industry. The state just beat the city over the defaulters's line.

The competition, however, was unfair, because Nelson's vehicle for insolvency was so much more high-powered. In 1968, he had invented a community crushing juggernaut called the "Urban Development Corporation" which had more functions than a Swiss Army knife. UDC borrowed vast sums, cleared out wide swaths of the city with eminent domain, overrode zoning laws, built thousands of units of upper-middle-class housing – Roosevelt Island was UDC's biggest project – and then simply collapsed.

I attended the Moreland Commission hearings into UDC's demise at the ornate New York Bar Association on W.44th Street, just across the street from the Yacht Club. Evidently, the prime culprit was Nelson Rockefeller. But none of the members of the blue ribbon commission chaired by Orville Schell, the head of the New York Bar, seemed terribly to anxious to discommode him. Rockefeller finished his testimony in a few hours.

Soon the press targeted UDC chief Ed Logue. But Logue was just a hired hand. Nelson had brought him in from Boston where he'd gained notoriety and experience pulverizing neighborhoods in the local urban renewal program. Along with aide Alton Marshall, who became head of Rockefeller Center, Inc., MTA chief William "Fido" Ronan, later head of the Port Authority, Logue was one of the state officials who received a regular stipend to be Nelson's friend. He wound up taking the blame. He'd been a bad manager, it was said. (In 1979, Logue was brought back by Mayor Ed Koch to run south Bronx redevelopment.)

Logue could have had the managerial skills of W. Edwards Deming and not avoided financial collapse at UDC. They teach you in first year finance not to borrow short and lend long. Any sensible person could have foreseen New York would collapse. Even Abe Beame, when he served as City Comptroller, warned of imminent disaster. Here, in fact, carefully coordinated across state and city lines, was one of the lamest urban development strategies ever concocted. Yet the elites who promoted the debt-propelled housing program were never targeted as fiscal crisis villains. That role was reserved for welfare moms, municipal workers, and incoming freshmen at CUNY.

If revolutions are festivals for the poor, New York's ever-recurrent fiscal crises are tailgate parties for the rich. Municipal workers' wages and pensions never recovered. Welfare allowances fell by one-third. The city imposed tuition on poor students at CUNY. It got rid of the stock exchange tax, halved the personal income tax, and set the real estate tax at a record low.

The New York's "fiscal crisis" stood as a world-class example of political unaccountability. The elites had made a terrible mess. But far from having to suffer any political consequences, they actually seemed to gain in prestige as the new ethic of austerity and *faux laissez-faire* took hold. The whole performance was highly reminiscent of the irresponsible, semi-authoritarian, one party regimes I'd studied as a graduate student in economic development at Berkeley.

Meanwhile, in a corner of the Uris Library, back in Ithaca, I stumbled on the Regional Plan of New York and its Environs – the 1929 Plan. Cornell just happened to have one of the few complete sets of the regional plan volumes in the U.S. It revealed an astonishing correspondence between its highway, parks and port plans and the shape and location of the networks we have today.

There snaking across Tremont, ran the infamous Cross Bronx Expressway. You could see the outlines of the Flushing Meadow Park, jutting down like an iron gate, protecting the estates of the long island barons from the advance of small working-class homes. Winding around the whole city was the great system of circumferential highways that the Regional Plan Association (RPA) had conceived to encircle the region. And sure enough, too, the Port of New York had been removed from downtown Manhattan and transferred to Elizabeth, New Jersey – just as recommended in the plan.

What made the similarities of more than geographical interest, was that the plans expressed a strong, single-minded desire to get rid of the city's blue collar industry and replace it with offices, apartment houses for the rich, and department stores. The RPA's chief economist observed:

Some of the poorest people live in conveniently located slums on high-priced land. On patrician Fifth Avenue, Tiffany and Woolworth, cheek by jowl, offer jewels and gimcracks from substantially identical sites. Childs Restaurants (the McDonalds of its day?) thrive where Delmonico's withered and died. A stone's throw from the stock exchange the air is filled with the aroma of roasting coffee; a few hundred feet from Times Square, with the stench of slaughter houses. In the very heart of the 'commercial' city on Manhattan Island south of 59th Street, the inspectors in 1922 found nearly 420,000 workers, employed in factories. Such a situation outrages one's sense of order. Everything seems misplaced. One yearns to re-arrange the hodge-podge and to put things where they belong.[3]

The RPA's directors not only had a yearning to put things where they belonged. As the region's philanthropic, social, financial and propertied elite – they had the power. The directors of the first Regional Plan included representatives from the House of Morgan, the Long Island "barons", the outer borough real estate developers like the Pratts, the William Sloane Coffins, the Cord Meyers, representatives from the Rockefeller Foundation, Russell Sage Foundation, the First National City Bank. Franklin Roosevelt's uncle served as the Plan's chairman.

And the great railroad interests – the New York Central and the Pennsylvania – were represented too. The railroads owned the land on both sides of the Hudson whose conversion from railyards and docks to office buildings and luxury residential towers would later prove so lucrative and strike so deeply into the heart of the city's blue collar economy.

Now the de-industrialization of New York – its conversion to FIRE industries and office buildings – has been presented as a strictly objective process. The unfolding of history's stern, impersonal and inexorable logic. It was accelerated, we are told, by the movement of industrial plants to the suburbs in search of more space on a single floor. As well as growing competition from cheap labor abroad.

Of course market forces exist. Decentralization and global competition are not myths. But the sudden destruction of New York's promising industrial culture of diversity starting in the mid-fifties after more than half a century of stability can't be explained as an objective, impersonal process. Those who took charge of planning the city – who decided where the subways and highways would run; who zoned its neighborhoods; and granted tax abatements and incentives to its real estate – they weren't indifferent as to whether office buildings displaced factories. They owned the land.

How could they be indifferent? There is a nearly 1000 percent spread between the rent received for factory space and the rent landlords get for class A office space. Simply by changing the land use, one's capital could increase in value many times. Presently, a long-term U.S. bond yields something on the order of 6 percent. An increase, say to 10 percent could probably draw capital from the outer planets. Imagine the incentive for increasing income by a factor of ten.

So if there is an inevitable path to de-industrialization, we have to note that the path of change follows a narrow and predictable route. Just look at the industrial land uses closest to the city's office districts – the west and south midtown areas and the areas around the two rivers downtown. They come under first and greatest pressure. As industry, docks, factories disappear, the path of conversion extends to more outlying areas – from the garment district to industrial Long Island City just across the east river where Citibank and Lazard Realty hold land. From the Water Street area east of the Chase, redeveloped in the fifties and sixties, to downtown Brooklyn just across the river redeveloped in the eighties with back office complexes like Metrotech.

Whatever the vagaries of the market, there is a strict real estate logic with spatial and temporal coordinates that has driven de-industrialization in New York. To generalize broadly, you can even say that the development history of the city since the fifties can be understood in terms of the efforts to conquer the twin real estate Golcondas of the downtown and midtown.

These are the goals of the RPA's 1968 Second Regional Plan financed by the Rockefeller Brothers and Ford. Read thoroughly, it provides all the maps you need to understand where the action will be; as well as a rough order of battle, targets and priorities.

Sent sprawling by the fiscal crisis and the overbuilding of the late sixties and early seventies, however, these plans had to be shelved until office leasing and business confidence revived at the end of the decade. Tremors of another building boom – albeit not the magnitude of the sixties – could now be felt.

The problem for those who'd been accumulating vast plots of west side property like the Dursts, the Rockefellers, the Tischs was that they could not get any developers to build on them. The wild west side had served as the graveyard of so many would-be prospectors in the sixties nothing could tempt them back. All the building in the early eighties was taking place on the east side. It was at this point that the Rockefellers, with a consortia of foundations including Ford and J.M. Kaplan intervened in the city planning process with consequences that continue to affect the life chances of every New Yorker.

They persuaded Bobby Wagner, Jr, then head of the City Planning Commission, to shut down real estate development on the east side, and make developers build on the west side. Overbuilding was destroying the east side, they argued. The west side should have a chance at being overbuilt too. For too long it had been real estate's stepchild getting no infrastructural attention at all. Wagner couldn't have agreed more. Nor was there any trouble persuading Mayor Ed Koch.

The RBF consortia negotiated the terms, timing and payment for the plan. City Planning agreed to withdraw zoning incentives and tax abatements on the east side, and put them all on the west side. The plan worked. In 1982 all the buildings in the city were built on the east side. In 1988 they were all built on the west side.

Developers weren't overjoyed. The Real Estate Board of New York initially fought the plan. But as powerful incentives drew the developers land values soared, the Rockefellers, Tischs and Times all sold their properties.

But there was a built-in problem for the purchasers. Rents hadn't risen. Just land prices based on generous tax abatements and the once-in-a-lifetime chance to be able to build towers as high as the sky.

Developers seeking to create as much office space as in the entire city of Pittsburgh all started construction on May 13, 1988. They ignored the Crash, the stagnating rents, and the collapse of the real estate market in downtowns across the country. Hey, no taxes! That was the attraction.

And the midtown market, which had held up better than any other in America, collapsed too.

Of course, corporate down-sizing and the steady shrinkage of the financial industry means that the office market would have declined anyway. But the city could have escaped the magnitude of the disaster which took place: 50 percent unemployment in construction, the collapse of the lending banks like Manufacturers Hanover; and a 50-year inventory of unused office space. New York stands 15th out of 16 as the worst market in the U.S. according to a survey by the Equitable. Overbuilding in New York was not price-driven, it was subsidy-driven. And the subsidies were the result of a plan.

The unfolding landscape of New York's real estate horrors contains not just one realm but two – downtown as well as west midtown. In many respects the performance of the planning elites is even more damning downtown. Efforts have been much more invasive, consistent, costly; results are even more destructive of resources, jobs, opportunities.

Comprehensive planning south of Canal Street begins in 1958 with David Rockefeller's Downtown Lower Manhattan Plan. David's planning group, the Downtown Lower Manhattan Association featured a complete post-industrial makeover for the downtown office district. To reverse the real estate tides pulling offices to midtown, David and his fellow FIREmen targeted the docks, the rail freight yards, the markets, in a word – the infrastructure of blue collar New York. In their place would arise office buildings, luxury residences, department stores. And if private developers were too cowardly to construct them, David and Nelson, the head of the private and public sectors, respectively, would get the State or the Port Authority to build them. In 1962, just to create the World Trade Center, the Port Authority got rid of 33,000 workers and small businessmen in the electrical district.

Expel the inhabitants, pave over the rivers, chop off the finger piers, drive out the manufacturing, ring in the post-industrial age!

In the eighties, downtown office development vacancies exceeded even the totals of the sixties and seventies. Throughout the 1980s Jones Lang Wootton estimated that the developers constructed 25 million square feet of space. (About 40 percent built under the auspices of the Port Authority and UDC's subsidiary, Battery Park City Authority.)

**As of September 1992, though, there was exactly 25 million square feet of empty space.**[4]

All the space built in an entire decade is empty. And the emptiness is growing.

Jane Jacobs predicted in 1960 that David's plan would never work. Downtown was a mixed-use area that could compete with the midtown office district only in a boom. Massive intrusive efforts to sweep aside the small firms that were already there and flourishing would simply destroy its diversity.

David was stung by the Jacobs critique. He insisted that his plan for downtown would in the end generate more jobs, more prosperity, more liveliness than those who advocated no clearances and pressed the virtues of smallness. He told an audience of Staten Island businessmen:

I believe in the old saying that, "You can't make an omelet without breaking eggs." I also believe that a city can't survive without constant rejuvenation. Frequently this involves major projects and major change – such as Lincoln Center, the United Nations, Rockefeller Center, Chase Manhattan Plaza, Rockefeller University, Morningside Heights and the World Trade Center. Most of these undertakings were at one time or another labeled disruptive white elephants. Yet the results seem to have eventually negated the allegations of even the harshest critics. Thousands of new jobs and small businesses have arisen and prospered because of the new economic activity.[5]

David had proclaimed that by the mid-seventies downtown would have over 550,000 workers.[6] And by the end of the century there could be as many as 800,000. It turns out though, according to the latest Department of City Planning (DCP) estimate that there are only about 375,000 workers. Probably the lowest number since the great depression.

But if jobs are scarce, there is no shortage of plans. The latest – designated the Lower Manhattan Plan – is a joint project of the city and the Downtown Lower Manhattan Association, now headed by Robert Douglass, Vice Chairman of Chase Manhattan, and the city.[7]

Instead of creating new office structures, however, the plan is to remove the ones they have. The Lower Manhattan Project aims at dismantling urban history's biggest real estate bomb.

Of the 300 office buildings downtown, a DCP spokesperson suggests that as many as "a couple of dozen" will simply have to be wrecked. What will go in their place? For a while parks were being considered, but grass is hard to maintain under the feet of hard-charging Wall Street traders. Probably, the DCP suggests, just open space, broad urban plazas.[8]

I have a suggestion for the name of the new Downtown Lower

Manhattan Plaza: It would be too cruel to name the empty space after David or Nelson. Instead they should call it the "Emily Latella Memorial Plaza" – after the Saturday Night Live commentator who constantly confused verbal signals and always wound up saying, goofily, "never mind!"

In Part II, I have greatly amplified the account of New York City's planning disasters and the Rockefellers' role in it. But before I do, in Part I, I try to present the meaning of the change: how the urban world's most lop-sided FIRE economy has performed in this latest downturn.[9]

Just how badly the new FIRE economy works, New Yorkers realize largely in personal terms. Most simply don't realize how aberrant the city's economy has become. Either compared to the rest of urban America. Or in terms of its own pre-post-industrial history.

New York today is a city without a private housing market – it has simply collapsed. Construction stands at a fraction of the rate built during the "good" years of the great depression. We produce fewer houses a year than in Las Vagas, Nevada. Retail sales for consumer durables – items like toilet paper and food are sinking. Consumer non-durables have fallen nearly a quarter since 1988. The problem is that after New Yorkers pay rent, they have less disposable income than any of the ten large cities but one. Worst of all, however, is the jobs market.

It's not just that New York City teen unemployment stands at record 40.9 percent. In a perverse sense these are New York's teen aristocrats. They are at least *in* the labor market. As Bureau of Labor Statistics director Sam Ehrenhalt points out, New York's labor force participation rate is only a "small fraction" of what it is in the rest of the country.[10] And it's not just blacks and Puerto Ricans. White teens have the lowest labor force participation rate of any whites in America. While the FIRE economy provides $850 million yearly income to currency traders like George Soros, who commute from Long Island mansions and pay a personal income tax of 0.0045 percent, it offers little opportunity for New York's neighborhood youth. They have become the principal casualties of urban planning.

No-one can explain the geography, much less the economy of New York city without taking into account the extraordinary impact of the Rockefeller family. From 1928 when they sign the fateful ground lease with Columbia University, to 1988 when they flip Rockefeller Center to the Japanese, understanding what the Rockefellers want is prerequisite to grasping what the city becomes. Not that they always get their way – there is no equivalent of Grand Central Station standing next to Rockefeller Center as Nelson envisioned. There is no subway station to Fort Lee. The World Trade Center had to be located on the Hudson River side of downtown, not the Chase Manhattan Plaza side. Indeed, the city is littered with failed Rockefeller family plans. Still, they have had a lot of successes and New York is simply unintelligible if their efforts are ignored.

A focus on the family may annoy academic Marxists for whom the capitalist is only the personification of abstract capital and who believe, austerely, that any discussion of individuals in economic analysis represents a fatal concession to populism and empiricism.

But New York is not capitalism in general, and the family's whole involvement in planning the city is the result of a series of astonishing accidents, blunders, awesome miscalculations. New York turned into a gigantic tar baby for the Rockefellers. So tightly were they tied to the terms of the Columbia ground lease and to the blighted neighborhood of west midtown, they found they could only tear themselves loose by completely reconfiguring Manhattan – and in the process, tearing apart the delicate web which joined the city's small interdependent manufacturers.

At the same time that I offend against the principle of grand abstraction, I am aware that my portrait of individual Rockefeller behavior is bereft of psychological complexity. "Journalistic cynicism", I can hear it said. No doubt the drama of the story would have been enhanced, had I been able to find some evidence of wrenching conflict between principle and expediency. I simply never found any . . . conflict that is.

This is widely true of the genus, big businessman, not just the Rockefeller species. Friedrich Nietzsche, among the shrewdest of psychologists once observed,

We must not ask the money-making banker the reason for his restless activity, it is foolish. The active roll as the stone rolls, according to the stupidity of mechanics.

The inherent interest in the story of the Rockefellers lies not in their psychological complexity but in their ingenious and audacious reactions to the external circumstances in which they find themselves. Once the family signs the $3.6 million Columbia lease, at the dawn of the Great

Depression, all dreams of graceful coupon clipping, easy returns from rentier investments disappear. To preserve the family capital, sunk in a bad neighborhood, with next to no mass transit, and crippling capital costs, they are forced to try one strategem after an another to extricate themselves.

The scope of their drive to retrofit New York so that Rockefeller Center will thrive within it is awesome. Who else but the Rockefellers would have sought and succeeded in having the city build a subway line – the Sixth Avenue IND – to their real estate development. Who else could have swung the whole pattern of real estate development from one side of town to the other as they managed in the case of the 1982 midtown plan?

But inner conflicts between principle and expediency, if they are present, must have been deeply repressed. To fill up acres of empty office space in Rockefeller Center, John D. Rockefeller Jr. tried to get Mussolini to rent "Il Palazzo d'Italia". But Jr. *admired* Mussolini, so there was no conflict. He also wanted to bring in the Nazis to rent the International Building. Despite long negotiations, they turned him down. (After all, for the Third Reich, New York was "Hymietown.") And while there is no evidence that Junior shared his aide Ivy Lee's enthusiasm for Der Fuhrer, neither is there any that he felt a pang of conscience over having them as tenants.

Anyone who attacks urban planning runs the risk of being identified as an economic conservative. An advocate of *laissez-faire*. My objection however is not to planning per se but to the narrow economic aims of New York City planning, the destructive content of the Plan. Lack of accountability for planning when it fails.

But democratic planning, planning in which the planners are accountable for their mistakes; planning that targets directly, and not through trickle-down mechanisms, the well-being of the city's working people; planning which recognizes the need for recreating productive industries, seems to be a prerequisite for survival. New York should be about more than just survival.

Every writer about New York is convinced that he is telling no local story, but one crammed with universal significance, deeply paradigmatic for our times. Just what it is that makes the city a paradigm however is often not as clear as it might be. In part this is because New York changes so fast. The city has swung from one economic pole to another. From a remarkably diverse economic structure, a model of flexible production, to an equally pure paradigm of urban monoculture based on the unproductive labor of FIRE elites. It's pretty clear which worked best.

My deepest conviction is that the city needs to restore and amplify its economic diversity in the full meaning of the term, if it is to fully express its genius – which is human diversity. Cultivated minds should not disdain a value just because it is fashionable – and thus taken up by cynics and manipulators. Long before David Dinkins' speech writers manufactured the "gorgeous mosaic" metaphor; Melville had cast Manhattanites as the polyglot crew of the Pequod:

> They were nearly all Islanders in the Pequod, Isolatoes too . . . I call such, not acknowledging the common continent of men, but each Isolato living on a separate continent of his own. Yet now, federated along one keel, what a set these Isolatoes were! An Anacharsis Clootz deputation from all the isles of the sea, and all the ends of the earth, accompanying Old Ahab in the Pequod to lay the world's grievances before the bar . . .[11]

It turns out that the modern owners of the Pequod recoiling finally from the polyglot nature of the crew, as well as the risks of enterprise, have sold their interests to the Japanese whaling industry, and whomever else would buy their shares, retiring to the coast of Maine, Pocantico Hills and points north. Still, the opportunities here – just like the grievances – remain as vast as ever. To seize them, we who sail on will have to federate or sink.

Since I began to work on the New York project, I've been transformed from an Ishmael, an outsider, to a resident member of the crew. Still, I am seventeen years late in delivering the assignment. And about 150,000 words over length. And there are always more interviews to do, more books and articles to read, more data to sift. Nelson's papers will be available in the next millennium some time. To wait until these materials are available would surely made the book more mistake-proof. But let adversaries find the mistakes. They inevitably will. And by so doing they will be forced involuntarily to widen the debate over the city's future.

The ultimate aim of this book however goes beyond a discussion of the city's ills. The point is to remove them. Part III presents a program for change. I would greatly appreciate comments. Please write me c/o New York Campaign for 1 million jobs, 211 E. 17th Street, Suite 4, New York City 10003.

*Acknowledgements*: In the several complete and total reincarnations of this book which nevertheless retained the same identity, I have piled up some conventional debts in some unconventional places.

This book received no grants or emoluments from giant foundations or think-tanks. Ms. Jane Latour, New York's premier political organizer, served as my Brooke T. Astor. Sam Farber and Selma Marks functioned as John D. and Catharine T. MacArthur. Loren Goldner substituted for the Rockefeller Brothers.

Among my fellow journalists, urbanists, and economists who helped at various stages with comments, data and criticism, I would like to mention Roger Alcaly, Jason Epstein, Doug Henwood, Don Guttenplan, Alvin Berke, Beth Glick, Phil Pochoda, Jim Sleeper, Elizabeth Kadetsky, Mike Davis, Bob Brenner, Annette Fuentes, and Ben Gerson. I would particularly like to single out the former editor of the *Village Voice*, Marty Gottlieb, who revived this project when it had gone into dormancy, by giving me a chance to write about New York planning for the *Voice*. And also Jim Dwyer who made me a celebrity in my building with his kind remarks in *Newsday*.

In academia, I owe special thanks to Columbia's Peter Marcuse whose thoughtful remarks and insights I valued very much. To Bob Brenner who helped find the publisher and Steve Bronner who encouraged me to publish in the first place. I would also like to thank SUNY Binghamton's Terry Hopkins and Immanuel Wallerstein for reading and commenting upon an early version of the manuscript. As well as Peter Kwong of Hunter College. I am particularly in debt to Jim Petras who did the most to free the Bird Man of Binghamton.

Sincere thanks to Tom Rosenbaum of Rockefeller Archive Center, Dr. Terry Rosenberg of the Community Service Society, Bruce Rosen, of the NYC Department of City planning, Marie Hall of the Real Estate Board of New York, and to the RPA for the use of the organization's private library.

In New York's trade union movement, I would like to thank Wing Lam of the Chinese Staff and Restaurant Workers Union; Sean Sweeney of District 65 UAW who reproduced an earlier version and made it available to members who made very helpful comments. Also Ed Ott, CWA 1180, Nick Ungar, ACTWU; Miriam Thompson, UAW, Jim Houghton, Harlem Fightback; Irving Lee, TWU, Local 100; Keith Brooks, New York Council of the Unemployed; and John Glasel of Local 802 AFM, whose legendary skills improved a previous draft. My deepest appreciation goes to President Arthur Cheliotes of Local 1180 CWA who showed unusual interest and concern in supporting research into the New York economy.

Former Bronx Borough President Herman Badillo illuminated the demise of the Koch Administration's plan to rebuild the Bronx. Congressmen Jerry Nadler and attorney John McHugh were patient in explaining the mechanics of freight and shipping to someone who didn't know TOFC from tofu.

There is one woman though whom I especially want to single out for gratitude: whose life of creativity and iconoclasm provided a model of action and commitment; who has given me love, encouragement and support at every stage of my life; and whose filing techniques, I seem to have inherited – my mother, Mrs. Jo Fitch, to whom this book is dedicated.

## NOTES

1. Roger Starr, quoted in Charles Kaiser, "Blacks and Puerto Ricans, a Bronx Majority," *New York Times*, April 19, 1976, p. 23. See also Starr's defense, "Making New York smaller," *New York Times*, Sunday Magazine section, November 14, 1976.
2. Roger Starr, *The Rise and Fall of New York City* (New York: Basic Books Inc., 1985), pp. 226–229. Starr in a very lucid analysis, blames the fiscal crisis on "imprudent borrowing to finance moderate rental housing." He says paradoxically, but correctly, that had there been no immediate crisis, the damage might have been even greater. "The only thing that kept the moderate-income housing program from continuing forever was the crisis itself."
3. Regional Survey, vol I, Major Economic Factors in Metropolitan Growth and Arrangement (New York: 1927), p. 32.
4. Jones Lang Wootton USA, "Manhattan Office Market," September 1992.
5. "Remarks by David Rockefeller, 'In Support of Catalytic Bigness,' Before the Staten Island Chamber of Commerce," February 27, 1979, pp. 10–11.
6. Downtown Lower Manhattan Association (New York: May 23, 1969), p. 3.
7. Office of the Mayor, "Mayor Dinkins and Downtown Business Leaders Announce Lower Manhattan Partnership," September 11, 1991. At the time John Zucotti was DLMA chief.
8. Phone interview, August 6, 1993.
9. New York City's economy – which as late as 1958 had nearly 1 million manufacturing workers, two workers in manufacturing for every one in FIRE. Now has about 275,000 manufacturing workers and about two FIRE workers for every worker in manufacturing. No city in America comes close to our lop-sided ratio.
10. U.S. Department of Labor, Bureau of Labor Statistics, Middle Atlantic Regional Office, New York-Northeastern New Jersey Mid-Year Report 1993, (New York: July 29, 1993), p. 4.
11. The footnote in my edition of *Moby Dick* reads, "Composed of men of different nations and races, like the motley deputation which Clootz led into the French National Assembly in 1790 to symbolize all mankind's support of the French Revolution," Herman Melville, *Moby Dick* (New York: W.W. Norton, 1967), p. 108.

MUNICIPALLY ZONED INDUSTRIAL AREAS
OF THE
CENTRAL PART OF THE NEW YORK REGION

0   1   2   3   4   5
SCALE IN MILES

1928

LEGEND

■ Heavy Industry        ▨ Undetermined or Unzoned
▦ Light Industry        ☐ Industry Excluded

Compiled from local zoning
maps and ordinances

REGIONAL PLAN OF
NEW YORK AND ITS ENVIRONS
ENGINEERING DIVISION

REGIONALLY ZONED INDUSTRIAL AREAS
OF THE
CENTRAL PART OF THE NEW YORK REGION
SCALE IN MILES
1928

REGIONAL PLAN OF
NEW YORK AND ITS ENVIRONS
ENGINEERING DIVISION

Suggested by the Regional Plan
of New York and Its Environs

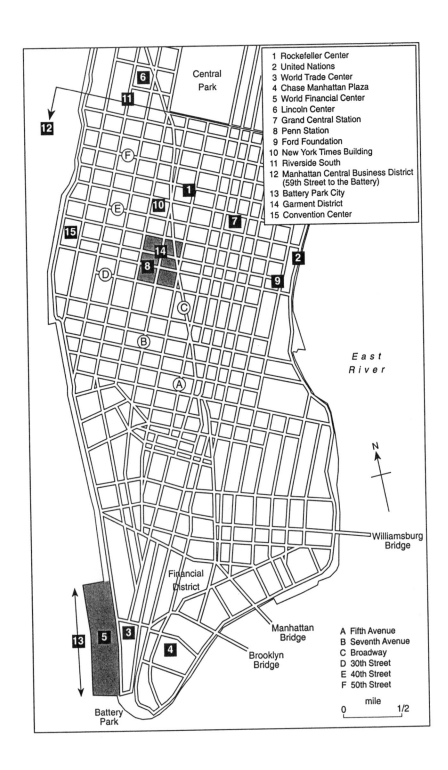

Central Park

1  Rockefeller Center
2  United Nations
3  World Trade Center
4  Chase Manhattan Plaza
5  World Financial Center
6  Lincoln Center
7  Grand Central Station
8  Penn Station
9  Ford Foundation
10 New York Times Building
11 Riverside South
12 Manhattan Central Business District
   (59th Street to the Battery)
13 Battery Park City
14 Garment District
15 Convention Center

East River

Williamsburg Bridge

N

Financial District

Manhattan Bridge

Brooklyn Bridge

A  Fifth Avenue
B  Seventh Avenue
C  Broadway
D  30th Street
E  40th Street
F  50th Street

mile
0            1/2

Battery Park

# ABBREVIATIONS

| | |
|---|---|
| CBD | central business district |
| CPC | City Planning Commission |
| DCP | Department of City Planning |
| DLMA | Downtown Lower Manhattan Association |
| FAR | floor area ratio |
| FIRE | Finance, Insurance and Real Estate |
| 421-a | New York City tax subsidy program for new construction |
| ICT | intellectual capital theory |
| UDC | Urban Development Corporation |
| ICIP | Industrial and Commercial Incentives Program |
| ILA | International Longshoremens' Association |
| IND | Independent Subway |
| IRT | Interborough Rapid Transit |
| J-51 | New York City tax subsidy program for "rehabilitating" buildings |
| LBO | leveraged buy-out |
| MTA | Metropolitan Transit Authority |
| LISC | Local Initiatives Support Corporation |
| PATH | Port Authority Trans Hudson Corporation |
| RBF | Rockefeller Brothers' Fund |
| RCI | Rockefeller Center Inc. |
| RPA | Regional Plan Association |
| SOB | speculative office building |

*Dedicated to my Mother,*
JO FITCH,
*artist, iconoclast, fighter for social justice.*

*PART I*

# NEW YORK CITY: WHAT WENT WRONG?

*CHAPTER ONE*

# THE FIRE THIS TIME

## NEW YORK'S SECOND SLUMP

In January 1993, New York City's official unemployment rate hit 13.4. percent.

The year before, when the official rate stood a bit lower, the city's Department of Employment Commissioner argued that the real unemployment rate – including discouraged workers and part-time workers who wanted to work full-time – had reached 28.7 percent.

But let's stick to the official figure of 13.4 percent.

Was it a lot or a little? New York City's rate wasn't as high as the level reported the same month in East Germany. In the former DDR, where the authorities acknowledged a near total economic collapse, the official rate there exceeded 14 percent.[1]

Nor was New York City's unemployment rate as high as the rate in the McAllen–Edinburg–Mission Texas metropolitan area – the hardest hit in the country with a rate of 18.2 percent. But McAllen's population was only about 5 percent of New York's. It would fit in one of New York's eleven Congressional Districts.

Of the 276 cities and metropolitan areas tracked by the U.S. Department of Labor only six had higher rates than New York City:

| | |
|---|---|
| McAllen–Edinburg–Mission, Texas | 18.2 percent |
| Modesto, California | 17.4 percent |
| Fresno, California | 16.4 percent |
| Stockton, California | 16.0 percent |
| Bakersfield, California | 15.8 percent |
| Vineland–Millville–Bridgeton, New Jersey | 13.5 percent |

The six metropolitan areas with unemployment rates higher than New York were primarily dependent on the farm economy. Of the U.S. cities based on industrial or post-industrial employment, New York's was hardest hit.

The rate in January 1993 was in the range of the milder years of the Depression decade. But it hadn't hit the levels New York City ran at the absolute pit of the Great Depression. In 1932 and 1933 it is likely the rate was nearly twice as high.

Still, 13.4 percent was nearly double the national average of 7.1 percent reported that month. Unemployment was higher than at any time in the history of New York City since the days of Fiorello La Guardia. If you counted all the people standing on New York City unemployment lines as well as the less visible jobless who couldn't qualify for benefits – a majority nowadays – the total reached 447,000 adults: a total equal to the entire *population* of Denver.

One month's bad economic news, by itself, may not mean a great deal. There are always seasonal fluctuations; revisions of preliminary figures; and in the case of New York City's unemployment, next month the figure did fall to 11.3 percent. But February's decline wasn't enough to undermine New York's status as the nation's big city unemployment capital which it had finally wrested from Detroit in the early nineties.

Viewed against the background of almost unrelieved economic malaise Gotham's 13.4 percent spike was no cyclical aberration. The cyclical shock had exposed the structural fragility of New York's newly re-built post-industrial economy. None of the ten largest U.S. cities had gone further than New York in concentrating its employment in finance, insurance and real estate (FIRE). And it was now this FIRE structure – not the old manufacturing-based structure – that led urban America in job loss, unemployment and "non-work."[2]

While in large parts of the rest of the country, a feeble recovery from the "contained" depression of the nineties seemed to be taking hold,[3] New York's FIRE industries still hadn't hit bottom. Job loss would continue.[4] And while during the "fiscal crisis" of the seventies it took New York eight years to lose 600,000 jobs, now after only three years of decline, nearly 400,000 jobs had disappeared.

Compared both with other central cities and its own post-war history, New York was experiencing record rates of unemployment, dependency, job loss, poverty, and labor force participation. At

56.4 percent, it had one of the lowest rates of labor force participation in urban America: nearly 10 points below Chicago, nearly 20 points below Dallas. And the rates for white residents were only marginally better than those for blacks. Teenage whites had a labor force participation rate of less than half the national average.

The city's income stratification resembled Mexico or Peru more than one of the Western European countries. In Manhattan 44,000 households, the top 6 percent, earned half of all the income in the borough. It is very likely the most unequal pattern of income distribution in urban America.

The housing market had completely collapsed, producing at less than half the rate of the great Depression. And manufacturing wages were lower than any other city in the top ten except San Antonio. (San Antonio, however, was catching up.) New York threatened to become the city with the lowest manufacturing wages with one of the highest costs of living in the U.S. Housing in New York costs four times more than the average of 286 cities surveyed by the American Chamber of Commerce Research Associates.[5]

Olympia & York, the city's largest real estate organization and its largest tax payer, had gone bankrupt and was now in a "work out mode" with the Department of Finance. How it would pay off the $300 million worth of Battery Park City bonds it had agreed to guarantee in order to beat out local developers for the right to build the World Financial Center was a problem no one wanted to think about. Macy's, the largest store in the city, had also gone bankrupt and cast a giant shadow across Seventh Avenue's garment industry. The city's largest newspaper, the *Daily News* along with the *Post* and its fifth largest bank, Manufacturers Hanover, had all either gone bankrupt or been reorganized. Citibank couldn't afford to keep its headquarters in the city: New York's largest bank sold off three-quarters of its signature building to the Japanese and moved to industrial Long Island City, where it owned property.

It was commercial real estate, however, that served as New York's leading sector of economic entropy. One of the biggest industries in the city had been throwing people out of their apartments – "condo conversion" it was called.[6] Even the MacArthur Foundation, bestowers of the famous "genius grants" got involved. A team from the John D. and Catherine T. MacArthur Foundation converted thousands of apartments in the boom years. MacArthur managed to unload its total inventory in 1985 for about $500,000,000. But the buyers, Equitable Life Assurance, the Mendik organization and Martin J. Rayes got stuck, finally selling the whole lot this year to a Mr. Bodini for about $26,000,0000.[7] By 1993, monthly sales of Manhattan condos had declined to double figures.[8]

Office building vacancy rates were twice those of the fiscal crisis years and threatened to last far longer. Between 1981 and 1990, real estate developers had thrown up 53 million square feet of office space: more than all the space in San Francisco, and certainly more than New York would need for a long time. About 65 million square feet – nearly 125 percent of the amount built in the eighties was vacant. The *Wall Street Journal* estimated that at current rates of absorption, to liquidate the downtown inventory of unrented office space – which was the highest of any central business district – would take 50.4 years.

In the winter of 1993 the market registered a new low when a downtown office building – just a block off Wall Street at 25 Broad – sold for less than $11 a square foot. Five years earlier you couldn't have *rented* a building at that address for $11 a square foot.[9] (It's hard to find a rent-stabilized apartment for $11 a square foot.) Office buildings cost $300–$400 a square foot to build. Now they were selling for a fraction of replacement cost. How was this possible? The answer is essentially, now, in the nineties, if you can afford to pay the taxes on a downtown office building, the owner will be glad to sell it to you just to avoid having to pay taxes himself.

As bad as conditions seemed, the city's economic elites seemed to be taking it all in surprisingly good spirits. Unlike the fiscal crisis years, when establishmentarians attacked the performance of the failing economy to justify their own restructuring program, conservative voices were no longer raised in full cry. There were no blue-ribbon commissions; no emergency coalitions of business and labor tops to save the city; no editorial questions about the city's survival. Just the usual mutterings about high taxes and low productivity in city agencies, and privatization as the city's salvation.

In part, greater equanimity was possible because, locally, the hard times of the nineties had produced an economic crisis, not a fiscal or financial crisis. The city's borrowings hadn't fallen due yet. So there weren't a lot of rich people worried about getting paid. Investment bankers weren't obsessed about the effects of default on the production of fresh securities. True, a lot of the city's erstwhile members of the Forbes 400 had negative net worth. Donald Trump had been put on short rations: the banks had cut his personal allowance to $200,000 a month. And some other developers had their toys taken away – Peter

Kalikow lost control of the *New York Post*. But none of these guys were driving cabs. Even a first generation developer like Ian Bruce Eichner, who lost every bit of equity in 1540 Broadway, and helped bring Citibank to the brink, managed to come out with a $10,000,000 consulting contract with the buyer by threatening to throw the whole project into Chapter Seven.[10]

The city's fiscal problems were politically manageable – municipal worker lay-offs were back-loaded and deficits never exceeded 10 percent of the budget. Unlike the seventies, city workers quietly accepted job loss and pay cuts. Only rank-and-file transport workers, with a tradition going back to Mike Quill, showed much fight. While nearly 200,000 were losing their jobs in 1991, the city's investment grade securities fairly flew off the shelves.

Essentially, this was not an investment bankers' depression, it was a people's depression. The Gross City Product had fallen more than 10 percent since the "recession" had officially begun in 1989.[11] Sales of consumer durables had fallen nearly 40 percent![12] Meanwhile however, salaries on Wall Street in 1992 shot up 49 percent. The average broker's salary had reached $91,000 a year.[13] Of the Wall Street yearly incomes publicly disclosed, Sandy Weil, head of Primerica startled many with total compensation of over $100,000,000.[14] But his income was dwarfed by currency manipulator George Soros who was estimated to earn $850,000,000 by *Financial World* magazine. Compared to Weil and Soros, Goldman Sachs' Robert Rubin, now Clinton's top economic advisor, who had served as Governor Cuomo's expert on urban poverty, seemed practically blue collar with a 1992 income of $28,500,000.

Under the circumstances, the city's opinion leaders didn't rate the performance of the economy highly, but they had no desire to question its fundamental structure. Indeed, in the nineties, even as the hard times wore on, those most in harmony with elite thinking seemed to form a kind of Hallelujah Chorus, hymning thanks for such economic blessings as were still being bestowed. Certainly, no one wanted to talk much about 13.4 percent unemployment. Or youth unemployment, which hit a record 40 percent.

## TONGUES OF FIRE

The two slick New York City weeklies – the *New Yorker* and *New York*, which increasingly function as slimmer, upscale local replacements for the defunct Sears' catalog – tend to ignore events which have a propensity to disturb wealthy shoppers' ability to concentrate. In February *New York*, owned by the legendary leveraged buy out (LBO) operator Henry Kravis,[15] had only one article on local unemployment. It probed the firing of Random House supereditor Joni Evans. ("Some say her list was weak. Others that she wasn't given time to make a go of the fledgling house. There is talk of personality conflicts, even conspiracy theories. Read on.")

But in the immediate aftermath of the World Trade Center attack, and the January unemployment report, it was the *New Yorker* which perfectly expressed the determined mood of the city's media elites who weren't going to allow any bombs – or an economic depression – to ruin their advertising parade. "Terrorists are on the attack, the gorgeous mosaic is cracking and the heat is on the mayor," headlined "Around City Hall", "but things may be looking up for New York."

Yes, a big bomb had gone off underneath the World Trade Center. And there was 13.4 percent unemployment in the five boroughs, the writer allowed. But the lasting news, according to the *New Yorker* was that the Democrat Clinton was in the White House and New York stood to get a lot of federal aid.[16]

The *New York Times*, alone among the print media, ran the story of the unemployment spike on its front page. But even the *Times* provided no accompanying analysis. No follow-up story. No editorial comment; no sense of how aberrant the city's economy had become.

The tabloids couldn't even feature the story for a day: they were busy flogging other civic issues: Heather's multiple mommies – a dispute over first grade gender education texts; the line of march in the St. Patrick's day parade – gays or Hibernians; the Woody – Soon Yi – Mia triangle; and the saga of teenaged Amy Fisher, whose shooting of Mary Jo Buttafuoco had catapulted her past aging tennis star John McEnroe as Long Island's most famous brat.

No publication is more pro-business than *Crain's New York Business*. Yet the somnolent self-satisfaction of the city's politico-business establishment disturbed even its conservative columnist James Brady. In early 1993, Brady attended an event organized by Lew Rudin, the scion of one of the few non-bankrupt real estate dynasties left in town. As usual, Rudin was feting the Mayor, the man from whom all variances flow, this time at a big breakfast attended by 1,200 business executives. The Mayor's speech, Rudin admitted, put everyone to sleep. "How did the rest of the meeting go?" Brady asked. "Splendidly, splendidly," replied

Rudin. No one seemed to want to challenge the Mayor or even discuss politics. And the Mayor offered up only his customary rhetorical air balls. "Where the hell are the issues in this election," Brady asked, "the things New Yorkers care passionately about: crime and lousy schools and the homeless and do the subways run on time and job flight and city taxes and drugs? Are parades and gay couples really the heart of the matter?"[17]

The Mayor's State of the City speech hadn't mentioned unemployment. Rather than discuss job loss, David Dinkins spoke expansively about all the jobs the city's economy would add during the rest of the century. Perhaps he thought the projections of paid consultants from imaginary trend lines were as real as the unemployment lines.

In New York there was simply no political accountability. In America, an election had been fought around Bush's failure to create jobs. It wasn't much of a fight, and the promises were forgotten, but at least Clinton was forced by the demands of electioneering to publish a very specific plan, "Putting People First", which detailed how he'd put people back to work. Here, although unemployment greatly exceeded the national average, there was no such pressure. Like 18th century mercenary armies that agreed to fight only during certain hours, and with certain types of ammunition, the major pols somehow reached a consensus to limit the mayoral debate to non-economic issues.

Rudy Giuliani's strategy seems to have been to turn the campaign into an unspoken referendum: "Do you like black kids who yell, 'Kill the Jews?' If not vote for me." And early in the campaign, the Mayor seemed to be listening to those who felt his best chance of getting re-elected was to make the election a quiet referendum on the Hasids. "Do you like men in long beards, black hats, and little ringlets, who call me a murderer? If not, get out and vote for me."

All in all, the reticence of media and the local political elites to say anything about the collapsed economy seemed to express a sort of cautious but affectionate regard for the city's business establishment. It was as if the facelift of one of the city's fabulous Park Avenue dowagers had suddenly fallen. And her loyal friends felt the best strategy was to let her find out for herself.

What was the city's business leadership thinking? How did they orient themselves to the big downturn? Did they even see a problem? 1991 had probably been the single worst year of the decline. During those twelve months, the city lost a record 213,000 jobs. Even during the fiscal crisis, when bankers were regularly predicting the utter collapse of the city, if their reforms weren't implemented, no more than 138,000 jobs were lost in a year. All in all, the downturn of the nineties, which still hadn't run its course, had already wiped out a total of nearly 400,000 jobs – 12 percent of the total. The downturn of the seventies, which lasted twice as long cost 15 percent. The big difference was that manufacturing had already been squeezed and had fewer jobs to lose. But already, of the seven major sectors of the economy, four had lost more jobs than during the "fiscal crisis" years: construction 46,000 (37.4 percent); trade 112,000 (17.3 percent); government 31,000 (5.1 percent); and even the highly regarded FIRE sector had lost 58,000 (11.0 percent). (See Appendix 1, p. 273)

In this subdued atmosphere, the New York City Council on Economic Education sponsored its 24th Annual Conference. Among the invitees was the head of the Port Authority of New York and New Jersey, Stanley Brezenoff, the former First Deputy Mayor in the Koch Administration. Brezenoff, evidently seeking to inspire confidence, reached into the back-courts of memory to invoke the apothegm of Herbert Hoover just after the 1929 Crash. The city and the region were strong, he insisted. And the regional economy "is fundamentally sound."[18]

Brezenoff's former colleague at the Ford Foundation, Vice President and chief economist Louis Winnick, seemed to agree with the diagnosis of "fundamental soundness". New York, he argued, is just going through another of its cyclical downturns. There is nothing wrong with its post-industrial structure. "Those who lament New York's transformation from a manufacturing to a service city are simply unaware of the superior entry and escalator opportunities attached to the service sector" he observed. "Even a chambermaid or a porter's job pays $10 or $11 an hour plus a standard package of fringe benefits."[19] FIRE, Winnick argued, had saved us during the downturn in 1981, and the present cyclical problems in real estate needed to be put in proper historical perspective: If you think 1991 is bad, Winnick pointed out, you should have been here in '71 – 1871. And 1837? Now, *that* was a depression!

Another year, another 100,000 lost jobs. When the Council on Economic Education held its 25th annual conference on "1992: A Quarter Century – Crises, Achievements and New Concerns" an invitation to Ronald Shelp went out as a matter of course. Shelp serves as a successor to David Rockefeller at the NYC Partnership.[20] By absorbing the New York Chamber of Commerce, the Partnership has become the leading voice of the local business establishment. And Shelp is their spokesman. He is a graduate of the London School of Economics, and the author of a number of publications on his specialty, business services. Shelp has also written a minor classic of the genre now in its third edition, *Beyond Industrialization*.

If there is anyone who sincerely believes that an entire population can make a living suing each other, it is Shelp, the Karl Marx of the elite service sector. Our economic future, Shelp believes, rests on further de-industrialization: continuing to export financial, legal, accounting services and importing the commodities we no longer produce. When you examine the city's exports and imports, what you see is that the biggest item that we ship out to the rest of the world is waste paper. The biggest import is alcohol.[21] This pattern of exchange only seems impractical, he argues, if you forget the large overseas investment stake the U.S. has built up and the steady increase in invisible income "we" receive.

The true problem, Shelp argues, is the lack of political power of the higher service providers. Their economic power has yet to be translated into political terms. This is because they lack self consciousness – a sense of their true identity. The investment banker, the lawyer, the ad man each advance their own interests without understanding the need for unity. "The United States is the only service economy," he notes, "where there are perceptible bare beginnings of a self-identity on the part of the service sector – an identity that transcends the parochial concerns of each individual industry and moves toward a more cohesive appreci-ation of mutual self-interest."[22]

Now if twenty years of declining wages, trade deficits and adverse balance of payments, along with a decade of declining U.S. currency values couldn't shake Shelp's confidence in the viability of the U.S. service economy you could hardly expect him to be moved by a mere disturbance of the local economy. "So at the outset," Shelp began, when his turn came to speak, "I must acknowledge the obvious fact that the current recession clouds any views one may have about attracting and retaining business for New York City." But it was important not to let concern cloud one's judgement. "Therefore," he said, "I propose for the purposes of our discussion we step back and *assume that there is no recession.* This will make it possible for us to have a more complete understanding of the challenges to our city."

Economists study the technique of *ceteris paribus*: keeping the variables and the coefficients in a problem the same, while perturbating just one. Shelp had learned the lesson well. He could look past the city's one out of eight unemployed; its one out of four living in poverty; over a million on welfare, the nine out of ten black youth not in the labor force. We must he urged, focus even more single-mindedly on "business services which are our engines of growth: financial, advertising, legal, accounting."

We must, Shelp insists, keep these "engines of growth" humming. But before more billions in real estate subsidies, tax abatements and exemptions which the Partnership seeks are granted to stoke the engines of enterprise, perhaps a few questions are in order. What does an "engine of growth" grow? Jobs for city residents? Since New York City converted to FIRE monoculture the job total has shrunk. The city is within a few thousand jobs of its all-time low. Growth of resident income? Between 1963 and 1987, New York City's income has fallen as a share of New York State's income from 47 percent to 37 percent. Growth of wages? New York has the lowest manufacturing wages of the top ten cities save San Antonio's. And what about the mighty FIRE engine itself? Since 1969, it's actually shrunk.[23] Admittedly, 1969 was a cyclical peak and 1993 is a trough year. But for the "engine of growth" to go 25 years without any increase says something about its horse power.

In the nineties, FIRE has found out how to grow profits while shrinking jobs. In 1992 Wall Street was still earning a fabulous $45 billion, with income actually doubling, and the average salary in the brokerage industry reaching nearly $100,000 a year. Certainly if Wall Street was trying to maximize jobs it was missing the mark. In 1992, a period of record profits, the finance sector lost 14,800 jobs in comparison with the same period in 1991. However, no voices on the Street could be heard arguing that Wall Street should be trying to maximize jobs rather than profits.[24]

But suppose you furnished Shelp with this information. Or pointed out further that the city's 700,000 commuters seemed to benefit disproportionately from the service economy, with a typical Fairfield County commuter earning about four times the average Bronx resident. Would any of this data have the slightest effect on Shelp's determination to pursue a FIRE-led strategy for the city? The question is really, what determines the Partnership's priorities? Was the Partnership promoting FIRE because it produced the greatest good for the greatest number?

A more plausible explanation for the desire of the FIRE folk to go "beyond industrialization" can be located in the imperatives arising out of the dynamics of the city's land and office space market. The conversion of industrial land to office, luxury residential or high grade commercial uses increases its value by as much as 1,000 percent. Then too, the members of the Partnership are connected with such institutions as Bankers' Trust, Mutual Life Insurance, Equitable Life, Prudential Bache, Rose Associates and the Real Estate Board of New York.[25] They provide construction loans, hold mortgages, syndicate equity in office buildings – and increasingly, albeit involuntarily, own large numbers of commercial buildings. To prosper or even survive, they must fill their office space with high paying tenants in financial, advertising, legal and accounting services, not with workers in the garment or food processing industries. However bad the local economy gets, they must continue to try to fill the space.

But despite total and unqualified agreement within the business establishment to continue stoking the "engines of growth" – carrying out more vigorously than ever the development strategy that brought about the present conjuncture – it's clear that the force of the downturn, as well as its concentration in the city's highly prized information industries, has come as a staggering surprise.

In the seventies, the city had gone through what was sometimes portrayed almost as a kind of mid-life crisis: an agonizing self-analysis about its true strengths and weaknesses. Like a patient in therapy the city asked itself, "What should I do with the rest of my life?" And somehow the answer boomed out, "Get into FIRE . . . and . . . 'producer services' . . . law, accounting, advertising."

The city jumped off the couch, thanked the therapist, and began energetically putting its life in order, discarding its garment cutting tools, its breweries, its freight connection with the mainland, its port. New York rid itself of everything that blocked its potential to become the biggest and best FIRE and producer services city in the world. Personal income tax rates were halved; stock exchange tax was effectively scrapped; real estate taxes fell from over $4.00 to $1.80 per $100 of market value – and the city said goodbye to 400,000 manufacturing jobs.

By the eighties, New York had emerged as the self-described economic capital of the world. Instead of the eastern terminus of the country's declining manufacturing belt, Gotham had re-invented itself. It was a sassy, self-confident globally-oriented center for post-industrial services. New York had become the most post-industrial city in the most post-industrial country in a world that was becoming post-industrial.

The big difference between New York City's first big post-war slump of the seventies and the present downturn isn't the severity or the scope of the damage. It's that whereas New York's economy of the seventies was transitional – going from manufacturing to FIRE, now we have a wholly FIRE economy. Look at what reliance on FIRE has done for us lately.

*Jobs.* The employment/population ratio in the rest of the U.S. is 62 percent. In New York it's 49 percent. In 1993, however, less than half of New Yorkers of working age were actually working. And it wasn't because the Bureau of Labor Statistics was being picky. You need to work only one hour a week to be counted as employed. Yet among young people aged 16–19 New York's labor force participation is less than half the national average – 12 percent vs. 36 percent for the rest of the country. New York not only has the lowest labor force participation rates for black and latino youth, it also has the lowest for whites.

Labor force participation showed the same historical pattern relative to the rest of the country as unemployment: below the U.S. rate prior to post-industrialism, higher than or at least comparable to all central cities throughout the seventies, and now completely pathological in the period of full-blown post-industrialism.

Why? New York City is not Japan, where cultural norms dictate that most married women don't work. Nor is it Palm Springs, where a sizable share of the residents are too rich to work. People used to argue that New York had such a low labor force participation rate because of the richness of educational opportunities here – that seems highly implausible given the standing of New York near the bottom in per capita spending for higher education. Nor is it plausible that New York has somehow acquired the laziest population in America. More likely is the hypothesis that post-industrial New York has too few jobs.

How many jobs would it take to bring the city up to the level of the rest of the country? Just take the 13 percent difference and multiply by the six million non-institutionalized New Yorkers of working age. To achieve this standard, New York would need roughly three-quarters of a million more jobs.

*Dependency.* Officials from the city's Department of Social Services used the round figure of one million on welfare. One million was as high a level of dependency as the city had run since the fiscal crisis of the mid-seventies. It compared with the levels reached during the thirties. But if you talked to Dr. Suwati Desai, the Department of Social Service's top statistician, you found there were more people receiving assistance that the city counted but didn't mention. According to Dr. Desai's unpublished figures, over 300,000 recipients of Supplemental Security Income (SSI) – disability, old age and blind assistance – didn't get included as being on the rolls. (Nor did the 1.3 million total include the recipients of food stamps or those who received medicaid – aid to the medically indigent.) As late as 1974, recipients of SSI were counted as being on welfare rolls. At the height of the fiscal crisis, removing them brought the total down from seven digits to six.

Today, if you included all three of the basic categories of assistance – to the disabled, to families with dependent children and to those recipients social workers can't fit into either program, so-called "general" assistance – the total was exceeded in this century only during the two worst years of the Great Depression. One out of every 5.6 New Yorkers was now on welfare. The rate of dependency even exceeded the totals run in the forties – the eighteen forties – the notorious hungry forties that sparked the Astor Place riots. At that time the number of paupers was only one out of seven.

*Poverty.* Welfare rolls surged, not because of the city's fabled liberalism – Dan Quayle's line about the failure of the welfare state to work even on twelve square miles of the richest real estate in the world had a wide circulation – but because there were so many poor people. In fact, all the while the city was getting poorer – roughly from the mid-seventies – it was getting less liberal. Benefits fell from 126 percent of the poverty level in the mid-seventies to 86 percent in 1989.[27] Even through the fabulous bubble years of the eighties, New York's poverty rate grew. (Given the way real estate speculation put pressure on the city's fast-disappearing factories, this was not as paradoxical as it seemed.)

When the crash came, in 1987, it relieved speculative real estate pressure, but then the lay-offs began. In 1990, the Census came out with a figure based on 1989. But the downsizing of the work force had just begun. The next year the Current Population Survey found that the city's poverty rate had soared to 25.2 percent.

This was an historic reversal. As late as the 1960 census, the city's poverty rate was about two-thirds the national rate. During the fiscal crisis years, it just about equaled the national rate. Now in the nineties, it had risen to nearly double the national rate. And the one-out-of-four poverty rate estimated in 1991 was before New York lost another 400,000 jobs. The rate in 1993 was probably closer to 30 percent than 25 percent. Detroit was substantially poorer than New York – nearly 60 percent of the children in Detroit were poor – but no other large city could make that claim.

*Housing.* In Roman antiquity, a pantheist aristocracy worshipped practically everything – especially their own fields and villas.[28] New York City's conservatives[29] don't worship their office buildings or condos. (Make them an offer.) Their god is the "market." No one, they believe, should touch, regulate or criticize this holy-of-holies. So to suggest that the New York City housing market had undergone a spectacular collapse that had lasted more than a decade would have been a gross impiety. It would have been like asking a vestal virgin for a date.

But in 1992, less than 10,000 units of housing were produced for 7.3 million people. This is about one-quarter the U.S. rate. And this feeble performance had become routine: even during the bubble years of the Koch Administration, the rate never exceeded 20,000. The city had pledged to create 252,000 housing units for middle, low income and homeless families.[30] And if press releases were housing units, and plans were mortgages, Koch Administration would have solved the city's housing crisis. But despite the constant housing hype, the average during the eighties was about 12,000 a year – that is, about half the rate produced in the city during the great Depression.

Opinion leaders had long adjusted to this low horizon, blaming everything on the city's rent control legislation. It was rent control that had destroyed the city's housing stock, impoverished the landlord class, and reduced a once proud citizenry to sheep, "going to the sheering for taxes that are 170 percent of the national average," the *Wall Street Journal* explained editorially. And *cui bono*? Rich yuppies, prima ballerinas, singers like Carly Simon with many platinum records, and city politicians who personally benefitted from the rent control legislation they supported.[31]

In fact, less than 2 percent of all the city's rent-regulated apartments were occupied by residents with incomes over $100,000.[32] And except for the La Guardia years, rent regulation had existed in one form or another since World War I. Rent regulation didn't even apply to the production of new units. And it existed in other cities where the housing output was many times New York's rate. How can rent control explain the collapse of the housing market? If it was really the undeserving rich who had taken over all the rent controlled apartments, how to explain the results of the 1991 Housing and Vacancy Survey published by the Bureau of the Census? It showed that whereas in 1981 one in five households spent more than half their income on rent, the figure today is one in four. If rent regulation is undermining the market, how to explain why rent-regulated apartments in many neighborhoods are *higher* than the market? Rent regulation did not stop landlords from raising the median rent between 1981 and 1991 from $265 to $509 – in inflation adjusted dollars.[33]

Ignored in the analysis of the city's housing market collapse were more relevant factors like the rising price of land, and the falling wages of New Yorkers. Almost as undiscussable as poverty and land monopoly as forces shaping the housing scene were the speculative forces which drove housing prices in Manhattan from an average of $80,000 in 1980 to $500,000 per unit in 1987.

The upshot was that average New Yorker had a better chance of getting AIDS than ever getting a new housing unit. And Las Vagas, Nevada with 741,000 people produced more units of housing than New York City with 7,300,000.

*Homelessness.* In the early 1980s, just as AIDS began to emerge in public awareness, the homeless began to be visible on New York City streets. Kim Hopper's 1983 estimate of 30,000 homeless in New York was roundly attacked as hypertrophic. And conservatives began immediately to blame homelessness on rent control.[34] Why rent control suddenly produced this phenomenon, especially when the number of units under control was falling, was not something conservative theoreticians cudgeled their brains trying to figure out. No doubt the same funding sources would soon help us to understand the connection between AIDS and rent control.

Today, few observers would contest the 30,000 figure. Since David Dinkins entered office the number of homeless families alone has grown from 3,700 to 5,600.[35] Nearly everyone agreed that State de-institutionalization of the insane had swelled the totals of homeless. But why again, was New York's share of the homeless higher than everywhere else? The city's potent combination of high rents, low wages and massive job loss would seem to account for much of the variance.

*Wages.* Asked in 1992 what constituted the biggest economic problem facing the city, the newly appointed Deputy Mayor Barry Sullivan, a former David Rockefeller protégé at the Chase before becoming a First Chicago executive, replied "high labor costs." Sullivan had been out of the city for quite a few years. Not yet "up to speed" as they say in hard charging managerial circles, he seemed unaware that the city no longer complained about high labor costs: it touted its low wages as a reason for manufacturers to move here.

In 1988, the city placed a sixteen-page advertising supplement in the *Wall Street Journal*. It headlined New York City's cheap labor, and provided the following table:

*New York City Industrial Wage Chart ($)*

| | |
|---|---|
| Detroit | 13.74 |
| Seattle | 11.77 |
| Columbus | 11.22 |
| Houston | 11.15 |
| Minneapolis | 10.99 |
| Denver | 10.79 |
| Stamford | 10.74 |
| Baltimore | 10.46 |
| Chicago | 10.46 |
| Philadelphia | 10.43 |
| L.A. | 10.37 |
| Westchester | 10.28 |
| Bergen/Passaic | 10.13 |
| Boston | 10.12 |
| Atlanta | 10.11 |
| U.S. Average | 9.73 |
| Dallas | 9.45 |
| New York City | 9.10 |

Since 1988, New York has maintained what the ad called its "competitive" position – New York is even "competitive" now with such cities as Little Rock, Arkansas. A New York City worker in manufacturing makes about two dollars a week more than his counterpart in Dogpatch country. Effectively speaking our only real rival among

America's large cities is now San Antonio, Texas where wages are about $50.00 a week lower.[36] San Antonio however, has a locational advantage: it's only about 125 miles from the Mexican border.

Nevertheless New York has been trimming San Antonio's lead. But in a world of global competition, there are always new competitors on the horizon – today San Antonio, tomorrow, San Juan, and someday, perhaps, Port au Prince.

*Inequality.* In 1848, at the peak of the "hungry forties", the Astor Place riots saw upwards of 20,000 workers attack the opera house owned by Jacob Astor, the city's largest land owner. "Burn the damned den of aristocracy," the crowd shouted. An editorialist observed later that the riots had left behind "a feeling to which this community had hitherto been a stranger." It was a feeling "that there is now in our country, in New York City, what every good patriot hitherto has considered it his duty to deny – a *high* and a *low* class."[37]

The post-industrialization of New York has meant an income structure like pre-industrial New York's. Overall, the city is becoming a poorer place relative to the rest of its suburbs, relative to the State, and relative to the rest of the U.S. This is an historic reversal of New York City's position.

Three of the five boroughs with more than 75 percent of the city's population have an average income substantially below not only the state average, but the national average. The average income in the Bronx is less than three-quarters of the state average. Brooklyn's is only slightly higher. These parts of the city, in income terms, have lower income than southern states like Georgia. They really conform more to the pattern of the poorest states of the South – North Carolina, Arkansas, Tennessee – rather than the North.

The 45,000 Manhattanites who make $15.6 billion dollars – an average of about $350,000 yearly – keep New York City from resembling a high rise tobacco road. These 6.7 percent make more than 50 percent of all the borough income. They constitute 1.5 percent of all New Yorkers. But they make nearly one-fifth (19.14 percent) of the City's income. Compared to the seven other leading industrial nations, the U.S. has the most unequal distribution of income – calculated on the basis of the ratio between the highest and lowest 20 percent.[38] So it can't be said that America is exactly mired in socialist equalitarianism. In Japan, in the mid-eighties, the top 20 percent received about 36 percent of the national income. But even in the good old unequal states of

America, the top 20 percent get to feed on only 43 percent of the national income. And the top 5 percent receive 16 percent.[39] In other words, income inequality here is somewhere between three and four times worse than in the rest of the country.

Just how aberrant de-industrializing New York has become needs to be further understood. While it is true that the eighties produced sharp income polarization in the country as a whole, with the rich growing in numbers and wealth richer and the middle class shrinking, this pattern has not imposed itself on New York. Here, the structure is better characterized by a simple downshift. (See Appendixes 5–8.)

Three generations ago, in the days of Henry James and Edith Wharton, New York, and particularly Manhattan, was *the* place for the wealthy to live in America. Fifth Avenue from Henry Clay Frick's at 70th Street to Andrew Carnegie's at 92nd was largely built up of the mansions created by retired robber barons – many of whom like Carnegie received checks from J.P. Morgan himself when he formed U.S. Steel, by floating a $1,000,000,000 bond issue. Now, lacking primogeniture here in the U.S., there are no more wealthy Morgans, Fricks or Carnegies. New York is losing its position as the place where wealthy people in the country come to live. Just how pronounced this movement has become is indicated by the most recently available New York State tax returns. In 1987, the five New York counties had 69,000 residents with incomes over $100,000. Three New York suburban counties alone, Westchester, Nassau and Suffolk with a little more than half the city's population had 79,000. The *average* Connecticut commuter, who earned over $90,000 a year, received *twice* the average Manhattanite.

New York City's non-resident workers – 723,000 of them – earn over $38 billion;[40] that is more than the entire population of Manhattan earns. It is more than twice what is earned by the Borough of Brooklyn which has 2.3 million people. The point here is not to suggest nostalgia for the lost polarization of wealth and poverty. It's simply to recognize that whereas the industrial revolution produced such a polarization, New York's de-industrial revolution is creating more poverty and less wealth.

Polarization of income can have different meanings depending on what's happening to the overall income structure. If the whole structure is growing, polarization may mean just that the rich are getting rich faster than the poor. People at the top of the income pyramid and those at the bottom are increasing their incomes – the problem is just that the rich are doing so at a disproportionate rate. It's extremely doubtful that this is the meaning of New York's Babylonian extremes.

The top income earners who can tap into the flows of fictitious capital that still run powerfully here are, indeed, getting wealthier. Whereas in 1987, the top 6 percent of Manhattanites earned more than 50 percent of the borough's income, in 1982 the top 9 percent earned 46 percent of all the income earned.[41] The preponderance of evidence, however, suggests that New York City as a whole is getting poorer. The city receives an increasingly smaller share of the State's income. In 1963, the New York City's income accounted for 47 percent of the income earned by State residents.[42] By 1977, the figure had dropped by a quarter – to 37.2 percent in 1977. And seems to have remained at this level throughout the next decade. (See Appendix 6.)

In 1993, almost a century and a half after the Astor Place riots, it would be impossible to organize even a token demonstration against Mrs. Brooke Astor, the kindly 95-year-old inheritor of the Astor fortune who looks absolutely marvelous and still regularly attends charity balls for her numerous philanthropic causes. But it is also hard not to recognize that the city's history has doubled back towards the past. The city's post-industrial economy has created a stratification pyramid sloped more like the pre-industrial 1850s more than the high industrial era of the 1950s.

*Job Loss.* In the early nineties, New York City had become the Bermuda Triangle of job loss. In January 1993 alone an astonishing 98,000 jobs had disappeared – a post-war record. Obviously, the city couldn't keep on losing jobs at the January rate: in less than three years New York City would have no jobs at all.[43]

New York City had 3 percent of the nation's population. But between 1989 and the present, Gotham suffered a decline equal to 40 percent of the nation's net job loss. Nor could it be argued this time, as in the seventies, that the problem was strictly regional. Back then, the argument ran that in addition to its fiscal problems, New York City had fallen on the wrong side of the snow-belt/sun-belt divide. It took too much oil to heat places like New York and Philadelphia. The future belonged to cities like Houston and Los Angeles, which had nearby oil and nice weather.[44]

The penchant for explanations which rely on a kind of thermal materialism has been blunted by the energy bust and the bi-coastal depression. But New York's job shrinkage still stands out. The state's other large cities – Rochester, Buffalo, Syracuse, Binghamton – have been shattered by major corporate down-sizings led by IBM, Bausch and Lomb, Eastman and Kodak. Poverty rates in these cities run in the twenties. But unlike New York, their economies seemed to have bottomed out. And, as in the rest of the country, modest job growth has begun. The result is that New York City with 40 percent of the population has lost over 100 percent of the state's jobs.[45] If you could somehow take all the jobs lost in New York City since the recession started and transfer them somewhere, they would furnish enough employment – assuming the national rate of labor force participation – for a city the size of Baltimore or San Jose. (See Appendix 7.)

In three years of recession, almost the entire job gain built up between 1977 and 1989, an advance so proudly hailed by the friends of FIRE as evidence of the city's re-invention, has melted away. Only 3,219,000 jobs remain in New York. That's just 31,000 from its all-time post-war low in 1977.[46]

You can't explain New York's de-industrialization process the way you explain manufacturing loss in the country as a whole. New York has lost too many manufacturing jobs. It lost them "prematurely," – that is, before the onset of the global forces responsible for them were brought into play. It lost them in industries like garment and printing that were comparatively immune to decentralizing forces. In fact, they required Manhattan's peculiar industrial ecology to survive. Just compare what's happened to New York with the rest of the country.

Between 1970 and 1993 in the U.S., the total of manufacturing workers fell from 19.4 million to 18.1 million. In the same period, New York's manufacturing jobs fell from 766,000 to 286,000. It's the difference between 6.7 percent and 63 percent. As far as other large U.S. cities are concerned, the pattern is surprisingly ambiguous. Some of the top ten cities have actually gained manufacturing – like Phoenix and San Diego. Some have stayed the same – like L.A. – essentially exchanging the old high wage jobs for new low wage jobs. Others like Chicago, Detroit and Philadelphia have lost big time. But no city has lost so many manufacturing jobs or lost such a large share of its manufacturing jobs as New York. (See Appendix 8.)

San Antonio stands as a partial exception. It has a lower share of manufacturing jobs than New York. But it never had many manufacturing jobs to begin with. Before New York's post-industrial transformation – in 1958 New York had 27 percent of its jobs in manufacturing – as of January 1993 the share is 8.6 percent.[47]

Or consider New York City's manufacturing loss within New York State. The state lost about three-quarters of a million manufacturing jobs between 1970 and the present. But of the state total, 62 percent were lost here in the city. With two out of five residents, in the State, the city has lost more than three out of five of the jobs. In fact, a lot of the reason *why* manufacturing jobs have been lost in the state is because they have been lost in the city.

At this point, instead of a summary or a conclusion, it may be more useful to turn the floor over to an imaginary critic. It needn't be someone who supports the general post-industrial direction the city's taken, it may just be a skeptic. Someone unwilling to see New York's problems as either unique or self-generated.

"Yes, New York is in bad shape," such a critic might say, " But why pick on New York? Aren't most cities doing just as badly or worse? What about Detroit? On Devil's Night, officials have all they can do to stop people from burning down the town. Moreover, your tone is inappropriately hostile and smart-assed. You sound as if you think it's someone's fault that cities are exposed to the global market, suburbanization, and post-industrialization. Cities are the objects of forces they can't control. Manufacturing capital has been leaving cities for decades and you're just finding out? Besides, people are literally dying to come to New York from China, from Haiti, and God knows where else, doesn't this show the continuing vitality of the city's economy?"

It's certainly true that from the perspective of an impoverished village in Fujian province, New York city still appears as a shimmering "Huangjingde shan", a golden mountain. But China also now has villages to the south, in Guangdong, which have a higher household income – over $20,000 a year – than many census tracts in the Bronx and Brooklyn. Manufacturing capital is flowing from Hong Kong into the city's garment sweatshops, not because of any tariff barriers but because wages here are lower than there. One hundred and fifty dollars a week is the going wage in the city's garment factories and Chinese restaurants. Hong Kong workers are even beginning to take retirement here because the cost of living is lower. Who could have imagined New York's FIRE economy would produce such an incredible reversal of economic fortunes?

Besides, people who argue that New York's steady stream of

immigration indicates the city's economic vitality downplay facts of history and geography. Immigrants can't just parachute into the country from the sky. They come across at the ports of entry like New York, Miami, and Los Angeles. Given New York's location, and its presence of existing immigrant communities, it's striking how our share has shrunk compared to the past: in the last great immigration wave, before World War I, the city received more than half the nation's total. Now the share is down to about one in ten.

Nor is it true, as we have seen, that most large cities in the U.S. are as badly off as New York. The 1990 Census – based on a survey carried out in 1989 – does show several cities with higher poverty rates. Detroit's poverty rate is substantially greater than New York's. But the results have to be put in perspective: Detroit is smaller than the Bronx and half the size of Brooklyn – which are comparably poor. And since 1989, New York has been growing poorer faster than the rest of the country. Eighty-nine was a fortunate year for the city to have its picture taken by the Census Bureau. It had benefited disproportionately from the LBO and real estate booms. But since then it's been disfigured by a disproportionate share of the nation's job loss. Besides, there are several indices of economic malaise in which New York stands out among U.S. cities: youth labor force participation, unemployment, office space vacancies, low manufacturing wages, inequality.

What's simply incontestable, though, is that in structural terms New York has moved further, faster in the direction of FIRE than any other city – probably in the world. You could argue that the problems of the seventies were the result of the old manufacturing structure. But the downturn of the nineties – New York's "second slump" – could only be identified as the product of its FIRE structure. Here is an industrial structure more skewed towards FIRE than any other city and it had produced what was demonstrably the nation's worst urban downturn.

Two really debatable issues emerge: (1) to what extent does the FIRE structure produce the urban pathology we see? And (2) to what extent did it come into being not just as post-industrial ideology argues through progressive, necessary and inexorable forces – global force and suburbanization – but of a conscious policy of structural transformation?

Post-industrial ideology explains New York's present FIRE-dominated structure as something progressive, necessary, inexorable. But it's not as if the de-industrial process we've undergone can be understood by the same explanation that is used for hollowed-out cities like Detroit,

Akron, Gary and Pittsburgh. New York was a lot harder to de-industrialize than the monocultural cities of the Midwestern heartland. In the late fifties, New York's economy was in crisis, but it had great diversity; flexibility; a magnificent, if depleted manufacturing infrastructure; a great port; a highly skilled working class. You could argue that the city was actually pre-adapted to the present day demands of "flexible production."

The problems of the cities of the Midwestern heartland like Akron, Gary and Detroit arise from the failure of urban economies built around one industry – cars, tires, steel. So when Detroit started exporting manufacturing capital overseas and U.S. consumers stopped buying Detroit cars, the fate of these urban monocultural towns was sealed.

New York's history is very different. It wound up as a one-industry town dangerously dependent on a single highly cyclical product: speculative office buildings (SOBs). But it didn't start that way. Until the 1950s, what characterized the city was an economy of diversity. Not only did the city maintain a balance between making, selling, transporting, storing and financing things – balanced growth. New York had diversity and flexibility built into its manufacturing structure.

In a profound sense, that was appreciated only by a few,[48] the city had actually pre-adapted to what would eventually be called the "post-Fordist" transformation in flexible manufacturing methods. That is, the city had already acquired the industrial structures and capabilities that would be required to meet world-wide competition in a later period.

Under vastly different shop floor arrangements and by means of very different types of industrial planning, these methods would soon permeate Japanese, Italian and German industry.[49] Even in the U.S. by the mid-eighties, hollowed-out industrially by capital export and urban de-industrialization, "flexibility" would become the main mantra for humbled managerial strata seeking to catch up to foreign competitors.

But New York City in the fifties was already "flexible." Because of the importance of the clothing trades, especially ladies garments, as well as the printing industry, the city's firms were highly attuned to shifts in styles and trends; experienced in adapting production to customers' needs. This sensitivity was linked to an ability to revise production routines, re-tool and re-style their products.

"Flexibility" here meant the dis-integration of production; external instead of internal economies – mutual dependence of small firms who essentially share the same capital base. Rather than capital-deepening technology; instead of the sub-division of the manufacturing process so that each operation can be performed on an assembly line with minimal skill – the redeployment among small shops with highly developed craft skills. "Flexibility" enabled firms to revolutionize inventory practice. Instead of maintaining huge stockpiles of goods, drawn from suppliers around the world, "konban" methods; instead of long production runs, "batch" production; instead of "one size fits all" – a product that is design-driven.[50]

In retrospect, New York can be seen not only as a pioneer in flexible manufacturing, it was also an incubator of industrial innovation – generating not only a disproportionate number of U.S. patents, but also a constant flow of new products, new industrial methods and new firms. The city's unique industrial culture of diversity and innovation has to be understood in terms of the scale and interdependence of its firms. Unlike Detroit, which rose to strength in the midwest on the basis of a few great automobile companies, New York had more than 70,000 firms at various stages of the product cycle.[51] So the city was constantly benefiting from the explosive growth of new, successful firms. New York's small companies, unlike giant, vertically integrated firms, needed each other's products and services. They needed a New York location for three primary reasons: to buy and sell to each other; to share facilities; and to be in the center of the world's greatest consumer market, with over 20 million people located within 25 miles of Columbus Circle.

New York's flexible manufacturing culture of the 1950s certainly could never have been mistaken for an economic paradise. Small firms failed at a high rate; the tendency of small firms to pay low wages – "industrial dualism" – was difficult to combat; crime family control of much of the city's transportation unions; the food distribution business; and the garment and construction industries on a scale unique in the U.S., made for a thoroughly violent and corrupt city – and a politics to match.[52]

But on the basis of what was then perhaps the richest and most diverse industrial culture in the world, a very wealthy city was able to support its own university system with free tuition, its own hospital system, as well as an array of public services envied by the rest of the nation and hardly imaginable today. Every day but Sunday, the city picked up the garbage and "flushed" the streets. The city had twice the number of park workers it has today. Libraries were open six days a week, even in the outer boroughs.

One of the few who spoke for New York City's economy of diversity and understood them thoroughly was Jane Jacobs, perhaps the pre-eminent urban thinker of our time. Jacobs lived downtown and knew it intimately. She loved her neighborhood, but not uncritically. Downtown in the late 1950s had serious limitations, with its paucity of amenities and services, the ring of stagnation, decay and vacating industries around the port and the financial center. But sometimes in some places, downtown's streets worked. And when they did it was precisely because the activity was based on an economic foundation of basic mixed uses. What she called "Hudson Street Ballet" deserves to be recalled in detail because although it has largely vanished, it sets a standard for economy and amenity we need to revive:

The workers from the laboratories, meat-packing plants, warehouses, plus those from a bewildering variety of small manufacturers, printers and other little industries and offices, give all the eating places and much of the other commerce support at midday. We residents on the street and on its more purely residential tributaries could and would support a modicum of commerce by ourselves, but relatively little. We possess more convenience, liveliness, variety and choice than we "deserve" in our own right. The people who work in the neighborhood also possess, on account of us residents, more variety than they "deserve" in their own right. We support these things together by unconsciously cooperating economically. If the neighborhood were to lose the industries, it would be a disaster for us residents. Many enterprises, unable to exist on residential trade by itself, would disappear. Or if the industries were to lose us residents, enterprises unable to exist on the working people by themselves would disappear."[53]

Jacobs showed that it was the diversity of economic uses of the neighborhood, spread throughout the day, not sheer numbers, descend-ing in one crush at 9 a.m. and sweeping out again at 5 p.m. that was crucial to downtown's residential development. The downtown central business district was never a true office center. That role had been played since the last quarter of the nineteenth century by midtown. Railroads and utilities chose not to locate downtown. They avoided its congestion as well as the ethnic populations and industrial activities of the loft neighborhoods of what is now called the valley. Midtown, which contained the residences of the very rich – J.P. Morgan lived on Madison at 36th – was the ideal spot for corporate offices which never locate too far from rich residential neighborhoods.

Since the advent of Grand Central Station, downtown had de-
liquesced into a second-class office center – but through its capacity for
diversity it had emerged into a first-class matrix for jobs. Not just
face-to-face communication for deal makers – but as a transportation
center; a locus for retail electronics; the machine tool center; the
produce markets; the preferred location for printers; as well as the link
for the storage, distribution and service sectors in the outer boroughs.[54]
Without this diversity she predicted, downtown wouldn't even be able
to remain a second-class office district. It would fail to compete
effectively with midtown for office space, except, perhaps, during
booms.

Naturally she was appalled by David Rockefeller's plan which he
promoted in 1958 as head of the Downtown Lower Manhattan Association to eliminate the port, the produce markets, and all local industry
from Canal Street to the Battery – and substitute office buildings and
luxury high-rise residences. She predicted:

The land clearance planned will clear out – along with empty buildings and decayed
work uses – much of the low-overhead services and commerce that does still exist to
serve the working population. Facilities already too meager in range and number for
the working population will be further subtracted. Conditions already inconvenient
will become intolerable. Moreover, the plans will foreclose the chance of reasonably
adequate services ever being developed, because no room, at economical rents for
the incubation of new enterprise, will exist for them.[55]

What the Rockefellers aimed at was simple: instead of a primary
central business district (CBD) in midtown and a secondary CBD with
mixed uses downtown, they aimed to transform the entire area from
59th Street to the Battery into one giant CBD. Besides downtown, the
family also had far-reaching plans for midtown CBD expansion. Rockefeller Center itself would soon double its capacity: jumping the Sixth
Avenue border, it would throw up another four million square feet. Nor
was this all: to "secure" the Sixth Avenue development, much redevelopment of the west side was necessary – since the western border of
Rockefeller Center was essentially a blighted area. Times Square
redevelopment, midtown zoning – essentially illegalizing development
on the east side and force-feeding it on the west with zoning bonuses
and irresistible tax abatements. It's an old story: if you subsidize
something, you get more of it. The greatest overhang of office space in
the city's post-war history – fully comparable to the inventory created by

the great depression – was policy driven. The result of efforts to stretch the limits of the CBD.

In David Rockefeller, whose family at the time was the city's largest landlord, Jane Jacobs found her most formidable practical antagonist. Rockefeller would not find the goal of economical rents terribly compelling. Whereas Jacobs looked at neighborhoods as a kind of ecologist, seeking to understand relationships and interconnections, Rockefeller saw big chunks of the city as an archaic jumble that needed to be cleared out. For every urban problem he had a practical solution: Build an office building. Attachment to small scale in urban places was just sentimentality. Instead he praised what he called "catalytic bigness": big real estate projects that served as catalysts for neighborhood transformation.

"My family, " he recalled one day in the late seventies before the Staten Island Chamber of Commerce, "has long been identified with controversial large projects" such as Lincoln Center, the United Nations, Rockefeller Center, Chase Manhattan Plaza, Rockefeller University, Morningside Heights and the World Trade Center. Most of these projects, he observed, were criticized at the time as disruptive white elephants. But then he noted "you can't make an omelet without breaking eggs." And his approach to urban transformation has stood the test of time. Today, New York is more diverse, there are more jobs, more housing. And as a result

basic economic activities such as finance, health and culture have been anchored here. . . . I hate to sound chauvinistic about Lower Manhattan, but it's well worth the cost of a ferry ride to go for Sunday brunch at the World Trade Center.

In conclusion, Rockefeller offered a list of projects that urgently needed to be put into the ground: Westway – more an office building park than a road; Battery Park City; the Convention Center; 42nd Street; South Street Sea Port. What all these projects had in common was that they were big and they would "stimulate significant ancillary activity."[56] Housing would flourish, Rockefeller predicted, and thousands of new businesses will be created.

At the peak of the Reagan Bubble, in 1987, the year the Koch regime produced its euphoric assessment and plan, *New York Ascendent*, most of Rockefeller's projects had been realized. But the total of businesses in the city had shrunk to 52,626. Housing production had collapsed.[57] Jane Jacobs' prediction however was right on the money. Downtown

Manhattan could only survive in boom conditions. By the 1990s its survival was in question. Wall Street itself had nearly two million square feet of empty space. David Rockefeller's Chase Manhattan Bank had lost its anchor tenant. In fact, downtown Manhattan with its 50.7 years of inventory loomed now as the empty space capital of capitalism. And not even the DLMA appeared to believe that the space would be ever filled.

In 1991, the head of the Downtown Lower Manhattan Association (DLMA), John Zucotti, the former City Planning Commission chairman, long-time real estate lobbyist, partner in Brown and Wood and chief of the soon-to-be bankrupt Olympia and York, proposed something called the "Lower Manhattan Project."[58] Convert the empty buildings to luxury residential apartments, Zucotti urged. Of course there wasn't much of a market for luxury residential space either, but at least it would alleviate some of the market pressure on the few salvageable buildings left.

The DLMA's proposal had a certain karmic logic: if the city could subsidize the creation of the office buildings in the seventies, why not subsidize their liquidation in the nineties? Nor could you argue with the urgency of the task: the original Manhattan Project sought to assemble the world's first atom bomb, the DLMA's Lower Manhattan Project aims at nothing less than the disassembling of America's most awesome real estate bomb.

What needs to be appreciated, however, is that while market forces proved too weak to allow New York to create a second office building district, as Jane Jacobs foresaw, the creation of downtown was not a simple response to market forces. The twin towers of the World Trade Center (nicknamed "David and Nelson" by downtown residents), the South Street seaport, Battery Park City, etc., weren't put there by the world market. They were all built by government – the state; the city; or various "authorities" which were created by government. These real estate projects continue to be subsidized by the institutions that created them: Battery Park City gets an $86.8million tax exemption; the World Trade Center receives $71.7 million, etc.[59]

The whole transformation of the city, its progress from diversity to office building monoculture was not a simple response to global market forces. New York designed a strategy for economic transformation. The strategy worked. What doesn't work is the new economic structure the strategy succeeded in implanting.

# NOTES

1. Unofficial estimates suggested that the east German rate has exceeded 30 percent, *New York Times*, March 8, 1993, B1.
2. "Non-work" here means a combination of unemployment and being out of the labor force. What the Bureau of Labor Statistics calls the "employment/population ratio," the ratio of those actually working to all those non-institutionalized people between the ages of 16 and 65.
3. Robert Heilbroner, "The Deficit: A Way Out," *New York Review of Books*, November 19, 1992.
4. In the one sector where hiring had begun, brokerage, the Shearson, Lehman–Smith Barney merger would shrink from 4,000 to 6,000 jobs. The merger would also put another million square feet of office space on the already saturated market. See Marcia Parker, "Shearson Deal Shrinks Wall Street's Job Gains," *Crain's New York Business*, March, pp. 15–21, 1993:1.
5. Cited by Stephen Kagann, "Why New Yorkers Pay More," *City Journal*, Spring 1993, p. 16.
6. The growing use of "non-eviction" plans in the eighties made it easier to co-op the property by lowering the voting threshold of tenants who had to approve the plan. But it also meant that fewer tenants were forced out of their apartment.
7. Alan S. Oser, "Perspectives: The MacArthur Portfolio," *New York Times*, June 13, 1993. LIR, 5.
8. *New York Times*, "'Pulse' Manhattan Condo Sales," March 17, 93, B1. In 1988, the owners of my building, the 211 E. 17 St. Associates offered me my 350-square foot studio for $92,000. Then, last year, they made me another offer: $23,000.
9. Peter Grant, "Bottom-fisher lands downtown Bargain," *Crain's New York Business*, March 8, 1993, p. 8.
10. Jerry Adler, *High Rise* (New York: HarperCollins, 1993), p. 388.
11. Office of the State Deputy Comptroller for the City of New York, Analysis of the New York City Economy, October 29, 1992; Technical Memorandum, February 93, p. 5.
12. Ibid, p. 24.
13. Office of the State Deputy Comptroller for the City of New York, Analysis of the New York City Economy, October 29, 1992; Technical Memorandum, February 93, p. 17.
14. *Wall Street Journal*, "Executive Pay Survey, " April 21, 1993, R15.
15. The magazine is owned by the K-III Magazine Corp. (See *Newsday*, April 1, 1993, p. 13.) Kravis's intellectual background includes a majoring in golf at Occidental College and a senior thesis on convertible debentures, Bryan Burrough and John Helyar, *Barbarians at the Gate* (New York: Harper, 1991), p. 131.
16. Andy Logan, "Don't Look Back," The *New Yorker*, March 15, 1993.
17. James Brady, "In this Mayoral Campaign, Issues are not the Issue," *Crain's New York Business*, March 8, 1993, p. 11.
18. Stanley Brezenoff, "The Long Term Economic Outlook," Challenges of the Changing Economy of New York City 1991, The New York Council on Economic Education at Baruch College, May 8, 1991.
19. Dr. Louis Winnick, "The Social Problems and Opportunities," Challenges of the Changing Economy of New York City, 1991, p. 59.
20. Not the immediate successor, Macchiarola.
21. Port of New York and New Jersey, Oceanborne Foreign Trade Handbook 1991, September 1992. The top seven imports were: (1) alcoholic beverages; (2) road motor vehicles; (3) coffee; (4) vegetables and vegetable preparations; (5) organic chemicals; (6) bananas; (7) alcohols. Of the top exports waste paper is far and away the largest – greater in long tons than the next five items.
22. Ronald Shelp, *Beyond Industrialization* (New York: Praeger, 1981), p. 2.
23. In the summer of 1969 FIRE reached a peak of 479,000 FIRE jobs. In April there were only 469,700 (unpublished figures, New York State Department of Labor).
24. Office of the State Comptroller, "Analysis of the New York City Economy," October 29, 1992. Technical Memorandum, February 93, p. 12.

25. Biographical material from *Who's Who*, October 24, 1990. Doug Henwood supplied me with this information.

26. Of course, not all those outside the labor force are poor. Some attend college. Some are supported by a spouse. Others have retired early and live off investment income, etc.

27. Elizabeth Durbin, "Public Assistance," in *Setting Municipal Priorities*, Raymond Horton and Charles Brecher (eds) (New York: New York University Press, 1989).

28. H.J.Rose, *Religion in Greece and Rome* (New York: Harper & Row, 1959), p. 235.

29. Americans call nineteenth century liberals – believers in the free market – "conservatives". This creates a dual confusion with actual conservatives – who value tradition, family, patriotism, etc. And with modern liberals who are actually social democrats and believe in the efficacy of government intervention. The term "conservative" in this context actually means nineteenth century Manchester School liberal.

30. See Bonnie Brower, *Missing the Mark: Subsidizing Housing for the Privileged, Displacing the Poor*, The Association for Neighborhood and Housing Development Inc. and The Housing Justice Campaign August, 1989, ch.2.

31. William Tucker, "A Model for Destroying a City," *Wall Street Journal*, March 12, 1993, A8. Tucker's general grasp of the city can be gauged by the fact that he thinks Ruth Messinger, the liberal Manhattan Borough President, is Andy Stein – the city's conservative "Public Advocate." On a federal level this would be tantamount to confusing Senators Robert Dole and Barbara Milkulski.

32. There were 1,095,000 rent-regulated apartments; 23,000 of them were occupied by residents who earned in excess of $100,000. (See Alan S. Oser, "For Almost All Tenants, Little Change," *New York Times*, July 18, 1993, R5.)

33. Andrew White, "Vital Statistics," *City Limits*, October 1992, p. 20.

34. William Tucker, *The Excluded Americans*, (Regenery Gateway, 1990).

35. Celia W.Dugger, "A Roof for All, Made of Rulings and Red Tape," *New York Times*, July 4, 1993, 1.

36. U.S. Department of Labor, Bureau of Labor Statistics, "Employment and Earnings," May 1991.

37. Edward Robb Ellis, *The Epic of New York City* (New York: Old Town Books, 1966), p. 265.

38. See Kevin Phillips, *The Politics of Rich and Poor* (New York: Random House, 1991), p. 15.

39. Frank Levy, *Dollars and Dreams* (New York: W.W. Norton & Company, 1988), p. 14.

40. Office of Management and Budget did not have figures available for 1987 – Wall Street's peak year. They did for 1988. But returns were unavailable for "approximately 600 millionaires." Since the average New York State millionaire makes approximately $3.2 million, figure the lack of this data understates the total earned by about $2 billion or about 5 percent. And thus, very roughly speaking, the average Connecticut commuter's yearly income is closer to $100,000 than to $90,000.

41. New York State Department of Taxation and Finance, Bureau of Tax Research and Statistics, New York Personal Income for Income Year(s) 1982 and 1987.

42. I have excluded the income earned by out-of-state residents. If it were included, New York City's share of total income would be seen to fall from 44 percent to 34.5 percent of all the income earned in the state. (See Appendix 6.)

43. The next month, preliminary reports suggested that the city made back much of the loss.

44. See George Sternlieb and James W. Hughes, *Post-Industrial America: Metropolitan Decline & Inter-Regional Shifts*, New Brunswick, N.J.: The Center for Urban Policy Research, Rutgers, 1975, p. 127.

45. In the case of the New York–Northeastern New Jersey area these have been declines in all its components; Long Island, the northern suburbs and Northeastern New Jersey have all suffered big job losses. But New York City's job shrinkage is the sharpest and the city failed to participate in the mild recovery experienced elsewhere in the immediate region. U.S. Department of Labor, Middle Atlantic Regional Office. "New York–Northeastern New Jersey Year-End Report, 1992: December 30, 1992. Payrolls began to increase at the end of 1992 in the rest of the region.

46. New York State Department of Labor (unpublished figures).

47. New York State Department of Labor (unpublished figures).

48. Jane Jacobs, *The Death and Life of Great American Cities* (New York: Random House, 1961).

49. Michael J. Piore and Charles F. Sandel, *The Second Industrial Divide* (New York: Basic Books, 1984).

50. As Adam Smith pointed out long ago, the division of labor is governed by the size of the market. So flexibility presupposed the fragmentation of the mass market for highly standardized productions and demanded the ability to respond to changes in demand and styles very rapidly. Gradually, General Motor's standard practice, its corporate structure, its notion of the division of labor, its "world car", became business school models of everything that was wrong with U.S. manufacturing.

51. New York City, City Planning Commission, *Plan for New York City: Critical Issues*, Vol.1, 1969, pp. 66–71.

52. New York State Organized Crime State Task Force, *Corruption and Racketeering in the New York City Construction Industry* (Ithaca: ILR Press, 1990).

53. Jane Jacobs, *The Death and Life of Great American Cities* (New York: Random House, 1961), p. 153.

54. Peter Hall, *The World Cities* (New York: McGraw-Hill Book Company, 1961), p. 196.

55. Jacobs, *The Death and Life of Great American Cities* (New York: Random House, 1961) 1961: p. 157.

56. Remarks by David Rockefeller, Chairman the Chase Manhattan Bank, N.A. before the Staten Island Chamber of Commerce, New York, February 27, 1979.

57. Census of Selected Services: 1977 and 1987, U.S. Bureau of the Census.

58. Shortly after Olympia & York's bankruptcy was announced Zucotti lost his position as head of the DLMA.

59. Message of the Mayor, 1992:84.

*PART II*

# HOW NEW YORK CITY
# BECAME POOR

CHAPTER TWO

# THE TREND BENDERS: NYC PLANNING (1929 – 1993)

Two maps face each other on leaves of the 1929 Regional Plan of New York and its Environs. The left-hand side shows New York as it was in 1928 – with the areas zoned for industry marked in black. Manhattan's west side from 59th Street to the Battery appears almost all black; most of downtown is black; both sides of the East River are covered with manufacturing zones. Outside of Manhattan, Long Island City, the north "coast" of Brooklyn, the Bronx all along the Harlem river, Flushing and Jackson Heights, Jamaica and Coney Island and part of the Rockaways – are all zoned industrial.

On the right-hand side looms New York as the directors of the Regional Plan envisioned it ought to be: almost all the areas zoned for manufacturing have been whited out. The map transforms Manhattan below 59th Street from the most industrialized area in the city to the least – the whole swath from 14th Street on the west side to the Battery has been completely de-industrialized. What industry that remains is confined to Hell's Kitchen, a little spit around the garment center and a small manufacturing corridor in what is now Noho and Soho. As far as the other boroughs are concerned, the south Bronx industrial area has shrunk more or less to its present dimensions around Hunt's point; a strip operation along both sides of the east river and in Long Island City – along with a little splotch around what is now JFK airport.

For the directors of the Regional Plan Association (RPA), the left side represented an unpleasant reality. The right, a vision.

A New York City purged of its manufacturing, and stripped of its port, was the dream of the Regional Plan's directors – Morgan bankers, Rockefeller Foundation executives, New York Central and Jersey Central railroad directors, outer borough real estate developers. Residential housing in the outer boroughs would replace manufacturing. Industry would lose its disturbing proximity to Wall Street. The port, the prime source of the disturbance, with its trucks, cargo and longshoremen would be transferred to Elizabeth, New Jersey. And thus the railroad interests on the RPA board would have the best possible of all worlds. The New York Central could concentrate on collecting rent on its west side property rather than freight cars. While the Jersey Central, represented by Jersey Central director and RPA chairman Robert De Forest, would get the benefit of increased traffic at its terminal at Elizabeth.

Today, of course, New York City does closely resemble the whited-out version. Bankers' dreams won out over a gritty manufacturing reality. The right-hand side prevailed over the left. Except for a fading five block patch along what is now the western edge of TriBeCa, all the industry from below 14th Street on the west side has disappeared. The port of New York, once the world's greatest – which handled over 50 percent of U.S. exports – has been shifted to Elizabeth, as recommended in the plan.

What explains the striking correspondence between the RPA's plans and their materialization? Was it their power or their prescience? Did the RPA men simply foresee how market and technological forces would operate? Did the RPA's port specialist, the eponymous Col E.H. Outerbridge envision containerization? Did Morgan partner Dwight Morrow realize that the world market would suddenly collapse, and then rise again? If so, they failed to mention these predictions in the many volumes of analysis and prescription that accompanied the Graphic Plan.

And what about the whole network of bridges, roads, and circumferential highways called for in the plan? The George Washington, Bronx–Whitestone and Verazzano bridges, the Cross Bronx Expressway and the entire circle of limited access expressways around New York City, Newark and environs.[1] This whole network has also been realized.

So have the main goals for shrinking manufacturing. It's not just that there is *less* industry. It's that there's less industry precisely *where* New York's FIRE elites wanted there to be less.

Isn't it plausible then to suggest that New York City planning elites who had the power to create a transportation infrastructure where they wanted, subsequently also had the power to shrink the city's manufacturing districts? True, the planners who realized the 1929 plan were a different generation from those of the fifties and sixties who formulated the Downtown Lower Manhattan and Second Regional Plans. But they aimed at the same primary object: the expansion and preservation of the Manhattan Central Business District. And without eliminating the port and manufacturing, the CBD couldn't be expanded. A common aim required a common effort.

In 1929, no one had heard of globalization, containerization or post-industrialization, the explanatory watchwords of present-day analysts. Yet the planners of the twenties pursued concrete objectives such as saving the downtown CBD, and removing manufacturing. These aims are identical to those of present-day elites, who claim that their goals are just conditioned responses to ineluctable modern forces.

Perhaps New York has been shaped by the planners' plans as much as by the ineluctable forces. At the very least, the closeness of the geographical fit between New York as it is and New York as it was envisioned – suggests a need for re-examination of the influence of New York City planning. In question are three generations of urban planners.

New York's Age of Plans begins with the great decentralizing highway and bridge plan of the twenties. It continues with the antithetical re-centralizing Second Regional Plan of the late sixties – a plan which called again, and more successfully, for the homogenization of downtown land use, and pointed the way towards development of the waterfront and the creation of outer borough office centers ("regional sub-centers"). It culminates in the initiatives of the Koch/Dinkins era – years that saw the CBD jump over the East River into Long Island City and downtown Brooklyn, and swing west and south towards Eighth Avenue and the Convention Center before shuddering to a stop in 1989. Did these planning efforts, each of which had as its stated goal the expansion of the CBD, have anything to do with our present state of de-industrialization?

Not in the slightest, if you believe the official version of New York history.

According to the Department of City Planning (DCP), for example, no one in New York had very much to do with manufacturing job loss: the factors were "in large part beyond the city's control."[2] There was the shift to the sun-belt, the emergence of a global market, that sucked out jobs. The invention of the truck and better communications made factories more footloose. Then there was the decline in the city's population and the shrinking of the northeastern market. Finally, the DCP concedes, there were some local factors – costs got out of hand, especially taxes; the kind of large tracts of land manufacturers like weren't available here as they were in the suburbs. And of course there was the high incidence of crime.[3]

In other words, says the DCP, the loss of three-quarters of a million manufacturing jobs, since the late fifties can be blamed almost entirely on (a) changing technology; (b) external and internal market forces and factors, i.e., other places became cheaper while NYC became more expensive. These factors, however, the study concludes, are "not unique to New York City."[4]

But New York is unique. Nowhere else have 750,000 manufacturing jobs disappeared. That's equivalent to the entire *population* of Baltimore. Nowhere else has the whole structure of employment shifted from a 2:1 ratio of manufacturing to FIRE to a 1:2 ratio. Nowhere else did land values rise simultaneously with the industrial job loss, from $20 billion to $400 billion. Nor were there any other cities where so many of developers crowded their way onto the Forbes 400 richest Americans by turning urban industrial land into components of the Central Business District.

The job loss in New York is all the more problematic when you consider that local industry wasn't of the footloose type. Compared with Pittsburgh or Detroit or Gary or Akron, the city had developed a remarkably diverse – and for a time, highly successful industrial economy – based on flexible production; on small interdependent firms which produced non-standard commodities and relied on the Manhattan CBD. Fledgling firms used cheap space in the CBD as an industrial incubator as they went up the product cycle.

For more than fifty years, up to about the mid-fifties, as the Harvard Study showed, while manufacturing declined in nearly every city in the great Northeast-Midwestern manufacturing belt, New York's industries thrived. The city had about 15 percent of the country's manufacturing workers in 1899. And about that many in 1956.[5] Then, much before the country as a whole began to be affected by de-industrialization, New York started to hemorrhage severely.

Official planning doctrine has portrayed the industrial bloodletting not as a problem but as an opportunity. Fresh FIRE and service jobs in an expanding CBD, we were told, would make up for those lost in the paleo-industrial sector. In *New York Ascendent*, released in June, 1987, exuberant planners predicted nearly 4,000,000 jobs by the year 2000. With the millennium only seven years away, there are only about 3,200,000 jobs – nearly 400,000 fewer than when the prediction was made.

In fact, the city has about 400,000 fewer private sector jobs than it did in 1958 when manufacturing was still strong. Recall too, that in the fifties, the city's employment and labor force participation rates were comparatively high. Today, New York has one of the highest unemployment rates in the U.S.; the city runs a labor force participation rate ten points below the national average; and it leads in low youth labor force participation with a rate of about one-third the national average. In New York, four out of five *white* kids aren't working. Poverty rates went from one-third below the national average to nearly twice the national average. While laboring in a city which has one of the highest costs of living in the U.S., workers receive the next-to-the-lowest manufacturing wages of the ten largest U.S. cities.[6] Our FIRE monoculture is highly unstable and subject to long downturns which continue whatever the performance of the national economy. To shore up a crisis-ridden CBD, over a billion in tax abatements is handed over to some of the richest people in the world. To keep the Old Greenwich crowd commuting to their tax-abated office buildings, the city essentially waives income taxes on them. As a result, the Bronx worker with a taxable income of under $15,000 a year will pay five times the tax of the average Fairfield County commuter who earns $100,000.[7]

Of course it may be that there is no connection whatever between manufacturing job loss and job loss, job loss and wage decline, wage decline and poverty, poverty and welfare, crime and social disintegration, etc. But common sense suggests otherwise. And our survival instincts should also suggest a need to grasp more clearly how those jobs disappeared.

Certainly an explanation which refers only to external, objective, impersonal factors can't account for the rate, timing and nature of New York's manufacturing job loss. New York lost too many jobs, it lost them at times when the rest of the U.S. wasn't losing them, and it shed types of jobs – those based on external economies – that are relatively hard to lose. It's not that New York wasn't affected by market and technological forces. But something different, something in addition to the decentralization and de-industrialization that's been going on in most of the rest of the country has happened here.

Can it be just a coincidence that de-industrialization and the 1950s push towards Central Business District expansion began at the same time? Between 1945 and 1957, a time of great manufacturing stability, exactly one office building twenty stories or larger was built downtown. Between 1957 and 1968, there were twenty-six[8] – and the city lost nearly 150,000 manufacturing jobs.

In the world of physics, two objects can't simultaneously occupy the same space. In the urban world, where the same principle must apply, how could the CBD have expanded without uprooting manufacturing? Aren't CBD expansion and manufacturing shrinkage simply two sides of FIRE's post-industrial coin?

What's intriguing, then, about the DCP's account of de-industrial-ization though is not that it repeats formulaic phrases about market forces and technological changes. Or even that it stuns common sense by recommending a strategy of expanding the city's "export industries" i.e., securities trading, lawyering, advertising, etc., as a way of nourishing manufacturing.[9] It is rather, that in considering New York's industrial devolution, the planners totally ignore their own role.

If the Commission were more capable of drawing on its institutional memory, we might learn quite a bit about how manufacturing was lost in this city.[10] But in its apparent reticence to recall those bruising battles, the Commission resorts to rhetoric that is oblique even by the standards of bureaucratic discourse. An exemplary passage emerges in the course of advocacy for its principle economic development recommendation, which is of course – "Facilitate the expansion of the Central Business District."[11]

The Commission – which doesn't explain why the CBD must expand further when there are already 65 million square feet of empty office space – then gives this account of how the CBD has grown so far. "Growth," it says, "expanded the geographic boundaries of the city's CBD to Battery Park City, TriBeCa, Midtown South, Downtown Brooklyn and Long Island City."

"Growth" created Battery Park City? Most would credit David and Nelson Rockefeller. It was David who first suggested "adapting" the Department of Marine and Aviation's idea for port expansion on the Hudson River – by simply getting rid of the port and using the space for upscale housing and the stock exchange. Then Nelson, in 1968, got the legislature to create the Battery Park City Authority to start paving over the river.

Not coincidentally, in arguing for Battery Park City in 1969, the Downtown Lower Manhattan Association used the same argument that the Commission uses today: CBD expansion was needed for "growth." There were 460,000 office workers downtown, explained David Rockefeller, and they were bursting at the seams. The city had to prepare for 5 percent a year growth in the white collar office corps.

Five percent! If David's prediction were on target we'd have 1.2 million office workers today just in the downtown CBD. Instead it is highly unlikely that today there are less than 400,000.[12] And the keystones of the DLMA's artificial growth strategy – Battery Park City and the World Trade Center – still receive $126.3 million and $101.1 million respectively in yearly tax abatements.[13]

"We're only following trends," says big FIRE. In the same way Roman generals used to say, "We're only following the cracks in sheep scapulae." Of course the generals had their favorite scapulomancers, just as the FIRE folk have their favorite planners.

What we have here are self-re-enforcing rhetorical strategies. First is the claim that the ends of action are dictated by the observation of trends. The second is the tacit denial that the actions taken by the planners have any effect. Both enable policy makers to avoid accountability. Either for choosing the goal of the plan. Or for evaluating whether or not the plan worked.

The rhetorical strategy of modern planning thus rests on complete self-concealment: the pretense that planning initiates nothing and is responsible for nothing. That planners merely follow trends and respond to forces. They have no particular ends that the rest of us don't share. And these ends are not the result of private interests, but precipitated out of the discovery of trends. Planners proclaim that they are just trying to promote jobs. And they present CBD expansion not as an end in itself but a means. How do we determine if planners are telling the truth about their real ends?

There are no knockdown tests. History isn't a science like genetic fingerprinting. But valid historical judgements are possible. Most would reject as imperial hypocrisy the various claims made to justify British expansionism: that the conquest of India was carried out to promote the welfare of the Indians; Joseph Chamberlain's argument that the Empire was maintained to promote the interests of British workers. Or the oft-repeated claim that "the British Empire was acquired in a fit of absent mindedness." British conquered large parts of Africa, India and America over the better part of three centuries because it had the power. And because British ruling classes directly benefited from conquest and exploitation. When these conditions no longer obtained the Empire dissolved.

If successive generations of urban policy makers promote a development strategy of which they are principal and direct beneficiaries; if the putative beneficiaries frequently resist the policy; if the nominal end is not promoted but damaged by the means, and yet it is still carried out – it is likely that the reasons are really rationalizations. The outcomes suggest that the means – CBD expansion – is really the end and that the rhetoric justifying it in terms of more jobs is discourse of deception, perhaps self-deception as well.

Before analyzing the actual ends of comprehensive planning and how it has shaped the city, let's look briefly at the other areas mentioned by the DCP: TriBeCa, Midtown South, Long Island City, Downtown Brooklyn. How did they wind up annexed to the imperial CBD?

*TriBeCa.* Was it "growth" that transformed TriBeCa – "the triangle below Canal Street" – into Robert Di Niro country? Just off Hudson Street, TriBeCa's main drag, you can find some of the city's premier expense account restaurants, like Bouley's, just a block from the old Washington Market and Chanterelle's located on the ground floor in the old Mercantile Exchange Building ( converted into an office building by Miele Rockefeller and now bankrupt). And by a mysterious process of urban magnetism, elite educational institutions pick up from other parts of the city and relocate there – like the new $300 million Stuyvesant High School, which used to be located on the lower east side.[14] But Hudson Street used be the urbanscape for Jane Jacobs' urban ballet of diverse industrial uses.[15] One of the city's prime "incubators of diversity," she called it. That was before the 1976 zoning change which stripped manufacturing of its protection. And before urban renewal: the flattening of the ten square block Washington Market. This clearance, called for by the 1958 DLMA was actually a "two fer": since the plans for bulldozing the produce market involved shifting it to Hunt's Point where the planners wrecked "Little Pittsburgh" just as the steel makers there feared.

*Downtown Brooklyn.* The implantation of office buildings in Downtown Brooklyn was no more market driven than the planning process which created Battery Park City and TriBeCa. It was also state-led, required massive subsidies, and the use of eminent domain, i.e., force. As Dinkins' own Public Development Corporation, (now the Economic

Development Corporation) says, "Downtown Brooklyn stands as a stunning example of how commercial areas throughout the city can be reborn or expanded through *planned development*"[16] (emphasis added).

Pierrepont Plaza, outerborough home to Morgan Stanley and Goldman Sachs and Metrotech, back office center for the Chase Manhattan Bank, were co-developed by Public Development Corporation (PDC) and Forest City Enterprises. "To help Morgan Stanley meet its very tight relocation timetable PDC structured the projects business terms and steered it through the public approval process in just three months' time;" PDC brags that it "also helped Morgan take advantage of a set of attractive city-sponsored financial incentives."[17]

But PDC takes too much credit for real estate projects that have been incubating for thirty years. Alair Townsend, former Deputy Mayor for Economic Development who confesses her eyes get misty when she sees these downtown office buildings growing in Brooklyn, gets closer to the truth when she credits "the dreamers" – the men of Regional Plan Association (RPA) and Howie Golden, the Brooklyn Borough President – for annexation of Brooklyn to the Manhattan CBD.[18]

But even before the RPA's Second Regional Plan which put downtown Brooklyn on the planners' map, there were the true pioneers of the fifties. It's comparatively easy to give away city money to tenants and developers and get the Board of Estimate to go along. The hard part was getting rid of the factories and working-class residences that were there in the first place.

One scholar of the city's urban renewal program estimates that in the ten years after World War II, 259 industrial and commercial structures along with about 8,200 jobs were bulldozed in the effort to create the Brooklyn Civic Center.[19] Aside from the prominence of the Brooklyn Dems, led by the appropriately named John Cashmore, and Robert Blum of Abraham & Strauss, most of those involved in what amounted to the creation of the Brooklyn CBD were familiar post-war players from the Manhattan CBD wars – Robert Moses, William Zeckendorf Sr., Corp. Counsel John P. McGrath. By getting on the board of the then somnolent Long Island University, and energizing Brooklyn Hospital's Board including slum land owner Nathan Straus[20] and General Electric's Gerard Swope, Zeckendorf and other developers used these institutions to purchase property contiguous to their own and turn them into sponsors for urban renewal, clearing out contiguous neighborhoods like Ft. Greene.[21]

The godfathers of the Brooklyn CBD faced two problems: land and capital. The land on which the new CBD was to be located was already occupied by factories, like the American Safety Razor Co., with 1,500 workers – presently the site of Metrotech. Working-class residences permeated the area. But through the liberal use of eminent domain, they were able to solve both problems. By taking a wide enough swath, Zeckendorf et al. convinced a consortium of financial institutions, including the Bowery, that the area could be made safe for upper-middle-class residences. And long-term mortgages. A Civic Center coordinating committee headed by City Planning Commission consultant Gilmore D. Clarke agreed to quick and extensive clearances. The legal challenges of the Ft. Greene manufacturers were easily disposed of. And the workers in the American Safety Razor (ASR) plant who tried sit-ins and violence to stop the dismantling of their factory were restrained by Brooklyn's finest. Eventually, University Towers got developed by Donald Trump's dad, Fred. The Rockefeller-funded United Neighborhood Housing Foundation took a chunk; the Bowery financed and took a piece of the action at Concord Towers; Long Island University's Title I expansion alone knocked out 20 acres of factories.[22] But it took two decades before the path for the SOB is really safe.[23]

*Midtown South.* Until just a few years ago, a traveller to Penn Station going up Sixth Avenue would find a startling oasis of flowers, ficus trees, and palms lining both sides of the street for blocks. This green patch, the residuum of a once-thriving flower market continues to shrink each year, a victim of what City Planning Commission (CPC) calls "growth." But while the conversion specialists and developers didn't have to advance behind police truncheons and Robert Moses' bulldozers, the case for spontaneous expansion of offices into "Midtown South" isn't very strong either.

A map on page 40 of Ed Koch's Year 2000 Plan, *New York Ascendent*, just after the text, recommends that we "expand the central Business District" – the Manhattan CBD itself is shown with three light green extensions. One is Downtown Brooklyn, another is Long Island City and the third is "The Valley", i.e., Midtown South: the area from 23th to 34th Street, from Sixth avenue to Ninth avenue.

As far back as the Second Regional Plan, Midtown South has been targeted for redevelopment.[24] But it's just been since the early eighties that the area, still densely packed with 40,000 industrial jobs,[25] has been sharply on the defensive. First the CPC re-zoned Sixth Avenue from

23rd to 31st Street to allow commercial and residential conversions and provided conversion incentives by creating the maximum FAR ratio – total floor area in relation land – to plus bonuses. Then, in 1982, the CPC created the Special Midtown Zoning District.

Effectively speaking, this planning device shut down east-side office development in order to encourage construction on the west side. Naturally rents rose on the east side. As leases expired, second tier publishers, lawyers, advertisers moved into Midtown South.

All this was not an unintended consequence of the midtown plan.[26] In 1985, the CPC wrote, "some of the flower market and plant wholesalers who do not own their own buildings may have to relocate." In fact they were supposed to relocate. The CPC had a program in place to put garment manufacturers and flower district wholesalers in the outer boroughs. Obviously they didn't want to go. Garment manufactures wanted to be close to the garment center. Flower merchants wanted to be where pedestrian traffic was high. How many people take a stroll out to College Point? By 1993, flower market operators still resisting a move to a reservation in College Point. And the Department of City Planning (DCP), which plays the role of the Bureau of Indian Affairs in these matters, had taken to calling the flower market a "flea market".[27]

*Long Island City.* The Bureau of Indian Affairs model also explains much of the development of Long Island City. As late as 1984, Long Island City, the part of Queens you can see from midtown just over the East River, still had nearly 50,000 industrial jobs – 44 percent of Queens total.[28] What the ordinary Manhattanite can see, however, is just what developers see, plus the opportunity for enrichment: more than 1,000 acres where land values are a fraction of what they are in Midtown, and just one subway stop away.

Manufacturers driven out of SoHo and NoHo by the DCP's J-51 policy of subsidizing factory conversion to luxury residences, began to migrate in the 1970s, moving east into the outer boroughs, just as the Indians continually moved west across the plains. What factory owners found in Long Island City was an area almost ideal for manufacturing. Indeed, during the debates over what land use should prevail, no one ever charged that Long Island City wasn't a thriving industrial area with low vacancy rates.[29] The Long Island Railroad Sunnyside Yards ran through the area. Water borne freight shipments, while not as important as thirty years ago, were still an option. And the buildings themselves were attractive. It's often argued that New York can't retain industry because it lacks the single-story buildings with large floor plates available in the suburbs. This is exactly the type of buildings and the kind of configuration available in Long Island City. Six subway lines converged there. Why not let it alone?

Because, as the DCP pointed out, it had "spectacular views of the Manhattan skyline."[30] Given the location, one stop from the midtown CBD, manufacturing could no more be left alone in Long Island City than the plains Indians after the discovery of gold in the black hills could be left alone in south Dakota.

In 1971 Citibank proposed to remove zoning protection from the Long Island City coast – Hunters' Point – and transform it into something called "City View." Nothing came of the plan. It was rejected by the CPC. But the World Trade Center wasn't built in a day either. As real estate interest picked up again in the late seventies, a series of zoning initiatives pushed back the industrial frontier. The DCP changed the waterfront zoning from heavy manufacturing to light. It created a special waterfront district. Zoning changes allowed Lazard Realty's conversion of the American Chicle and the Bucilla Needle Work Company Building in Long Island City into the (now bankrupt) International Design Center which meant the loss of about 1,000,000 square feet of manufacturing space.[31] Another zoning change allowed Lazard to add one million more square feet.

Citibank, reeling from its bad real estate loans, forced to sell off its signature midtown headquarters to the Japanese, shifted to its LIC property to build a new tower. To speed development, Urban Development Corporation (UDC), PDC and the Port Authority were brought in: UDC to over-ride zoning laws; Port Authority to float bond issues that don't have to be approved by the voters for infrastructure; PDC to "help Citicorp take advantage of an array of city-sponsored financial incentives."[32]

The whole state-led de-industrial movement culminated in 1991 with the announcement of Governor Cuomo's plan – the centerpiece of his economic revitalization strategy for the city – a $2.3 billion waterfront project in Long Island City, with 6,000 apartments, 2 million square feet of office space.[33] To give unity to the different agencies' efforts, Cuomo created something called Queens West which would operate as a subsidiary of Urban Development Corporation (UDC) but be headed by someone from the CPC, which would still allow participation by the EDC and Port Authority. These, in turn, would smooth the way for The Trotwood Corp. – a private investment vehicle owned by William Zeckendorf, Jr. and the Dreyfus Corp. Former CPC chief Herb Sturz is nominal head of Trotwood, enabling him to appropriate in private life in the nineties the plans he developed in the eighties in the public sector.

Essentially, over the last three generations, the city has had a real estate strategy – expand the CBD/shrink manufacturing – which it has presented as a jobs strategy. This is what makes the whole insistence on purely objective factors so particularly hypocritical. It's not as if the heads of the CPC haven't made careers out of the real estate-driven planning process they've designed.

Herb Sturz gnawing away at LIC for the Dreyfus interests is no isolated phenomenon. It's the old in and out. James Felt, a land package assembler and urban remover who worked for Metropolitan Life at Stuyvesant Town and David Rockefeller at Morningside Heights, Inc.; Don Elliott, Lindsay's CPC chief who took up a real estate law practice at Webster and Sheffield; John Zucotti, head of City Planning under Beame, who moved from Brown & Wood to chief of Olympia & York, the city's largest taxpayer, and head of DLMA until the Olympia & York bankruptcy required his exclusive efforts; Victor Marrero who suc-ceeded Zucotti and also wound up at Brown & Wood.

Let me try to clarify and narrow the argument. To highlight the existence of a FIRE-oriented planning elite is not to assert that this elite is seamless or all-powerful. Or that its aims can be understood in terms of a "growth coalition." It's not a matter of simply inverting planners' claim that they are simply *responding* to growth by asserting that the planners create growth.

"Growth" is not the aim of large-scale urban planning. What's really at stake is making certain parcels of land worth more, which is something very different. The value of my parcel depends entirely on what you are able to do with your parcel.

Why is Leonard Stern, the Prince of Petfood and the owner of the *Village Voice*, considered a bad boy in *haute* planning circles? Because he also owns great chunks of the Meadowlands and persisted in developing his property with offices when the RPA called in both the First and Second Regional Plans for leaving it as marshlands and factory space. The growth of the Meadowlands as an office space makes it that much harder to develop the Manhattan CBD just across the Hudson.

Call it the principle of "disjunctive planning." Either/or. To develop the west side, the DCP had to shut down the east side. East-side owners protested. But the Rockefellers, Citibank, the Equitable et al., as well as the private foundations Rockefeller Brothers Fund, and Ford, all supported the west side shift. The promotion of the World Trade Center by the Downtown Lower Manhattan Association brought howls from midtown owners like Larry Wein and Harry Helmsley.

In another example of the disjunctive principle, David Walentas sought to transform Fulton Landing – the Brooklyn manufacturing area between the two bridges – into office buildings at the same time the RPA was trying to attract tenants and get infrastructural support for Downtown Brooklyn just a few blocks away. Walentas made the right moves and said the right things. "Manufacturing is a dying industry," he proclaimed in press conferences in front of his factory buildings as he prepared to rid the area of 4,000 mainly black and Puerto Rican workers. "The unions made it too expensive for them. The real issue is economic development." Former CPC chief John Zucotti, Brooklyn boss Andrew Fisher, PR wizard Hank Sheinkopf were all pressed into service. But the CPC insisted that Walentas hold off for 15 years.[34]

To assert that the principle of disjunctive development is fundamental to urban planning helps to define its nature. *Urban planning is the coordination of land monopoly.* It is to the higher real estate interests what the Judge Gary dinners were to steel manufacturers. Both steel makers and FIRE folk seek to maximize their return on investment. Not to achieve growth in steel production or office building production per se.

A land monopoly? True, one individual doesn't own all the land in New York anymore than Judge Gary or J.P. Morgan owned all the steel. Call it oligopoly, if you will – competition among the few. Olympia & York owns 8 percent of the city's office space. And half a dozen control interests own about one-third of the office space in the CBD. The concentration ratio is more substantial if just Class A office space is considered.

The SOB oligopoly operates like any producers facing imperfect competition. Unlike small producers whose supply can't affect the price, the big guys can co-ordinate their output to match supply with demand. When demand is slack, they try to ensure that supply doesn't get out of hand by restrictive zoning, floor area ratios, greenbelts, landbanking, ULURPing, etc.[35] When demand picks up, the same oligopolistic interests may seek to vastly expand production – especially by introducing a new expansionary plan. But production itself – "growth" – is never their the goal.[36]

Urban oligopolists differ from steel makers in that, while the latter try to fix prices and keep the state out of their business, the SOB people must bring the state in. Without the government laying down new transit, transportation, utility infrastructure, no big increase in supply is possible. Without the use of eminent domain, developers can't get rid of those standing in the way of expansion. Without zoning, planning, etc., it's impossible to stop competitors from developing their property and increasing supply.

The existence of comprehensive planning on behalf of FIRE's oligopolistic goals, however, doesn't mean that there's an omnipotent FIRE elite that always gets its way. There has never been more than sporadic resistance to comprehensive planning. Since black and Puerto Rican activists disrupted the RPA's fortieth anniversary in 1969. But there have been notable examples of successful neighborhood resistance to planning. In the late fifties, Jane Jacobs led the movement against the renewal of Greenwich Village.[37] In the seventies, Marcy Benstock led a coalition of ecologists and neighborhood activists in a stunning defeat of Westway, backed by a united FIRE phalanx.

Nor is it the case that the topmost elites always agree among themselves. The play of real estate interests, fiscal stringency, the turn of the business cycle, often means that plans have to be altered or scrapped. Much of New York's CBD development has been dictated by resistance from New Jersey, or efforts to compromise with New Jersey real estate interests. Nelson Rockefeller succeeded in getting the city to build a Sixth Avenue IND, but he failed in the effort to get the city to build a subway from Rockefeller Center to New Jersey. Battery Park City, the great landfill project on the Hudson River got built, but David Rockefeller's landfill plan for Manhattan Landing in the East River is still on paper. The initial plans for the World Trade Center called for it to be sited next to the Chase Manhattan Bank – on the East River, not on the Hudson River side where it is presently located.

Such deviations and setbacks notwithstanding, the city's development process – the struggle to expand the CBD and shrink manufacturing – is totally unintelligible unless you realize what the FIRE elites are consistently aiming at. In the early eighties, Westway sinks under the blows of the ecologists. But it rises a decade later as the "Hudson River Conservancy."

*Conclusion.* Until recently, the DCP has presented itself as the Janus of New York's household gods. Looking backward to preserve the old order while at the same time looking forward to promote the new post-industrial age. It is always the honest broker. In the battles over Loft zoning, Lower Sixth avenue, Union Square, the Midtown Garment Center, the Convention Center, Chinatown, Clinton, Midtown planning, Fulton Landing, Hunters' Point, City Planning presents whatever it does as the golden mean between preservation and modernization.

Now, with its seven volume apologia for an explicit course of de-industrialization, the DCP doesn't say, "We tried to save jobs but the objective forces were just too great." Or "Our predecessors were wrong to have wasted all that effort." It simply argues as if none of its interventions had ever happened.

Indeed, de-industrialization doesn't seem like a public policy, because no one ever announces it as such. No one ever says simply, "We're going to get rid of those goddamn factories!" Even now, the DCP argues that it is simply compelled by objective forces to withdraw protection from land uses incompatible with the expansion of the "export industries." What we appear to have is a series of piecemeal changes, that deal with this or that neighborhood. Or even if the changes are more comprehensive, like 1961 zoning or the zoning changes suggested by the 1993 DCP studies, they are not presented as efforts to reduce the amount of manufacturing in the city; rather they are offered as responses to a changed situation in which manufacturing is no longer needed.

But there's a big difference between New York's de-industrialization and the manufacturing job loss that took place in cities like Detroit, Gary, Akron. These manufacturing-belt cities didn't lose them in the course of pursuing an explicit strategy of maximizing FIRE jobs. Nor did the Mayors of those cities – like Koch and Dinkins – commit themselves implicitly to the elimination of manufacturing. (That is what the primacy of waterfront development entails – the waterfront being the prime location of the city's remaining industry.) For the last three generations, New York City has had such a strategy. But while the strategies generally wind up at 22 Reade Street, they don't begin there.

What happens here is not a simple response to market forces. It is social action. As Weber points out, two bicyclists colliding can be understood in terms of physics. On the other hand, their effort to avoid each other; the blows, insults, excuses and understandings they may exchange as a result of the collision have to be understood in terms of social action.

The understandings and collisions of planners – with each other and the rest of us – can't be understood unless you grasp what it is they're actively aiming at. Thus to fully explain New York's planning process requires both that we understand its objective impact on the city – and also the subjective dimension: what the planners are aiming at when they plan.

# NOTES

1. Regional Plan Association, "What Has Regional Plan Accomplished," n.d., pp. 9–13, Rockefeller Archive Center, Box 92, Folder 13.
2. DCP/NYC, "New Opportunities for a Changing Economy," Summary Report of the Citywide Industry Study, January 1993, p. 9.
3. Department of City Planning/New York City, Citywide Industry Study, Industry Trends Technical Report, January 1993, pp. xii–xiii.
4. Ibid., p. xiii.
5. Robert Lichtenberg, *One Tenth of A Nation*, (Cambridge, MA, 1960) p. 73, chart 3.
6. Good New York City cost-of-living data aren't available. But substantial evidence suggests New York City's costs are among the highest, if not the highest. The New York, NJ, Connecticut area outpaces all others in cost *increases* (U.S. Department of Labor, Middle Atlantic Regional Office, May 13, 1993). For data suggesting New York among the highest in absolute terms, see Stephen Kagann, "Vital Signs," *City Journal*, Spring, 1993, p. 16. Kagann cites a study by 286 U.S. cities conducted by the American Chamber of Commerce Research Associates. The study shows that the city's cost of living is twice the national average. A limitation of the study is that it measures living costs for city dwellers in middle management jobs. So the average rent for a two-bedroom apartment is pegged at $1,935 per month. Kagann's claim that these high costs are caused by high taxes strains credulity and he provides no evidence.
7. In New York the commuter tax is set at 0.0045%. Whereas the top resident rate is 4.46% (*Message of the Mayor*, 27 April 1993, p. 56). Meanwhile, in Philadelphia, they think their system is unfair because residents pay 4.96% and commuters pay 4.31%.(See Carolyn Adams, et al., *Philadelphia* (Philadelphia: Temple University Press, 1991), p. 160.
8. Downtown Lower Manhattan Association, 3d report, 1969, p. 10.
9. DCP/NYC, "New Opportunities for a Changing Economy," January 1993.
10. As in chapter 5, where we saw how the DCP ignored its own previous studies showing how manufacturing job loss hurt blacks and Latinos.
11. New York City Planning Commission, "Shaping the City's Future," Spring 1993, pp. 21–22. Or why it would recommend expansion as its principal goal when the very next goal is to find a new use for the office buildings that have already been built. The Commission's other four recommendations for economic development all involve promotion of office districts: Re-use and Retrofit Existing Buildings in the Central Business District; Upgrade the Public Environment of the Central Business District; Improve Central Business District Accessibility; Support Export Industry Growth Outside the Central Business District, (pp.21–26).

12. I interviewed the executive director of the DLMA in 1988. I asked him then, when the figure would have been more impressive then it is today, how many workers there were below Chambers Street. He said he didn't know and didn't know how to find out. The highest estimate of downtown space would be about 100 million square feet. Of this an estimated 28% is vacant. At 200 square feet per worker, this would be well under 400,000.

13. Message of the Mayor, April 27, 1992, p. 84.

14. Actually a block north of the "border" at 15th Street and First Avenue.

15. Jane Jacobs, *The Death and Life of Great American Cities* (New York; Vintage, 1961), pp. 166–167.

16. New York City Public Development Corporation, Arthur Levitt, chairman (brochure), n.d., p. 6.

17. Ibid., p. 5.

18. Alair A. Townsend, "Brooklyn Downtown Rebirth More Than Field of Dreams," *Crain's New York Business*, December 7, 1992, p. 11.

19. Joel Schwartz, *The New York Approach* (Columbus, Ohio: Ohio State University, 1993), p. 238.

20. In 1934, when Moses was running for Governor as a Democrat he attacked Straus for selling land he owned to the State Housing Board which he headed: "If Senator Straus made no claim to be anything more than a very slick trader . . . I should have a good deal more respect for him. When, however he pretends to be a philanthropist, civic champion and uplifter, it becomes a little disgusting." Caro *defends* Straus on the grounds that the price was low and Straus' motives were high. See Robert Caro, *The Powerbroker* (New York: Vintage Books, 1975), p. 417.

21. Ibid., ch. 9.

22. Joel Schwartz, *The New York Approach* (Columbus, Ohio: Ohio University Press, 1993), p. 244.

23. Ibid. pp. 239–246.

24. Regional Plan Association, *Urban Design Manhattan* (New York: Viking Press, 1969), p. 11. See also New York City Planning Commission, "Plan for New York City, 1969. A proposal," vol. 1, Critical Issues, p. 31.

25. Department of City Planning/New York City, Citywide Industry Study, Geographic Atlas of Industrial Areas, Part Two – Study Area Profiles, January, 1993, p. 180.

26. Citywide Industry Study, p. 181.

27. See below.

28. New York City Department of City Planning, Hunters Point, "Recommendations for a Land Use Policy," March 1984, NYC DCP 84–06, table 2, p. 78.

29. Department of City Planning/City of New York, Plans, Programs and Policies, 1980–1985, pp. 26–29.

30. Ibid., p. 26.

31. Hunters Point, "Recommendations for a Land Use Policy," March 1984, NYC DCP 84–06, p. 34.

32. New York City Public Development Corporation, "Promoting business expansion and job growth in New York City through commercial, industrial and waterfront development," n.d. 1990(?), p. 4.

33. See *Newsday*, September 25, 1991. Cuomo also called for the completion of the Second Avenue subway – delayed since the late 1920s.

34. Michael Henry Powell, "Brooklyn's Great Fulton Landing Debate," *City Limits*, November 1983, pp. 7–10.

35. See Rockefeller Brothers Task Force, "The Use of Land." William K. Reilly (ed) (New York: Thomas Y. Crowell Company, 1973).

36. Bill Domhoff and Harvey Mololtch are both gifted observers of urban politics. I disagree with their claim, however, that politics of urban development can be understood in terms of a "growth co-alition." They aren't simply wrong. But they have over-generalized from observations of small operators in the suburbs, or small university town developers, who face a different demand curve. Little guys always object to "planning" (i.e., oligopoly).

37. It was precisely to counter Jane Jacobs community organizing in Cobble Hill that Pratt Institute successfully appealed to the Rockefeller Brothers' Fund to finance a pro-urban renewal community movement in Central Brooklyn. Pratt assisted movements against factory expansion on the part of S&S Corrugated Box; for the de-industrializing of Fulton Ferry area; and argued for the elimination of Brooklyn's Piers 1–6 as working piers. But unless the nature of the plan is understood, neither the resistance nor the counter-resistance is intelligible.

# CHAPTER 3

# "A SENSE OF ORDER": THE FIRST REGIONAL PLAN

The release of New York's First Regional Plan in the late spring of 1929, only months before the October Crash, appears on the face of it as an unfortunate case of bad timing. Just as the city's economy was poised to shrink by a third, New York's planners grandly proclaimed the need for real estate to spread out across the region. Who could have imagined?

A year before the Crash, as the long negotiations dragged on between John D. Rockefeller's real estate advisors and Columbia University over the leasehold of its giant midtown estate, the *Real Estate Record* described a boom so frenzied that by the time an office building got built, it was time think about tearing it down and building a bigger one. "Comparatively new buildings being discarded." the *Record* headlined. These buildings were structurally sound, they were built only a few years ago. Since then, however, the market had soared to such heights that they had to be torn down "to assure an adequate return on land values." If a building were more than a decade old, it stood in the way of progress. "No twenty-five year old building on lower Broadway adds anything to the value of the land."[1] No wonder, John D. Rockefeller Jr. felt fortunate to be finally able to lease six square blocks of land for $3.6 million yearly

"Overbuilding of Offices is Impossible." headlined the *Real Estate Record*, the city's authoritative real estate journal, just a few months after the collapse. It was true that the *older* buildings would have a problem. "But this situation does not call for the lessening of building activity," one expert observed. A developer "must only bear in mind that his new building must be so much better than its neighbors that it will create its own demand."[2]

Real estate boosters insisted the crash posed no problem for Manhattan real estate investors. The difficulties were all confined to the stock market. Charles F. Noyes, the renowned real estate broker, bravely maintained that "New York City real estate is giving a glorious account of itself during a period when happenings in Wall Street have shaken confidence in our security and caused paper losses or real losses." It turned out that the events of November were actually a blessing in disguise.

Why? Because now we can get back to work, real work. No more easy money. All the idle money can now go into sound investments: such as real estate mortgages – safe, conservative 5 percent to 6 percent, well-located parcels of real estate growing more valuable, if properly selected, with the birth of every child.[3]

No one should worry about too much space. There was not enough. "The U.S. is far from overbuilt," explained the *Record*. "New building construction during the past three years has not kept pace with the growth of population. The population of the United States is increasing at a rate of more than 1.5 million persons per year. This means housing accommodations annually for that number of persons and, in addition, business accommodations and public institutions to care for their needs."[4]

Between 1921 and 1929 developers had added 30 million square feet of office space to the Manhattan inventory – an amount and a rate of increase that approaches the eighties office boom. But commercial real estate men didn't believe the depression applied to them. Living in their own version of *Fantasia*, they behaved like the Sorcerer's Apprentice. Instead of helping Mickey to bail out the overflow, they kept increasing the flood of overcapacity. Between 1929 and 1937, 30 million more square feet piled up. Nearly a quarter of the post-1929 office space was added by John D. Rockefeller who found he couldn't sublease his ground lease to builders and was stuck with the $3.6 million yearly payments for money-losing tenements if he didn't replace them with offices himself.

In 1929, office vacancies had ranged from 0 to 5 percent, depending on the neighborhood. But in 1930 alone, however, developers erected 17 major office buildings – with over 7 million square feet. And the year 1931 matched 1930: including the Empire State Building, five others uptown and 11 downtown. The momentum barely flagged in 1932 which saw the erection of Bankers Trust and the Cities Service Buildings. And in 1933, the first installment of Rockefeller Center rose – 4 million square feet. By 1933, vacancy rates exceeded 30 percent throughout the city – a rate that wouldn't be approached again until recently, and then only downtown. Real estate wars broke out between the Rockefellers and the Du Pont's over the dwindling supply of tenants. The Du Pont's hired Al Smith to pull in new tenants, while John D. Rockefeller Jr. passed over Johnny, his eldest, putting son Nelson in charge of the Rockefeller Center sales battalions. It was Rockefellers vs. Du Pont's, each using whatever corporate leverage they could to dragoon tenants into their buildings.

The 1929 Plan, rather than containing any measures which would have mitigated the output of unneeded office space, has to be understood as a direct expression of blind market forces. Consider the timing of the plan – indeed the timing of all the major New York City plans. Strikingly, each has come out a season or so before a major crash: the May 1929 Plan. The Lindsay Plan, based on the November 1968 Second Regional Plan, came out just as the market collapsed in 1969. And Ed Koch's *New York Ascendent* appeared in June 1987, again, just months before the 500 point downturn signalled the end of the eighties boom.

The consistently inappropriate timing of the plans – which presumes a need for more space just when investment ought to be checked – can be explained in simple business cycle terms. At the peak of the boom, the existence of the business cycle itself is pooh-poohed by academics in learned articles and tacitly by bankers with their safe, sound, "no-brainer" mortgages. A Depression? Irving Fisher insisted in 1929 that America had arrived at "a permanent plateau of prosperity." Milton Friedman paraphrased him just before the downturn of the sixties.

High optimism and low credulity both spring from a conjuncture in which real estate is awash with capital, the newspapers are full of ads, the wealthy are endowing new chairs for economics professors and the stock market is creating overnight wealth. The stock market and particularly New York real estate receive growing amounts of capital from the rest of the country that can't be invested in normal channels because consumer power has tapped out. (U.S. auto production peaked in 1926.) At the end of the cycle, manufacturing profits are still being earned, but there's no need for new investment in auto factories. So the uninvestable surplus gets diverted into "adventurous channels" like the stock market and real estate speculation. Downtown developers become especially ebullient, because Wall Street is hiring more brokers to sell more stocks. Not only is there a big supply of surplus capital, but plenty of apparent demand for office space. So real estate feels the need to spread out. It is hemmed in though, by the existing transportation, utility, infrastructures. A new structure is needed to create outlets for the uninvestable surplus capital that has built up from the clogging of the pores of normal capital accumulation.

So it's no wonder that, in 1928, the leading beneficiaries of America's old auto–petro complex – Walter P. Chrysler, John D. Rockefeller II, and the Du Pont's, the leading share holders in G.M. with a quarter of the stock – are each planning speculative gigantic office buildings in New York City within a few blocks of each other. Nor is it a co-incidence that at the same time, New York's FIRE industries feel the need for an expansionary plan.

Essentially, the RPA proposed a government-financed highway, bridge and tunnel network unprecedented in size and expense to "decentralize" the region. The men of the RPA, the great decentralizers, included early plan proponent Charles Norton of First National Bank, who died in 1923; Long Island land baron and philanthropist Robert De Forest, director of the Jersey Central; Dwight Morrow of the Morgan Bank, director of the New York Central and the reorganizer of the IRT; George McAneny, the former chief lobbyist of the Pennsylvania Railroad; and Frederick Delano, FDR's uncle, director of half a dozen railroads, who resigned from the presidency of one of them to take the chairmanship of the RPA.

Together, they devised the architecture of decentralization: three giant circumferential arteries around the city – a total of 630 miles in length. The inner circle, or "metropolitan loop", built at a radius of 14 miles from City Hall would run 114 miles. And the city – which is made up of three islands plus the Bronx – would be spanned by five crossings. Three of them the RPA conceived itself: the Bronx–Whitestone, Triborough and Lincoln Tunnel. In other words, just about every highway and bridge credited to Robert Moses was conceived and planned by the RPA. Moses simply poured the concrete on the dotted lines indicated in the plan.

What was so important about "decentralization" that it required millions of tons of concrete to be poured all over the regional landscape? Actually, the RPA was touchy about the word. In a 1926 memo written on the plan's "Basic General Assumptions", it was suggested that directors "avoid use of 'centralization and decentralization.' Use terms like 'better balance,' 'distribution of building,' 'less friction of space.'"[5]

Apparently, "decentralization" had something of the odor of

"planned shrinkage" today. Chief economist Robert Haig explained that "when city planners speak of decentralization, they usually have prominently in mind the decentralization of factories. Manufacturing seems to many of them one thing which certainly does not 'belong' in the center of the metropolis."[6] Haig certainly agreed with his colleagues.

Some of the poorest people live in conveniently located slums on high-priced land. On patrician Fifth Avenue, Tiffany and Woolworth, cheek by jowl, offer jewels and jimcracks from substantially identical sites. Childs restaurants thrive and multiply where Delmonico's withered and died. A stone's throw from the stock exchange the air is filled with the aroma of roasting coffee; a few hundred feet from Times Square with the stench of slaughter houses. In the very heart of this "commercial" city, on Manhattan Island south of 59th street, the inspectors in 1922 found nearly 420,000 workers employed in factories. Such a situation outrages one's sense of order. Everything seems misplaced. One yearns to rearrange things to put things where they belong."[7]

Decentralization meant putting people – i.e. "things" – where they belonged. But who exactly would put whom where? By what means and using what criterion? Unquestionably, the men of the RPA would do the putting. Who were they? Essentially bankers, railroad men, foundation executives, very large property owners and developers, plus the various specialists in housing, planning, zoning, and landscape architecture who were employed to do the actual work in what was sometimes called "the movement". They had the social cohesiveness of a Millsian elite. And the shared economic focus of a Marxist class.

The world of New York City urban political reform in the 1920s was unvexed by problems of intellectual, ethnic, institutional diversity. There was essentially one foundation – Russell Sage – to which urban activists applied for money. The Rockefeller and Carnegie Foundations had bigger endowments, but the Russell Sage Foundation had an urban focus whereas the other, larger foundations concentrated on national and international issues, peace, science and health.

Similarly, there was one ethnic group – Anglo-Saxon Protestants. Jewish developers and financiers who founded the Bank of the United States – the Tishmans, the Rudins, the Ravitches – were very much involved in Manhattan CBD development, converting not just factories but synagogues to office buildings.[8] But in a city polarized by ethnic rivalry as well as class antagonism, these Jewish bankers and real estate men were not seen as plausible partners for the task. The Morgans, who tried to have their German Jewish rivals incarcerated after World War I, weren't the only passionate anti-Semites in New York City.[9]

Even the leading charitable foundation in the city, Russell Sage, systematically excluded Jews from its model housing programs. Forest Hills Gardens, built in mid-Queens just before World War I by Russell Sage Realty permitted no "Hebrews" whatever in its quaint English-style homes. Russell Sage's directors advertised as much, noting that

there will be no discrimination whatever against or in favor of any race or religion except insofar as may of necessity be involved in considerations vitally affecting the success of the development, the value of the experiment, and the interests of the greater number of persons likely to reside there.[10]

One of the few exceptions to the exclusion of Jews from "the movement" was Jacob Schiff who, as managing partner of Kuhn Loeb, a substantial rival to Morgan, as well as its co-manager on some bond syndicates, sat as banker to the Pennsylvania Railroad; and who also occupied what appears to have been the "Jewish seat" on the Board of the Charity Organization Society. Schiff financed Lillian Wald's work at Henry Street on the lower east side. But he also invented something called the "Galveston Plan" for the elimination of lower east side poverty – it consisted in sending poor immigrant Jews to Galveston, Texas. A Jew like Schiff, the Protestant charitable interests could work with.

The Protestant philanthropists read one social philosopher, William Graham Sumner, the social Darwinist whose ideas permeated twenties urbanism through the widely read work of the Chicago School of urban ecologists.[11] The Chicagoans, Robert Park and Ernest Burgess, believed that the city expressed true human nature – a pitiless struggle between in-groups and out-groups over territory. The men of the RPA agreed perfectly, citing the authority of the Chicago School. While the professors of the Chicago School cited the authority of Sumner:

The insiders in we-groups are in a relation of peace, order, law and government and industry to each other. Their relation to all outsiders, or others-groups, is one of war and plunder, except as far as agreements have modified it. The relations of comradeship and peace in the we-group and that of hostility and war towards other groups are correlative to each other. The exigencies of war with outsiders are what make peace inside, lest internal discord should weaken the we-group for war. These exigencies also make government and law in the in-group, in order to prevent quarrels and enforce discipline.[12]

The lines of intellectual and confessional influence among this highly self-conscious "we-group" all seemed to intersect at one point – Yale University – the University which served uniquely as the incubator of the higher New York philanthropoids.

Robert De Forest and several others who served on the Board of New York City's Charity Organization Society – including its chairman Otto S. Bannard of New York Life – as well as many directors of the Regional Plan Association all seemed to have attended Yale. De Forest and Bannard actually took classes with William Graham Sumner. The prophet of social Darwinism remained American favorite philosopher in business circles until the Great Depression. When Yale-man Morgan Partner and Regional Plan director Dwight Morrow wanted to give a fellow Yale-man an impressive gift he presented him with a leather-bound volume of one of Sumner's books. "I've already read them," said Calvin Coolidge.[13]

In a far less specialized world, the paladins of "good government," charity administration, tenement reform, population decongestion, and zoning seemed to go from one meeting to the next. Their worlds intersected like circles in a Venn diagram. No matter what weighty reform was on the table, the same mix of very rich real estate and financial people and non-rich professional activists tied to them by salaries and recommendations kept turning up around the table.

Lawrence Veiller, the tenement house reformer; Edward Bassett, the "father of zoning," Frederick Lewis Olmstead Jr., the landscape architect, Lawrence Purdy, the tax expert were the ancestors of today's professionals who go back and forth from think tanks to governmental agencies. They turned out position papers, ghosted books and speeches for busy lawyers, bankers and real estate developers. Veiller, for example, wrote the classic "Tenement House Problem" with future Russell Sage Foundation chief Robert De Forest, the godfather of New York urban reform. It was Veiller who seems to have been the actual author of New York City's first zoning law passed in 1911.[14] He was chief executive of the City Club. He also recommended cheap lots for De Forest's brother Johnston to purchase.[15] Veiller had to move into the background of philanthropy however when his employment by Allied Real Estate interests, the slum property owners, came under fire while he was working for election of progressive gubernatorial candidate Charles Evans Hughes.[16]

Of the non-barons, George McAneny was probably the most well known to New Yorkers. He had been a Manhattan Borough President, head of the Board of Estimate. And before that chief lobbyist for Pennsylvania Railroad, in the days when the Pennsylvania and the New York Central were the two most potent factors in city politics. Historically in the U.S., railroads interests were mixed up with property development and nowhere was this more true than in New York City where the railroad financiers also controlled the elevated and subway lines. Actually, throughout the 1920s and 1930s, the Rockefellers controlled the elevateds.[17] And railroad terminals created central business districts.

Whereas the Morgan–Vanderbilt interests controlled substantial property in the Bronx and west side Manhattan, all the way down to the Battery, the Pennsylvania controlled the Long Island Railroad (LIRR) which in turned owned land along the route of the road, as well as much real estate in Long Island and Queens. And each of the two rail giants owned midtown property around its terminal – Penn Station and Grand Central. In fact, it was the creation of the midtown terminals, especially the first of the two, New York Central's Grand Central, which established midtown over downtown as the premier corporate and financial location.

The same interests that ran the railroads created the New York subway system. The Morgan–Vanderbilt New York Central rail interests faded into the Morgan–Belmont Interborough Rapid Transit Co. (IRT) – at one time the second largest corporation in the U.S. – after U.S. Steel. The Brooklyn Rapid Transit Co. (BRT) overlapped with the Pennsylvania.[18] Jacob Schiff served as investment banker for both lines.

To have been the chief lobbyist of the Pennsylvania, then, like McAneny, meant not just to represent transportation interests, but to serve as power broker for one of the city's two big property holders and developers. As a principal RPA director, he shared fund-raising duties with De Forest. He was elevated to the chairmanship of the RPA after Delano moved to D.C. following his nephew's election to head the National Planning Board. McAneny held his RPA chairmanship at the same time that he served as Chairman of the Board of the Title Guarantee and Trust Company. A generation later, however, McAneny turns up in the principal account of New York's power politics as "an old line idealist" and the leader of "the reformers."[19] If the Pennsylvania Railroad, the RPA and the Title Guarantee and Trust Company represent interests on behalf of reform, what institutions make up the status quo?

Landscape architect Frederick Lewis Olmstead Jr., son of the designer of Central Park conceived much of the intellectual framework of the 1929 plan. Of the independent professionals hired by the RPA, he was perhaps the most eminent. Olmstead Jr., the favorite landscape architect of the Long Island barons, seems to have designed half the bird baths in Oyster Bay. More lucratively, he specialized in plans for real estate subdivision, highway placement, park design. For example, in May 1911, Frederick Lewis Olmstead Jr. was employed by Robert De Forest to landscape, survey and subdivide about 100 acres in Little Neck.[20] It was just a small job, one of many, but it enabled De Forest to sell land he'd bought for $2,500 an acre to fellow baron and New York Central heir W.K. Vanderbilt for $3,500. About the same time, Olmstead laid out the Forest Hills Garden development in Queens for Russell Sage Realty which De Forest originally conceived as a charitable project for workers, but which wound up a profit-making project for upper-middle-class home owners who paid as much as $25,000. It was De Forest who recommended Olmstead to John D. Rockefeller II when Jr. was trying to develop his Washington Heights property. Later, when the market soured for subdivision, it would be Olmstead who designed Ft. Tryon Park. Olmstead became the head of the city planning school at Harvard when it was inaugurated in 1929.

Along with the professionals, a group of very rich property owners, all of whom had spent decades in urban reform movements, formed the initial core of the RPA. F. B. Pratt inherited much of what is now central Brooklyn from his father Charles, who had been Rockefeller I's partner in the Standard Oil Trust. Like other big Brooklyn land owners – e.g., Alfred T. White and Seth Low, Brooklyn's largest individual landowner and the first Fusion Mayor of New York – he owned selected chunks of downtown Manhattan. The Pratts owned land on Pearl Street. They also controlled the Pratt Holding Company, whose properties included 111 John Street Corporation.[21] The Pratts were also highly active in Brooklyn real estate – Edward Bassett worked for them buying and selling South Brooklyn property. They established the Pratt Institute that still bears the family name and on whose Board the Pratts have continued to sit. Through the Institute, which served in the late fifties as a sponsor for the "urban renewal" of north central Brooklyn, the Pratts have quietly shaped Brooklyn development for a century.[22]

Two other developers helped create and consolidate the RPA. Alfred T. White like Charles Pratt was a big Brooklyn landowner, developer and philanthropist. Both participated in Brooklyn charitable works and local housing reform. The Pratts, Charles and James, served as vice presidents to White's president of the Brooklyn Bureau of Charities. The Alfred T. White apartments were the first Brooklyn buildings constructed under the reviewed housing law which White helped pioneer. He would construct 300 more.[23] Just a year after the formation of the Regional Plan, however, White died in an ice-skating accident. But his influence with the Sage Foundation – he had worked with De Forest for decades – was critical in shaking loose initial funds. And of course White was a reformer too. He served as President of Improved Dwellings Association of Brooklyn; with De Forest and Veiller he served on the first New York City Tenement House Commission.

Charles G. Meyer of Cord Meyer Development Co. attended the earliest RPA meetings and stuck with the organization through the publishing of the plan and after. His company helped develop central Queens, especially Forest Hills and Jamaica. Cord Meyer actually co-developed Forest Hills Gardens with Russell Sage Realty, controlled by De Forest. As RPA director, Meyer's role was that of the organizer, speaking before local business chamber of commerce groups in Queens and Brooklyn. No family had better entree into the world of Queens transit companies, Queens political utilities, Queens real estate, than the Meyers, Cord and Charles.[24]

The idea for a comprehensive New York regional plan is generally credited to Charles Norton, the First National City banker who had helped bring off the great Chicago Lakefront Plan designed by Daniel Burnham. Norton, together with real estate developer Charles Wacker and Wabash Railroad President Frederick Delano had been the principal officers of the plan which had been sponsored by the Chicago Commercial Club. The idea to duplicate Chicago's comprehensive planning in New York may actually have come from George McAneny who persuaded Norton to approach De Forest at the Russell Sage Foundation.[25]

Whoever gets credit for the initiative, what they sought to create is indisputable: a plan for circumferential highways around the city; with radial wedges and parks segregating high grade areas; expanding and beautifying the CBD. But at first, De Forest turned Norton down. The project was altogether "too vast", De Forest later recalled, for Sage to fund. But Norton persisted. He got Alfred T. White to put up some seed money. He hired Nelson P. Lewis the land value expert to analyze the tax implications of the plan. He persuaded his friend Delano to come to New York and take part in the plan. After striking out at other foundations, Norton tried again to get De Forest's support, bringing White and Delano along for the meeting. This time he succeeded. And the funds – eventually over a million dollars – began to flow.

Having made the heavy initial commitment, De Forest decided to limit other foundations' help. (And credit.) The Regional Plan bears the Russell Sage imprimatur. Directors like Darwin James of the Rockefeller Foundation, Frederick Keppel of the Carnegie Foundation and Dwight Morrow of Morgan also served on the board, but the project was 80 percent funded by Sage. The balance came from individual families like the Rockefellers and the Pratts plus the public utilities – which assumed a prominence that Rockefeller Foundation executive Arthur W. Packard would later find disturbing. More generally, what the narrow source of cash, ideas, and aims meant was that De Forest and his friends, the outer borough and Long Island barons, and their valued retainers like Olmstead and Bassett, would shape the spatial structure of New York region for the next two generations.

Although he only played a small role in the physical planning process itself, and according to one of his aides was "never fully convinced of the value of the plan",[26] probably none of the directors or professionals of the RPA was as critical to the success of the 1929 plan as the man whose name has become totally obscured. In 1929, there was no one more powerful and renowned in New York City good government circles than Robert De Forest. By profession, De Forest had a trust and estates practice with his brothers. They also dabbled and plunged in real estate. But like no one else Robert bestrode the New York and even the national world of urban reform and charitable organization.

The creation of Forest Hills Gardens, Russell Sage Realty, as well as the funding of the Regional Plan and the creation of the Russell Sage Foundation itself were largely due to the efforts and initiative of Robert De Forest. His books and articles appear to have been ghost written; he left no memorable statements on reform.

De Forest spoke, rather, through directorships, money, peer networks and memos. He served as head of the New York City Parks Council, as a member of state parks organization. He was Chairman of the Board of the Metropolitan Museum of Art. And for a generation, he headed the city's protestant charities movement. He was the city's first tenement house commissioner. And from the turn of the century throughout the 1920s, he was perhaps the leading funder of movements in housing reform,[27] planning, parks and charities.

It was through charities and charitable foundations that De Forest exercised his leverage over the other areas of reform. As a trust and estates lawyer, he wound up controlling the property of deceased clients. It was through his profession as a trust attorney, apparently, that he convinced Mrs. Russell Sage to endow the foundation, which he then controlled. He was frequently in the position of directing bequests to particular institutions. Then, as head of the institutions, he could shape the form of the gift. For example, as head of the Metropolitan Museum of Art, he received the gift of the Munsey estate. "I am really in a position to control this situation," he wrote to Olmstead, whom he gave ten days to provide a plan, and directing that the plan contain no "rectangular streets and negative small twenty-foot lots."[28] De Forest also wanted the overall plan of development cleared with the RPA.

De Forest was the J.P. Morgan of charitable accumulation merging, leveraging, rationalizing, centralizing money and power, creating inter-locking directorships. He founded New York School of Social Work. He headed the Charity Organization Society – the leading protestant charity in the city in an age when protestants were the dominant civic leaders and federal welfare hadn't been invented. He built United Charities Building (UCB) which still stands today on Park Avenue – now serving as the headquarters of the Community Service Society. Just what regal appointments the world of charity offered in De Forest's day, can still be seen, in the interior of the "Directors' Room" on the top floor of the UCB. And his influence even reached to the editorship of the single national magazine that exclusively covered urban reform movements, the *Survey Graphic*.

When De Forest died in 1931, no estimate of his wealth appeared with his obituary. It must have been quite considerable – at least before the Depression. If you look at the map Robert Caro provides of Long Island in 1929 to illustrate the great Robert Moses – Long Island barons battle over the routing of the Northern Expressway, you see that of all the estates – Vanderbilt, Morgan, etc. – De Forest's is quite a bit the largest.[29] Still, De Forest himself made no substantial charitable gifts, unless they were anonymous, which wasn't the style of the age. It was through the control of other people's money that De Forest was able to exercise his pre-eminent influence. Very rich people trusted him.

Edward Devine, a social work professor, helps explain how De Forest became the founder of the New York School of Charity.

Mr. De Forest called me to his office and said: "A friend of mine has just offered to give $250,000 for any good cause which I recommend to him. I think I know what you would say." My reply was "I think you do." "Well," he said, "I have already told Mr. Kennedy that we want it as endowment for the School and he agreed to give it for that purpose."[30]

In addition to Kennedy, a local construction company executive, De Forest was Rockefeller's attorney. Russell Sage was also his client. When the famous transit stock manipulator died, it was left to De Forest to advise his widow, 78-year-old Margaret Olivia Sage, what to do with the $60 million fortune she'd just inherited. De Forest, her counsel and personal adviser, thought up the idea of the Russell Sage Foundation. She would be the president. He would be the vice president. Her first gift amounted to $10 million. When she died in 1918, Russell Sage Foundation got $15 million more.[31]

With De Forest in control of the old robber baron's millions, the table was set for a generation of urban reform. The money was there. Essentially the same generation of real estate barons and retainers that reformed tenement housing at the turn of the century; invented zoning in 1911; then, in the 1920s, they made the leap into the most comprehensive level of urban control: regional planning.

They did so from the perspective of a class of very large closely knit outerborough and Long Island landowners from the North Shore to Hempstead. Somehow, Robert Moses got the idea in the late twenties that he would run his Northern Expressway through the Dix and Wheatley Hills, where De Forest, the Stimsons, Morgan, Whitney and Phipps held property. Altogether, 270 members of the committee that formed to oppose Moses owned 17,000 acres. This was an amount greater than the total acreage of Manhattan.

But the battle was not simply between Moses, "the Highwayman" and insular Long Islanders who didn't want highways, as Caro portrays it. After all, De Forest and Phipps[32] – at the time, were promoting through the RPA the biggest highway plan in history. The struggle was rather about who would structure the development of suburban land. Moses or the barons.

## PARK POWER

As a class, the Long Island barons didn't simply want to enjoy land. They wanted to profit from it. The barons, and none more than De Forest were deeply involved in subdividing property and selling it for the best development. De Forest brothers – Robert W., Henry W., Johnston, Robert Throne and Henry L. carried out the subdivision of Little Neck and Huntington. Naturally they were concerned that their property not be spoiled. The owners' committee, represented by former secretary of state, Elihu Root, had Moses suing for peace and re-routing his highway according to the plans of the Nassau property owners. Grenville Clark, Root's partner (of Root, Clark Howland and Ballantine) wrote to Henry V. Hubbard of Olmstead Brothers. The Nassau property owners demanded a four-mile detour.

Moses has said up to now that this four miles was impossible. He now says that he will be responsible for constructing it if we will lay off our activities.[33]

De Forest and Clark were also longtime members of the New York State Parks Council. Their exercise of power and influence have been so little understood that Robert Caro, one of the acutest students of New York politics, can write of them

Parks were a source of power now, but the old park men didn't want power. They just wanted to be left alone to preserve and pass on beauty to other generations.[34]

Notes from a meeting of the RPA's engineering committee, chaired by F.L. Olmstead Jr., who worked for De Forest, indicate a very different perspective:

Mr. Olmstead pointed out that there was a chance for unlimited growth in the New Jersey part of the district where (industrial) sub-centers would naturally occur rather than in Westchester or on Long Island. He believed that Long Island and Westchester country would have to be largely reserved for residences for the business workers in the New York City business district which must continue to grow. A large proportion of the population now working in Manhattan might logically move to outlying centers of industry and commerce. Their places could then be taken by business employees.

Ample and unrestricted means of communication are a necessary requisite for the development of sub-centers, he concluded.

Olmstead, in another memo analyzing Queens and Long Island land use for the Regional Plan, offers a grand perspective which reveals the strategic use of parks; the choice of mass transit vs. auto; the role of zoning. And the concerns that lay behind the choices. "The direct thrust of the mass of the city's growth into Nassau County," Olmstead observed, had only recently begun to show itself. It took the form of a straggling line extending out from the direction of Jamaica. The fringes of the mass he described as highly undesirable, consisting of detached houses, poorly built, easily converted into slums. Once these homes were in place, little could be done. Zoning and construction codes couldn't help, because the people who inhabit them can't afford a higher standard. At the same time, he wrote,

the incoming type of cheap development and still more the type into which it will tend to change as small industries follow the labor supply, do not mix well with those which have been up to the present typical of the sector.

This incoming type of development "would almost certainly be fatal to the continued maintenance of the latter." The business commuter would have to shift further out. This would make his commute much less satisfactory.[35]

In sum, the westward movement of cheap housing threatened the existing Long Island residential neighborhoods of downtown commuters; if allowed to continue, these affluent commuters would be forced to move east; extending their commute and threatening the CBD itself by prolonging and making more onerous the businessman's journey to work.

Urban planning to the rescue! What needed to be done, according to Olmstead, in light of this threat, is a pattern of restrictive zoning, road and park development to block the continued westward movement of low-grade homes. It would be necessary to protect the Nassau residential areas – with safe corridors. Zoning would have to be carried out not in the form of a "target" with bands, but radially. Olmstead explained (in connection with selected radical transportation routes)

I mean . . . wedges or sub-sectors of relatively open residential use with relatively high standards of amenities should be protected by every means as corridors from outlying areas.

These, he urged, must be guarded from the expansion of industrial and residential areas of a more intensive sort, the occupants of which are much likely to be engaged in work which *must* be done in the central business district. These people and their work

should be directed into separate and distinct subcenters and more *outlying expansion which might even approximate to industrial satellite cities.*[36] (Olmstead's emphasis)

Parks were especially needed in Queens to block the expansion of working class housing and keep it from spoiling the property for higher use to the west. Olmstead proposed parks to block the advance of low-grade housing from Jamaica into Flushing and Bayside; and the movement up from Queens Village into Nassau County. Flushing Meadow would have to be drained and made into a park. And Alley Pond too. If you look at a map of New York City, these parks today come down like daggers, cutting through central and eastern Queens. Flushing Meadow Park walls off Jamaica from Bayside; Alley Pond park protects Nassau County from the incursion of 20-foot lots and rectangular streets found in Queens Village. The park is thus the modern planning equivalent of the medieval moat, protecting the barons' castles.

Caro, in *The Powerbroker*, preserves something of the filiation of ideas from RPA President McAneny's mouth to Moses' ear, without grasping at all what's at stake. Speaking of Moses, in 1939, he writes,

The mind that could grasp an idea in an instant, expand it, fill in its details, sees its relation to other ideas, lunged at the idea of the Fair as it fell from George McAneny's lips. "By God that's a great idea!" he had said, pounding the table; he would sell it to La Guardia, and he himself "would stop at nothing to help" – if the fair was held on Flushing Meadows, and if "from the beginning the project was planned so as to ensure a great park" on the meadows after the Fair closed."[37]

Moses' more florid account of the origin of Flushing Meadow parks, in his autobiography, shrinks McAneny, and presents it as a kind of semi-religious epiphany: "Then the miracle happened," he exclaims, "the idea of a world's fair." The miracle touched two wise men and a child: a Belgian engineer, his daughter and a remote relative of the Roosevelt family. Together, somehow, *they* conceived the idea for a World's Fair, Moses insisted, on the site of the Brooklyn Ash Company's Corona Dump. With the little girl leading them, says Moses, "they sold it to George McAneny, a bewhiskered leading citizen who in turn sold it to me to sell to Mayor La Guardia."[38]

Moses presents the execution of the park project, save for the miraculous idea, as the product of his mighty will. He says he resolved to stop at nothing in order to transform this formidable rat's nest in the middle of Queens into a little girl's dream of sylvan beauty. The twin implications of this account are first, that Moses turns himself into the Babe Ruth of regional planning, with his promise to go out and hit the equivalent of an infrastructural home run for the little Belgian child. And the RPA's purpose and priority – which go back to before the girl was born – are both lost. But the whole layout of the Flushing Meadows park can be seen in the pages of the Graphic Plan of 1929. And the RPA people privately claim Flushing Meadows as one of their principal accomplishments.[39]

A principal RPA imperative – keeping lower-income workers at a safe distance from upper-income businessmen – also goes far to explain why, when the Long Island Expressway was built in the early fifties, no provisions for mass transit were ever made, an outcome which Caro blames squarely on Moses.[40] While the second generation RPA urban philosophy, which serves as the basis for Caro's critique, promotes mass transit, the first generation opposed it on the grounds that it created new forms of concentration of low-income people. There was enough mass transit already. Long Island and Westchester were to remain redoubts for "business workers" in the CBD. From the perspective of the barons, who worried both about the viability of the CBD and the upscale residential neighborhoods where CBD commuters lived, it made no sense to build more mass transit out to these areas.

From the RPA perspective, there was simply no need to have industrial workers riding around on mass transit. Why expend all that capital and operating expense when you can simply relocate the industry and have the industrial workers live next to the factories? Anyway, the new industrial areas that the RPA planned were to be located in New Jersey. Not Long Island. And certainly not anywhere near Long Island's north shore, along Oyster Bay or in Huntington where De Forest lived.

Thus, the real reason why the Long Island Expressway turned into the "world's longest parking lot" isn't simply because of Moses' narrow concept of transportation alternatives. But rather because the early RPA planners believed mass transit would create population "congestion" on Long Island. Such concentration of population would have drawn employers. And spoiled the prime elite residential area in the region with factories.

Naturally, for the second generation RPA figures, like Larry Orton and Paul Windels who served as Caro's prime sources, a scapegoat was required for traffic congestion. Especially after the urban party line changed from the auto to mass transit.[41] Similarly a scapegoat had to be found for another program which didn't work: urban renewal. In both these respects, Moses is absolutely indispensable to the now-standard version of New York history.

De-industrialization can be plausibly explained in terms of global markets and decentralization. But someone and not something mapped out the transportation system. And someone did decide to level big swaths of the city. But it turns out that the protestant elites – the planners, the real estate interests, the banks, the foundation leaders, who coincidentally overlapped with the biggest landowners, mortgage makers, and developers – had nothing to do with either urban renewal or New York-style highway building. It was all the fault of one man: the loud, boastful, obnoxious guy with the big nose and the name of Moses.

The criterion for decentralization is what promotes development of the CBD and the enhancement of residential stability and values in the regional suburbs. The latter is a fundamental condition of the former. The vehicles of decentralization are roads, and bridges with parks as brakes. The two principle objects of decentralization would be the garment industry and the port.

# THE PORT OF NEW YORK OR NEW JERSEY?

Considering that New York's principal reason for being has been its matchless port, it comes as something of a surprise to realize that for the last three generations, the city's establishment has been anxious to get rid of it. But port transfer would, from the establishmentarian standpoint, confer three principal benefits.

First, it would free the space docks and rail yards take up for more lucrative uses – on both sides of the river. The impetus for redevelopment is obvious on the Manhattan side. But since the Port Authority has been the super-agency of control, and the instrument of transfer, and New York can't act without New Jersey consent, it's important to observe that there were nine New Jersey railroad interests who owned the land from Hoboken to Bayonne who would also benefit from converting the Jersey Shore to their highest and best use – just as the New York Central would find the value of its below-14th street property appreciating when the port itself disappeared. Second, ridding the city of the port's capital expense would lower property taxes. No stronger advocate of port transfer could be found than the watchdog of big property owners, the Citizen's Budget Commission, created by John D. Rockefeller Jr., and his fellow owners, to limit city expenditures and taxes. Like other advocates of scraping the docks, the CBD loved to talk about how port facilities were obsolete and rotting. But capital expenditures to get rid of the rot were always fought as unsound. Finally, even if there weren't big real estate profits to be made in redeveloping the waterfront; even if big tax savings weren't to be gained by off-loading the capital expenses, privatization is reason enough for the urban establishment. Keeping city property and city functions small keeps city politicians small. Who wants to face big people across the negotiating table? Relieving the city politicians of port control would reduce a rival elite's source of power and patronage.

With all these good reasons, it's not surprising that port riddance is advocated as early as 1922. Or that it was a consistent goal of the city's establishment. The relocation of the port and how it could lead to a new regional order are explained in physical terms in the 1929 Plan. The actual intent to transfer is translated into legislative language in the form of a 1947 bill passed in the state legislature creating a World Trade Corporation. Headed by Winthrop Aldrich, chairman of the Chase Bank, and David and Nelson's uncle, the WTC was empowered to clear the Washington Market and shift it to the Bronx; to build a world trade center; and to help effect the transfer control of the New York City port to the Port Authority.

The full legislative intent of the bill was not realized however until after Nelson became Governor, in the late fifties, and the formation about the same time of David's Downtown Lower Manhattan Association – a merger of the old downtown real estate organization headed by John Butts, with David Rockefeller's FIRE folk – Keith Funston of the New York Stock Exchange, Henry Sturgis Morgan of Morgan Stanley, et al. Nelson could then use his leverage with the Port Authority. And the DLMA provided the comprehensive plan for higher real estate development that was the principal reason for shifting the port. So for thirty years, well before containerization had been invented, there were well-conceived plans by the city's establishment to shift the port. So that the explanations of the transfer in terms of containerization and the lack of upland space has a distinctly *post hoc* character.

Even without these successive efforts and the paper trail they've left which illustrate intent to shift the port, port riddance could be deduced however from the RPA's passion for "decentralization" – i.e., de-industrialization. A key premise for de-industrialization pops up in the section entitled "New Port and Industrial areas":

Industries locating within the New York region do so because of the advantages of the Port and the large consuming population. Hence the reciprocal of the distance from the center of the region is an indication of the proximity to that center.

In other words, given that the port served as the rim around the city's hub, relocation of the port was a fundamental precondition of the success of RPA's decentralization. This may in fact be the reason why the Port Authority was invented: to do what it eventually did do: take the port away from the city and put it in Newark.

As early as 1922, *New York Times* editorialized:

It is plain that Newark has the railways in greater competitiveness (sic) than the city has the ships. Newark's competitive effort is to get access to the ships, just as the competitive effort by the City Administration is to get access to the railway feeders of its docks. (But) Newark has better access to deep water than New York city has to the railways across the Hudson.[42]

By all reckoning, Manhattan had one of the two or three greatest ports in the world in physical terms because of its capacity for all weather use; its depth; its proximity to Europe – closer by almost a day than any other spot on the east coast. But it had a single geographical weakness which the *New York Times* editorialized upon: Manhattan's lack of a suitable rail freight connection to the rest of the country.

All the railroads had their terminals across the river in New Jersey. The Port of Manhattan, failing an expensive freight tunnel underneath the Hudson River, could only be served by what John Dos Passos would later make famous – the "Manhattan Transfer" – the "lighters" that plied the Hudson with railroad cars from the Jersey side which transported them to the Manhattan side of the river.

In 1922, Newark, didn't have much of a port. But you could build a great one there, the argument went, and it would be better located in relation to the New Jersey freight yards. Why invest more millions in the city's port, the argument went, when the same capital could be put to better use in New Jersey? For large property holders, the freight efficiencies were probably secondary to tax concerns. If the port were in New Jersey; if it were run by the Port Authority, instead of New York City, the costs of maintaining it would be spread out across New Jersey and New York state taxpayers – New York City property holders could lay down their disproportionate burden.

From a tax-minimizing as well as a topographical perspective, there was nowhere in the city – not even Staten Island (too hilly) – that could compare to the Newark–Elizabeth area in New Jersey as a potential port location. Only the short-sighted Hylan regime, reluctant to yield control, the *New York Times* pointed out frequently, prevented rationalization of freight costs and overall space efficiencies. But the way to overcome local political opposition was simply to vest control of the port in the Port Authority.

Of course, there was one primary reason to keep the port in New York: jobs. The Port of New York Authority itself argued that about one out of four jobs in the city depended on the port. A detailed analysis showed that nearly 430,000 jobs were directly at stake:

> marine transportation – 66,000
> auxillary maintenance – 65,000
> marine construction – 34,000
> land transportation – 40,000
> port trade and finance – 96,000
> port industries – 127,000

Add to these figures, secondary employment effects, and the estimate seems plausible.[43]

Raymond Vernon, chief of the Harvard study carried out for the RPA's Second Regional Plan and financed by the Rockefellers and Ford, would later publicly challenge the notion of a city dependent on its port.[44] But even the Harvard port expert estimated that 90,000 manufacturing jobs in the city were tied directly to the port.[45] And that figure of course didn't include cargo handlers, like the 34,000 longshoremen. Benjamin Chinitz argued that containerization would soon shrink these numbers. Assume on the most conservative premises, that there were only 10,000 port jobs for a round total of 100,000, that was still 3 percent of the labor force. And for every port-dependent manufacturing and port job, there were somewhere between two and four times that many in secondary employment.[46] So a loss of the port would have meant a total job loss on the order of 300,000–500,000 – 10 percent–15 percent of the private sector jobs. Any administration in which labor had leverage – Hylan's probably represented a peak – couldn't easily pack the port off to New Jersey.

The RPA approached the problem quite tentatively. This is from the "basic general assumptions", a private 1926 memo:

> point #6. There is ample room in the Upper Bay North River and East River. Therefore . . . Jamaica Bay and Newark Bay should be developed on the basis of making the most of the existing port [crossed out is "retaining and developing"]; but in such a manner as not to preclude the extension of major facilities to Jamaica and Newark Bays in the future. This involves numerous changes in outlook as the treatment of Manhattan Waterfront and Jamaica Bay, the development of New Jersey railroads.

This language is reproduced almost verbatim in the Plan itself. But now, instead of just asserting that the future of the port belongs in Newark or Jamaica – the RPA adds language downplaying existing plans for port expansion in Manhattan. Such proposals, say the RPA,

> while not seeming to be too visionary when considered as separate schemes are seen to be unnecessarily ambitious and therefore extravagant when they are studied as part of a comprehensive plan.

The RPA had in mind more modest plans for the New York port: proposals that would enable port functions to harmonize better with commercial and residential development: double-decking the Brooklyn Heights piers; and building a Parisian-type quay to spruce up the East River docks.

In keeping with their primary economic assumption that manufacturing follows the port, the RPA suggests that areas near the proposed port areas be reserved for workers' residences and factories. The language seems a bit tortured, because "de-centralization" – i.e., de-industrialization – has to be called "reducing the friction of space." So the RPA plan now reads:

> from the point of view of distribution of population, of reducing the "friction of space" within the metropolitan district, and of best serving the needs of industry, it is considered desirable to provide residential areas as near as practicable to places

where the people are employed . . . For these reasons, Hackensack Meadows should be reserved for residential purposes as well as for industry.

This would involve a shift in the volume of freight traffic. One that De Forest, director of the Jersey Central, could hardly have found displeasing: from the Manhattan side where the railroads were carrying about 88 million tons, to the Newark–Elizabeth area where the Central Railroad of New Jersey with 13.5 million tons was one of two lines carrying three-quarters of the traffic.[47]

The RPA suggested that the Port Authority's power be increased. The Port Authority should be vested with the power to create a comprehensive port-industrial planning authority. One that would organize the reclamation of the Meadowlands for industry, dredge a new channel for shipping and co-ordinate between government and the railroads. The RPA argued

The whole Port depends for its future growth and prosperity on the proper utilization of the enormous asset which New York City (in Jamaica) and certain New Jersey counties possess in these large areas of marsh and water which are capable of reclamation.[48]

It took a generation for the RPA port vision to be realized. But the difference between the perspective of the city's political elite and the city's planning establishment is time frame. At best, the short-winded politicos think in terms of the next election, if not the next press release. The planners reckon things in generational time so what Junior's people fail to accomplish is simply left to be carried out by Nelson and David's.

## SHMATAS

Two sets of feelings normally shape the outlook of aristocracies. The first is optimism, basking in being beloved of the gods. Second, is the love of battle, especially against the lower orders, trusting that the odds favor the extravagantly armed. Because of the increase in the electoral franchise, however, prudence dictated that the social Darwinists of the RPA could rarely express themselves publicly like happy Homeric warriors or even like their parents' generation – the Robber Barons. They couldn't portray the battle for urban space as they saw it – as a battle between urban in-groups and out-groups. Instead, their chief economist described it in terms of a struggle between "functions".

But since human groups, rather than bodily organs carried out the functions, it's easy to see the point Columbia economist Robert Haig was driving at in his analyses of New York City economic succession. He showed historically that the groups which began the battle for urban space were not those which survived after a few generations of adaptive struggle. Then he rated the functions, showing that those which tended to survive were the fittest in terms of intelligence. The battle for urban succession was won by functions involved in transmitting intelligence. (An astonishingly modern perspective!) And he identified these intelligence-transmitting functions precisely as do modern prophets of the "Info City".

Indeed, there is hardly any distinction to be drawn between Haig's insistence on the urban primacy of "intelligence-transmitting" functions and the recent academic discovery that cities are chiefly engaged in "information processing."[49] Haig's intelligence transmission and modern information processing, in urban terms, both take place chiefly in the same "industries" – the traditional business professions of finance, accounting, law, plus advertising. In both scenarios, high real estate values, success in spatial competition are all identified and justified in terms of high intelligence.

Then, as now, the analysis carried a strong tincture of ideology and wishful thinking. The semi-credulous insistence on the rapid growth of intelligence transmission just like those more recent claims predicting the nearly vertical growth of information-age employment led, in both instances, to more investment in centrally located offices. And more office space than anyone could use for decades.

The RPA's wishful thinking was especially evident in such confident predictions that downtown real estate wouldn't have to worry much about corporations moving to midtown; that the retail section near 32nd Street (Penn Station) wouldn't decline (it can't move above the 59th Street "border", ran the argument); and that downtown will become more elite as second-tier businesses move out and big corporations and big finance – investment bankers and insurance companies – increase their presence.

All in all, the RPA believed, the market forces in the New York Metropolitan area were tending to produce a nearly ideal outcome. The higher, intelligence-transmitting functions were gravitating towards the center. The baser, more routine functions in the periphery. Specifically, heavy industry, together with light industry producing for export, was headed to New Jersey; industry producing for local markets was moving to Brooklyn and Queens. This left Manhattan CBD to retain the higher functions.

The only exception to the grand convergence of the actual urban spatial order with the ideal order was the garment industry. It was actually increasing its hold on the central business district. And making dresses was not intelligent in the true sense. It did not involve decision-making at its most significant. "A decision as to whether the Kingdom of Norway shall be loaned $25,000,000 of American capital and whether the rate shall be five or six percent is obviously more important" than mere haberdashery. [50]

But in the heart of the CBD, the rag trade was outpacing banking and even lawyering. Between 1900 and 1922, the number of investment bankers had increased 58 percent; the number of insurance brokers 90 percent; lawyers 108 percent. But men's furnishings increased 365 percent; knit goods 263 percent; embroidery 242 percent. Perhaps most significant, because it started from a higher base, was the growth of employment in ladies' garments – from 16,000 in 1900 to over 50,000 in 1922.

It was axiomatic that competition for space produced the best results. But the garment industry, under-capitalized, small-scale, dominated by foreign races, was winning out too, even increasing. This was not as it should be. Nor could the results be shrugged off as a mere anomaly. The garment industry was too huge and too expansive to dismiss this way; the consequences too vast and threatening.

Because garment jobs were multiplying in the CBD, the residential population of garment workers was increasing in Manhattan. The peculiar food requirements of these workers for kosher products – their meat had to be freshly killed within 72 hours before being eaten – meant the east side along the waterfront was crowded with slaughter houses. Worse, as the industry moved uptown, and the workers continued to live downtown, they took mass transit and pre-empted its use by business people. Finally, there was their overwhelming presence in the midtown CBD, right next to the highest-grade shopping Manhattan had to offer. It had been this complaint in particular, by the President of the Fifth Avenue Association, against garment workers mixing with elite shoppers at lunch hour, that had provided much of the top-down impetus for the 1911 Zoning Act.[51] The RPA concluded,

Obviously, the clothing industry should not be allowed to spoil the character of the choice shopping district by flooding the shopping street with throngs of non-buying pedestrians.

Nor should it be allowed to clog the streets with vehicles that slow the pace of those with money to spend and payrolls to meet.[52]

"It would be a tragic waste to turn Times Square into a potato patch," the RPA observed.[53] But what to do? Haig did not underestimate the difficulties of decentralizing the garment industry. He suggested

With radical changes in the transportation system a large part of the fabrication might be moved away from the center of the city.

But ladies' garment manufacturing with its ability to use space in obsolete buildings and with the advantages of close contact with salesrooms

will probably be among the very last of the factories to yield in the competitive struggle for sites in the center of the metropolis.

Even this is no sure bet.

Fabrication in the branches where style is less of an influence may be expected to offer less resistance to a policy of decentralization, particularly if the transit plans are so arranged as to encourage the movement.[54]

In the meantime, while transportation alternatives were being prepared, rather than a frontal assault, which was definitely to be avoided, Fabian tactics were called for. A series of measures could be imposed. If the garment industry is going to pre-empt space for higher business uses, subway cars for more strategic passengers, and clog the streets with its deliveries, then the industry will have to pay a premium. A tax on the use of streets, on the use of transit facilities for its workers, special construction requirements for its buildings were the appropriate remedies for such damages.[55]

The protestant planners attitude towards the garment industry beautifully expresses the in-groups sense of when the results of competition are to be accepted; and when planning must take the initiative. Competition is an ideal. A value. It is very much like the attitudes of modern Christians towards peace. But neither peace nor peaceful competition are absolute values. Peaceful competition is to be pursued as long as the policy pays dividends. But when the out-groups' profits begin to come at the expense of the in-group, then planning must be brought in to rectify the results of competition. "Planning consists not merely of beautiful pictures of civic centers or interesting projects for pleasure boulevards," the RPA observed. Planning decides where things go and by what means of access. "It seeks to achieve its ends by both voluntary co-operation and legal compulsion." And if the planners have conceived a plan that is in "conformity with the true values of the community" the RPA warned, "'compulsion' can be carried very much further than would otherwise be feasible."[56]

## FULFILLING THE PLAN

It would be hard to deny that the RPA founders were disproportionately rich men, linked by common material interests, who formed an experienced, well-articulated social and political network, sharing common beliefs, with full command of able, dedicated specialists, capable of steady, co-ordinated work towards clearly defined aims. It would be even less plausible to deny the fulfillment of the plan – the city planning commission by 1938; the parks, most of the highway and bridge plan by the forties. (Re-zoning and the shift of the port took longer.)

None of this, however, proves that the RPA drove the political process that fulfilled the 1929 Plan. Putting in place the elements of the plan may have been, as Caro suggests, all Moses' doing. Caro's testimony is diminished, however, by his failure to recognize that there even was an RPA plan. He seems unaware that the mass transit mavens of the sixties and seventies were the highwaymen of the thirties and forties. This perhaps explains his uncritical attitude towards RPA sources; he doesn't see that his principal sources for the period, Orton and Windels, are using Moses as a scapegoat for their own organizations' failures. They resemble the Stalinists who used to blame all the problems of the Soviet Union on their former collaborator, Trotsky.

Unwittingly, though, Caro provides a lot of evidence against the idea that Moses could have prevailed against the will of the men of the RPA. He shows that Moses' biggest triumphs come, as in the case of the 1939 World's Fair, and the creation of the Queen's park system, when he listens carefully to the plans of RPA chief McAneny and makes them his own. Moses' biggest setbacks come, as in the case of Northern Expressway fiasco, when he fights De Forest and the barons. Or when he battles McAneny instead of following his lead in the famous Battery Bridge fracas. Moses had insisted in 1939 that Battery Park should be linked with South Brooklyn by a bridge because it was cheaper. McAneny, the RPA and downtown landowners insisted it be a tunnel, to preserve the view and the value of their property. Today there's a tunnel. Not a bridge. And fifty years later, the RPAers are still beating their chests.[57]

For the 1929 plan to get realized, power needed to be turned on from two primary sources: La Guardia in Gracie Mansion, and FDR in Washington D.C. had all the money for the public works. La Guardia had the power in the city to acquiesce in building them; to create a charter commission to create the city planning commission; to name the right people. There is a paper trail from both places, giving something of a sense of how the RPA and its funders fulfilled the plan.

La Guardia towers in our official history as the scourge of the powerful and the friend of the little guy. But that's not how the powerful saw him. Where Governor Roosevelt doubled state income taxes to provide a fund for the jobless, Mayor La Guardia froze real estate taxes, while imposing the city's first sales tax. Then, to meet the terms of the 1933 Bankers' Agreement, he tossed thousands of city workers out on the street, calling them "chair warmers and parasites."[58]

The Rockefellers could be decisive in city politics when they threw their full resources – personal and foundational – behind a candidate. But they had been out of city politics for a generation when Nelson explored the question of supporting La Guardia in a 45-minute meeting with the Fusion candidate for Manhattan Borough President, Langdon Post. Post was seeking $400,000. Nelson insisted he was only interested in "fairness."

Both sides understood the value of discretion. Nelson explained that if knowledge of a contribution leaked out it would be embarrassing "because of our large real estate holdings in the city." Post, who became La Guardia's Housing Commissioner recognized that publicity about receiving Rockefeller money wouldn't boost La Guardia's reputation as a reformer. So they pledged to say nothing.

Nelson recommended to Junior that he back La Guardia. He thought a La Guardia victory would be a blow for what he called "honest and efficient government." So it turned out. Raymond Fosdick, Junior's chief advisor, was so impressed with Fiorello's "fairness" on real estate matters, that they considered scuttling their newly founded watchdog agency, the Citizen's Budget Commission.

The chief obstacle to RPA-style planning is the residual accountability that ties public officials to the public. Representatives who vote for highly unpopular projects – like highways that go through the neighborhood or urban renewal – can get unelected. Thus the passionate preference of the higher real estate interests for unelected commissions, appointive authorities, public development "partnerships." This is also why the RPA had as a principal aim the creation of a city planning commission that obviated legislative accountability.

As agreeable as New York City legislative bodies had been to some of the most destructive real estate projects, they generally used the neediness of the higher real estate interests to exact a price. Selling in this market for permits, franchises, variances constitutes the whole point of elective office for the machine pol, and more recently, the blow-dried, self-crafted politicians who rely on campaign contributions rather than a pre-existing campaign organization. Thus, pols insist on their legislative prerogatives. And they refuse to simply acquiesce in their own demise.

Nor was it possible to take planning power out of the hands of the legislature and concentrate capital budget decisions in mayoral appointees simply by mayoral decree. Nothing would have suited La Guardia more. But any sweeping change of this sort required City Charter changes. And voter approval of the Charter changes.

La Guardia made firm pledges to the RPA to deliver a City Planning Commission through the charter process. Unlike his customary humiliations of subordinates including Moses, his tone with the RPA was always decorous and sober. He gratefully thanked the RPA for drafting the make-up of what the City Planning Commission should look like. He promised to institute their outline. And he delivered on his promises. He even put Larry Orton in charge of the Commission staff.[59] None of this was acknowledged publicly.

Rockefeller Foundation Trustee Henry James, who served on the Board of the RPA wrote to staffer Arthur W. Packard to complain.

The main trouble with the work of the (Regional Plan) Association is that we are seldom shown credit for what we have done. Some of the best part of work has been helping public officials who not only like to take credit for whatever was done but are in a certain sense entitled to because it is they who carry the responsibility for the ultimate action.

James noted that the amount of public money "that is being spent hereabouts in work connected with the planning of the region has vastly expanded our own budget."[60]

Larry Orton, who had to submit regular reports to Russell Sage project officer Shelby Harrison to keep the money flowing, obviously couldn't say that their project was a big bust. But given the outcome, his report on unofficial co-operation seems genuine enough. "Unusual official co-operation has contributed to the success of our work," wrote Orton, just after the Charter Revision Commission had trimmed back city council power and created a basis for a City Planning Commission. Orton explained that the RPA was

acting through a committee appointed by the Administration . . . [we] have also had access to and co-operation from practically all of the city departments and agencies. Although undertaken in confidence that there would be some official agency to carry it on, there was no expectation that the set-up would be so favorable as is the case under the new Charter.

Orton advised that the Commission would be set up next January. And it would open up a new phase of their planning activity. "Our association and the City have never had such an opportunity and must not fail in this one."

In fact, the expectations for the CPC were never fully realized. More than half a century later, the CPC has never delivered on its mandate to produce a Master Plan for the city.[61] The true significance of the Commission is that it pre-empts planning by any responsible elective body. The existence of this non-functioning Commission allows private planning agencies – like the RPA – and even private developers and their publicists to set the planning agenda and frame the public debate.

Following the official creation of the CPC in 1938 with Orton as chief of staff, Delano, now head national planner in his nephew's administration, sent his congratulations on the creation of the formal body. Delano had kept in touch. He not only made requests to the Rockefeller Foundation to support RPA grant proposals, he helped steer Work Projects Administration money to New York to advance RPA projects. He wrote

At last, you have got a commission which looks very good. You have Lawrence Orton who is an old Russell Sage associate attached to the Commission; you still have George McAneny on the sidelines helping out, and I dare say [Nelson P.] Lewis and some of the men on the staff will still be working on it. . . . All those who have been associated with it including myself are delighted with what you have accomplished.[62]

What *had* the RPA accomplished? The institution itself sought to measure its success in terms of how much of the paper plan got turned into concrete. By this criterion Delano's rush of institutional pride was fully justified. But outside the RPA, among urban real estate men of substance there was a growing sense that something had gone drastically wrong. "Had decentralization gone too far?" they asked.

Not decentralization in the abstract – no one questioned the value of getting rid of industry or factory workers. But decentralization in the sense that the means had begun to conflict with the end. If decentralization didn't result in higher real estate values, what was the point? If the wrong people were staying and the desirable people were moving to the suburbs the whole strategy had to be re-evaluated. Evidently there had always been slums and people moving to the suburbs. But by the late thirties, with housing construction in the region booming again, both the rate of exodus and inner-city decline were alarming.

Nelson Rockefeller was one of the first to articulate this fear. In addition to heading the Rockefeller Center sales corp, in 1936, Nelson helped his father develop apartments on family-owned land right across from the Museum of Modern Art on 54th Street between Fifth and Sixth Avenues. On completion of the project, he made a speech pointing out the growing problems of real estate investment in a decentralizing city. He observed

Property owners in Manhattan for many years, lulled into a false sense of security by rising land values, have awakened to find those values declining while adjacent suburban residential communities have experienced an increased demand. A decentralization movement has set in which unless it is checked will involve the very future of this great island.[63]

Nelson's biggest concern was obviously not the apartments, but Rockefeller Center – the family's most important investment which still had enormous vacancy rates – depending on the building, occupancy rates ranged from 30 percent to 60 percent. The *Herald Tribune* planned to run an article on the speech in its Sunday supplement. Nelson had his uncle Winthrop intervene with Vincent Astor, who happened to be summering in Bermuda at the time, to kill the piece.[64]

Beginning about 1937, the *Real Estate Record*, however, carried many thorough articles analyzing the problem. Herbert U. Nelson, the Executive Vice President of the National Association of Real Estate Boards, expressed his disillusion with modern urban planning. Nelson complained that planners had overstepped their role. Instead of simply serving metropolitan traffic needs, providing parks, getting enough arterial roads in place to keep down congestion in the central business district, the planners had gone too far. "The new roads," he observed, "shortening driving time from rim to hub entice people to live further and further out." The new highways were precipitating a ring of blight around the city's heart. And high taxes on open land was forcing it into premature development, he observed, competing with central city investment.

Federal Housing Administrator Miles Colean focused on New York City's decentralization problems. According to Colean, a protean development of transportation infrastructure was carrying real estate development into new areas.

All forces have combined in the acceleration of this outward movement; and the generous provision of new utilities and the competition of cheap land favorably situated, the pressure of funds seeking investment.

But by doing so the movement was

leaving behind a broadening area of neglect – areas which are increasingly unprofitable for its owners and unproductive to the city.

There was nothing new in this phenomenon, he allowed. It happens in waves, but the amplitude this time this had outstripped previous outward movements. "It represents an actual draining of population from the older areas" and is creating a "greater certainty of neglect and loss." What's good for the suburban areas receiving the new roads, is bad for the city. Colean pointed out,

From the point of view of the city as a whole and of the investment in urban real estate, the benefits of the new expansion may not outweigh its detrimental effects. The city is forced to pay for new utilities and added services while . . . the older areas become idle.

Oscar Wilde suggests that the worst possible nightmare is the realization of our dreams. By successfully carrying out the gigantic highway plan, the RPA created hundreds of thousands of acres of new land in the periphery to compete with centrally located land. Not only had too much office space been built, at the beginning of the decade, but the planners had over-produced the amount of available land at the end. But by so doing, the men of the twenties had bequeathed the next generation of planners a task that would last for the rest of the century: undoing its first plan with a second.

# NOTES

1. Even much younger structures had to be wrecked. At the corner of Seventh Avenue and 39th a 12-story building that cost $2 million dollars to construct 9 years ago, was replaced by a 35-story building that cost $10 million. *Real Estate Record and Builders' Guide*, September 1, 1928.

2. *Real Estate Record and Builders' Guide*, February 8, 1930.

3. Ibid. January 11, 1930.

4. Ibid., November 14, 1931.

5. Russell Sage Foundation Papers, Box 32, file 251, Rockefeller Archive Center.

6. Robert Haig, "The Assignment of Activities to Areas in Urban Regions, Regional Plan of New York and its Environs," p.33.

7. Ibid., p. 31.

8. Tom Shachtman, *Skyscraper Dreams: The Great Real Estate Dynasties of New York* (Boston, MA: Little Brown), p. 112.

9. See Ron Chernow, *The House of Morgan* (New York: Simon & Schuster, 1990), pp. 215–17.

10. Frederick Law Olmstead Papers, Russell Sage Realty, Library of Congress.

11. The term "social Darwinist" libels Darwin, who explained infrahuman adaptation as much in terms of cooperation as individual struggle and who wrote extensively and insightfully on the difference between human adaptation – which is mediated through culture and adaptation through genes. I am perpetuating the injustice in lieu of a whole essay which would be required on Darwinism and culture.

12. Cited in Robert E. Park and Ernest W. Burgess, *The City* (Chicago: University of Chicago Press, 1925, 1967), p. 36.

13. Ron Chernow, *The House of Morgan* (New York: Simon & Schuster, 1990), p. 288.

14. Veiller to Olmstead March 31, 1919. "I have been presently and quietly (and this I must ask you to consider strictly confidential) working out a plan by which I think we may get a proper building code for New York City and which would be a standard or model code for the entire country." Olmstead Papers.

15. Veiller to Johnston De Forest, November 9, 1901, Charity Organization Society papers.

16. B. Aymer Sands to Lawrence Veiller November 1, 1906. Charity Organization Society Papers. Sands of Bowers and Sands and Allied Real Estate interests reminds Veiller that his employment came about entirely as a result of his decision and the recommendations of Cravath and De Forest.

17. See Robert Fitch, "The Family Subway," in *Research in Political Economy*, vol. 8, 1985.

18. Later the Brooklyn and Manhattan Transit Co. (BMT).

19. Robert Caro, *The Power Broker* (New York: Vintage Books, 1975), pp. 567, 683 et seq. Robert Dowling, head of City Trust Company – later City Investing Company, a real estate organ of Citibank – one of the largest money raisers for the Democratic Party in the 1950s and 1960s and a force within the RPA is identified by Caro as a financier for "reform". p. 685.

20. Olmstead said that De Forest "hoped to sell the rest as a whole but the market seems to be mainly for small pieces of 1 to 5 acres or so and they had not wanted to take the trouble of selling it off retail . . . they are inclining now to the view that they had better 'lot it up'." (i.e., subdivide the property), Olmstead Papers, (Box 286).

21. See *New York Times*, May 10, 1931, II, 8:4.

22. And they continue to exercise city-wide influence – notably through the Rockefeller-funded Pratt Community Institute. Director Ron Schiffman sits as a mayoral appointee to the City Planning Commission.

23. *Brooklyn Daily Eagle*, January 21, 1921.

24. Unless perhaps it was the Coffin family. By a curious coincidence both sons of these prominent Queens families wound up as prominent CIA agents: William Sloane Coffin, Jr., and Cord Meyer Jr.

25. See John Glenn to Frederick Delano, February 3, 1938, Box 39, RAC.

26. Glenn to Delano, February 1938, Box 39, RAC.

27. See Veiller to Olmstead, December 13, 1909. "Strictly confidential" Veiller acknowledges that Russell Sage underwrites expenses of the national conference of the National Housing Association. Attendees included Jane Addams from Chicago, De Forest, Paul D. Cravath (the founder of the Cravath firm), John M. Glenn, Alfred T. White, who would later participate in the RPA, and Henry Phipps, Olmstead Papers, Box 309.

28. Robert W. De Forest to Olmstead. February 1, 1927, Olmstead Papers, Library of Congress.

29. Robert Caro, *The Powerbroker* (New York: Vintage Press, 1975), pp. 302–303.

30. Edward T. Devine, *When Social Work Was Young* (New York: Macmillan, 1939), p. 130. The "Kennedy" was developer John S. Kennedy, who also contributed to the United Charities Building "in the belief that intimate contact inevitably promotes cooperation."

31. Russell Sage Foundation Papers, Box 40, Folder 344, RAC.

32. The Phipps family was a steady financial contributor.

33. Grenville Clarke to Henry V. Hubbard, Olmstead Papers.

34. Caro, *The Powerbroker* (New York: Vintage Press, 1975), p. 256.

35. November 21, 1923, "Plan of New York and its Environs" (Long Island) "Sector I," Olmstead Papers.

36. Frederick Law Olmstead Jr. "Plan of New York and Its Environs" (Long Island) "Sector I," November 21, 1923. Olmstead Papers, Library of Congress.

37. Caro, *The Powerbroker* (New York: Vintage Press, 1975), p. 1085.

38. Robert Moses, *Public Works. A Dangerous Trade* (New York: McGraw-Hill, 1970), p. 538.

39. Regional Plan Papers, Box 40, File 335, Rockefeller Archive Center.

40. Robert Caro, *The Powerbroker* (New York: Vintage Press, 1975), pp. 941 et seq.

41. See chapter 4, 'Getting Centered.'

42. *New York Times*, January 3, 1922.

43. The Port of New York Authority, "The Port and the Community," 1958, p. 5 et seq.

44. Speech at City Club November 18, 1958.

45. Benjamin Chinitz, *Freight and the Metropolis* (Cambridge, Massachusetts: Harvard University Press, 1960).

46. Dean Baker and Thea Lee, "Employment Multipliers in the U.S. Economy", Working Paper No. 107, Economic Policy Institute, March 1993.

47. The other line was McAneny's Pennsylvania Railroad with 17.7 million tons. See The Graphic Plan, "Transit and Transportation," p. 148.

48. Ibid., p. 327.

49. Manuel Castells, *The Informational City* (Oxford: Basil Blackwell, 1989). Castells paradigm is grander, involving more sweeping claims about society, "the social meaning of the space of flows", etc., but his strictures about the city and its space don't diverge all that much from Haig's. Both present FIRE's occupation of the city as a consequence of technology and competition.

50. Robert Haig, Regional Survey of New York and its Environs – Major Economic Factors in Metropolitan Growth and Arrangement, (New York: Regional Plan of New York and its Environs, 1927), pp. 41–2.

51. Robert Fitch, "Planning New York," in Roger E. Alcaly and David E. Mermelstein (eds), *Fiscal Crisis of American Cities* (New York: Random House, 1977).

52. Robert Haig, Regional Survey of New York and its Environs – Major Economic Factors in Metropolitan Growth and Arrangement, (New York: Regional Plan of New York and its Environs, 1927), p. 43.
53. Ibid.
54. Ibid., p. 87
55. Ibid., p. 44.
56. Ibid.
57. In a brochure advertising their 1993 meeting the organization shows a picture of what the Moses Bridge would have done to downtown.
58. Thomas Kessner, *Fiorello H. La Guardia: and the making of Modern New York* (New York: McGraw-Hill, 1989), p. 266. The quote, not the interpretation, is from Kessner. Kessner argues that La Guardia had no choice but to obey the powers that be. Of course by the time he'd taken their money for his campaign, this was true. Kessner misses this.
59. La Guardia to Stacy, May 4, May 1935, Russell Sage Foundation Papers, RAC.
60. Henry James to Arthur W. Packard, October 5, 1934, Russell Sage Papers, RAC.
61. The Lindsay Plan (New York City Planning Commission, Plan for New York, 1969) lacked a physical dimension.
62. Delano to Glenn, January 26, 1938, Box 39, Russell Sage Papers, RAC.
63. Transcript of radio talk on station WJZ, June 16, 1936, RAC.
64. Nelson Rockefeller to Vincent Astor, July 27, 1936, RAC.

*CHAPTER FOUR*

# GETTING CENTERED:
# THE SECOND PLAN

## RE-PLANNING THE RPA

Addressing his fellow planners at a post-war conference in Newark, RPA President Paul Windels stood at the crest of his career. In 1934, he'd been elevated from the RPA staff to become New York City's corporation counsel; from there La Guardia appointed him to the City Planning Commission, and now he'd returned to run the organization he had once served. Windel's impressive credentials as a professional planner and a political insider gave him the authority to pose a stark choice for the entire New York region.

Nearly vertical real estate growth was inevitable, he argued, after the flat years marked by war and depression. At least two million extra people could be expected to crowd into the region by the year 2000. How would this growth be accommodated? New Yorkers, Windels insisted, faced a fundamental decision:

Is this metropolitan region to become finally and permanently a massive and monolithic structure keyed largely to a few centers with a daily ebb and flow of millions of people to those relatively small areas, or is it to develop as a metropolitan region of many centers of housing, trade, industry and recreation, each closer to places of work and possessing greater opportunities for intimate participation in home community life?[1]

By the mid-fifties, Windels would be thundering *against* his positive alternative – decentralization.[2] And embracing the "monolithic structure" he had offered as the grim alternative. What Windels portrayed fondly in the forties as "intimate participation in the community life of small communities" would become in the influential RPA rhetoric of the later fifties and sixties "urban sprawl", "spread city" – a threat to the very possibility of urban civilization. The RPA highwaymen of the thirties and forties would become the region's principal institutional foes of the population-scattering freeway, the main advocate of "centering" the region. And Windels, a prime source for Robert Caro's Pulitzer prize-winning *The Powerbroker* – he's cited more than fifty times – would go down in urban history as a lonely fighter against highway building and sprawl, "an old giant of the reform movement," as Caro calls him.[3]

Men and women change their beliefs all the time. Often for the better. Keynes had a saying, often quoted, "When I discover new facts, I change my mind. What do you do?" Paul Windels' namesake, on the road to Damascus, underwent the ancient world's most famous alteration of belief. It was a conversion that kindled in him the spiritual power to transform a dying world. But if Windels and the men of the RPA made some new spiritual discovery; if they suddenly discovered new facts about the region which caused them to scrap their most basic premises about what makes a good community, the public was not informed.[4]

Second generation RPA leaders like Paul Windels and W. McKim Norton, and their successors, were often eloquent in exposing the lack of any broad principles implicit in the work of City Planning bureaucrats: Reade Street's total immersion in petty details, its narrow "curb cut focus" at the expense of any larger notion of goal or agency. The RPA by contrast, constantly invoked broad planning principles. But where did they come from? How deeply held were they? Indeed, were they for sale?

You have to wonder, given how the old principles were abandoned with such unseemly haste and complete absence of public discussion for the very opposite principles. Clearly, planner Windels was no man of ideas like Lewis Mumford who also supported decentralization. After all, Windels had been La Guardia's corp counsel, the City's top lawyer. He was good at finding reasons.

If decentralization was desirable, so too, he had argued, in 1943, was centralization, under certain circumstances. When RPA financial supporter Met Life sought city assistance to sweep out 11,000 working-class tenants between 14th Street and 23rd Street, from the East River to First Avenue, and build a segregated, all-white middle-class development, Windels thought this a worthy effort. Otherwise, he asked, "How can we stop the drift away from the city and maintain valuations in older areas?"[5]

Windels raised all the right questions: what kind of urban form the region would take; the type of transportation the region would emphasize – the car or the subway; whether jobs should be centered or dispersed within the region – but he and his successors seem to have subordinated them to questions of organizational survival.

By the early fifties the organization, as RPA official W. McKim Norton acknowledged, needed to produce a new plan or disappear. Whether the plan emphasized decentralization or centralization seems to have been less important than that there be a plan. It was, he said, "a do-or-die" matter.[6]

For there to be a plan, there had to be a payroll. For the better part of two decades the organization had nourished itself from the ample breast of Russell Sage Foundation income. It moved forwards as the result of the momentum and ideas of the De Forest generation; prospering from the whole network of funding, contacts and energy provided by the Long Island barons and the suburban and outer-borough developers – the Cord Meyers, the Sloane Coffins, De Forest himself. But real estate men on the island didn't require a new plan. They were profiting mightily from the one in place. They didn't need a dating service. They'd found the party. Brooklyn donors like the Pratt family were no longer concerned with extensive development; they were desperately trying to maintain their properties in the "gray areas" of the outer boroughs against advancing urban blight.

The RPA did manage to eke out some income doing small studies for utility companies. (In the early thirties, Rockefeller Foundation staffer Arthur W. Packard had noted the share of income the RPA received from public utilities with disfavor.) AT&T's Harold Osborne had served in the fifties as the RPA's chairman.[7] But besides the utilities, there aren't a lot of institutions which both need and are capable of paying for the long-run projections that become the basis of a regional plan. Banks and insurance companies come to mind as obvious consumers in the urban research market. But like the utilities, they're only secondary players, surprisingly lacking in money and the outside staff that's required to evaluate funding requests. Legally, there's nothing that prevents Citibank or Chase or Morgan from giving away large sums to a foundation, which in turn could fund the research and plans they need. In fact, they do. But the amounts of capital financial institutions mobilize in the eleemosynary sphere are comparatively small. Even when all the big New York City banks come together in the New York Community Trust their assets are dwarfed by Ford and Rockefeller Foundations. Competition demands that bank capital be used either for dividends or reinvested in banking. This leaves the foundations created by individuals of great wealth, particularly rentiers, as the big players in the funding of urban and social science research in general.[8]

So it may be more than a coincidence that the same year, 1952, the Rockefeller Brothers Fund got a $58 million grant from their father, John D. Rockefeller II, propelling the Fund to no.2 in the foundation world, David Rockefeller got an invitation from the RPA to speak at their annual banquet. David represented a new generation of the real estate rich who were predominantly focused on the Manhattan CBD. Whereas the De Forests, the Lows, the Pratts, had owned outer borough, suburban and centrally located property, the Rockefellers had gotten rid of nearly all their non-CBD property and in real estate terms were concerned primarily with New York City. Not the 'burbs. The same narrower focus was true of William Zeckendorf, Sr. and Robert Dowling – head of City Investing Company – a large real estate holding company associated with what's now Citibank – who were among the most prominent of those to break with the decentralization orthodoxy of the 1930s.[9]

As early as the 1930s, while the RPA was promoting decentralization as an urban panacea, the family had come to see it as the principal threat to their interests. Nelson had spoken out on municipal radio against the highway programs that were taking affluent customers out of the Rockefeller Center concourses that he was trying to rent out during the pit of the Depression. It was Nelson who had digested the results of the transit study which the family had commissioned to find out why Rockefeller Center was empty. The principle reason, the consultants explained was that Rockefeller Center lacked access to mass transit. It was too far from Times Square. Too far from Grand Central. Mass transit was the key to healthy office development. The automobile was killing it.[10]

David naturally agreed. The youngest of the brothers had become head of Westchester's planning council. But as early as 1947, his vital planning energies were flowing in the city itself, through the vehicle of Morningside Heights Inc., a typically vast and surprisingly futile plan-

ning effort David headed for nearly two decades. Rockefeller knew the
upper west side university neighborhood well. He had gone to school
there. Not to Columbia – he was a University of Chicago Ph.D. – but to
the Lincoln School, a Deweyan experimental institution funded by his
father which he and Nelson attended. David had also gone to church
there, since Junior, in a break with his father's provincial baptism had
endowed the universalistic Riverside Church, "the God Box", with its
non-Baptist iconography – including portraits of Buddha, Confucius,
Hegel and Darwin. And at the same time the family had bought up
blocks of tenements along 123rd and 124th Street, only to wreck them
during the 1930s to save taxes.

Now, as part of the effort to "renew" the city, David would cultivate
Manhattan's core uptown institutions – as well as the family's Rockefeller Center landlord[11] – by leading the effort to thin out black and Puerto
Rican poor from the Columbia University area. But while causing lots
of misery to the tenants forced to relocate, the mid-fifties removal of
5,935 people failed in its immediate object.[12] The new prison-like
structures, "General Grant Houses," had hardly arisen when it turned
out, planners discovered, that many of the residents who'd been forced
out just wound up moving *closer* to the elite Morningside institutions
which sought to rid themselves of their poorer, darker neighbors. This
of course, required another round of urban renewal and so forth until
the great Columbia University uprising of 1968, and its after shocks,
which put an end to Morningside Heights, Inc.[13] But not to David's
efforts in upper Manhattan which continued through the New York City
Partnership, an institution which remained dedicated to David's vision
of recentralization and renewal.

Had the family been the only powerful advocates of re-centraliza-
tion, the focus of New York City's planning institutions would probably
not have changed at all – much less so abruptly and decisively. Family
leadership through the two Rockefeller foundations, Rockefeller
Brothers' Fund and the Rockefeller Foundation, Nelson's governorship,
linkages with other important FIRE figures were all decisive. Bill
Zeckendorf, perhaps the most famous and flamboyant developer of
the period was another powerful advocate of urban renewal and
recentralization whom the family cultivated. He was the Rockefellers'
favorite real estate developer, chosen by the Chase Manhattan Bank to
build Chase Manhattan Plaza.[14] The family invested in his firm, Webb
and Knapp, which specialized in office development. It was also to Bill

Zeckendorf that the Astor family had turned after World War II, to manage their enormous, but low-yielding investment in midtown real estate.[15] Zeckendorf publicly urged a curb on suburban growth to keep New York City from being choked by an "endless chain of suburbs."[16] The *Times* gave lots of space to Zeckendorf's views. They were shared by the paper's Executive Vice President, Amory Bradford, who would become President of a reoriented RPA.

Up until the 1950s, the Rockefeller family, despite the contributions of the Rockefeller Foundations and Junior's own small subventions, had played next to no role in the RPA. The Rockefeller Foundation – which had a certain autonomy from the family – sent the publicist Darwin James. But the family's influence was so small, the RPA backed a plan that would have driven a road right through the middle of Rockefeller Center – a north–south avenue from Bryant Park at 42nd Street to Central Park running through what is now the RCA Building. Carole Krinsky suggests that it was to forestall this plan, which had begun to gather support, that in April 1931 the family began rapidly clearing the thousands of residents who would be replaced by empty buildings.[17]

It's fairly clear why the hard-pressed, post-war RPA wanted the Rockefellers as patrons, whatever their views on decentralization. But why would the Rockefellers want to invest millions in research and planning for the New York metropolitan region? What did they need to know? What did the RPA have to teach?

Staffers at the Rockefeller Brothers Fund, who evaluated W. McKim Norton's request for money, were skeptical that the RPA had either the competence or the skill to carry out comprehensive research. Their advice was to find real experts to do the research and let the RPA carry out a plan based on it. Why not hire Harvard's Graduate School of Public Administration to do the study, they asked?

It was on this basis, with Harvard undertaking the research and the RPA devising the plan, that Rockefeller Brothers Fund, together with the Ford Foundation, decided to fund the project. Otto Nelson, of New York Life, who was supervising construction of Lincoln Center for John D. Rockefeller III, recruited a new board. It included Arthur H. Sulzberger of the *New York Times*, James Felt, head of the City Planning Commission, who was helping David with his urban renewal program at Morningside Heights, and Henry Heald, who would become chief of the Ford Foundation.[18]

There were at least two reasons why Rockefellers must have keenly felt the need for authoritative analysis of New York's economy. First of all, they were locked into a long-term and extremely constraining lease with Columbia University for the land underneath Rockefeller Center. It provided for a series of renewals and renegotiations. What the lease was worth depended on the future demand for office space. Then, too, the Family had been assembling land on the periphery of Rockefeller Center – especially in west midtown. And they were considering a giant leap across Sixth Avenue. Naturally, they didn't want to make a leap in the dark. What they had to know was the capacity of New York's office district for expansion.

Again, two questions loomed. First, since the renting of office space depends on the number of office workers, what were the prospects for white collar office growth in New York? Second, and somewhat less obviously, they had to know what the prospects were for the blue collar work force.

What really limited the westward and southern expansion of the midtown office district, both in physical terms and in terms of competition for transit use was the vast manufacturing district that surrounded the office district. Just think of the situation from the standpoint of a Rockefeller. It must have been so tantalizing: On the eastern side of Rockefeller Center, Fifth Avenue, where Columbia owns the land, you have the best commercial location in the city. But on the Sixth Avenue side, especially across Sixth Avenue, where you own land, on the west side of the street, the situation is very different, "blight" is everywhere. The change in values is so extreme. – just a few hundred feet between real estate heaven and hell. Even as late as 1981, the year before City Planning instituted its program to pump up values on the west side, land values on the east side of midtown were about seven times higher than land values in west midtown.[19]

The problem with the west side wasn't transit. If anything there was an *embarrassment de richesse* – an Eighth Avenue line, a Seventh Avenue line and a Sixth Avenue line. Nor was the fall-off simply due to the highly publicized forms of "blight", like Times Square, the block between Seventh and Eighth on 42nd street. These were just the squalid expressions of a classic zone in transition – an area poised to change from manufacturing to office use. But "the transition" was lasting an unaccountably long time. How to move it along?

In 1959, the RPA estimated that there were 650,000 manufacturing jobs in the Manhattan CBD. Plus 640,000 other non-white collar jobs.

The obstacle was the garment district which had moved up from downtown after World War I to Seventh Avenue and the upper thirties to be near the big department stores. And even more formidable, was the wall of factories, warehouses and docks on the far west side which had grown up around the port of New York. What was the future of these blue collar districts? As subsequent RPA studies would illustrate, there is a zero-sum game going on in Manhattan between manufacturing and offices. Land speculation can't thrive unless it can expand into cheap manufacturing zones. Blue collar industries can't survive if they're under speculative pressure. Thus the weaker the future for blue collar industries, the stronger the prospects for real estate speculation and development.

The Rockefeller Foundation had underwritten scholarly studies of industrial location in New York. In 1955, their grantee, John I. Griffin of City University, published his work. Griffin's study, although articulated in academic language, is startling for its concerns and its iconoclasm – especially given the period. While McCarthy may have been terrifying New York intellectuals, it was urban renewal that most frightened poor and working people. Dissenters were few.

Vast urban renewal schemes were as popular as deficit reduction and budget cutting today. It wasn't just real estate developers like Bill Zeckendorf, but good government people like Ira D. Robbins, President of the City Club, who were calling for broadscale industrial clearance in Manhattan. Robbins, attacking City Planning's "lack of vision" thought that everything south of Canal Street and east of West Street all the way down to Park Place – about 150 acres – should be levelled and redeveloped.[20] And the American Institute of Architects was proposing, on aesthetic grounds, the elimination of an even larger chunk of downtown – the entire loft district between Chambers and 23rd Street.[21]

Griffin's study went entirely against the elite sentiment for urban clear-cutting. Before Griffin, industrial job loss was a buried issue. But he inventoried the loss of over 100 large manufacturing firms between 1946 and 1954. And he insisted de-industrialization could and should be stopped.

Most strikingly, Griffin's research identified city planning as the principle reason for de-industrialization. He carried out the widest and most thorough survey ever undertaken up to that time to determine manufacturers' reasons for leaving New York. The businessmen whom Griffin surveyed furnished the usual complaints about high rents, no room for expansion, high taxes, congestion, unco-operative unions. But one reason manufacturers mentioned with some passion, which struck Griffin as decisive in explaining job loss, was city policy. New York public officials, businessmen insisted, seemed not to care that manufacturing was leaving the city. Certainly they did little to retain it.[22] And under Title I of the urban renewal program, the city was busily plowing under factories and sowing middle class housing. Nor was the city, whatever it might declare publicly, really concerned with finding new locations for the displaced manufacturers.

Griffin's most dramatic example of city-led de-industrialization was the battle over the American Safety Razor (ASR) plant, located in Brooklyn where Metrotech now stands. With 1,200 workers, a relatively high percent of them black, ASR was one of the borough's largest factories. The plant was doomed, however, because it was located in an urban renewal zone: along with hundreds of other plants, it sat on land designed for the revival of downtown Brooklyn. Initially, ASR tried to find another city location, but when city officials proved obstructive, and offered no suitable land in New York, management settled on the least costly alternative – Staunton, Virginia. Only the workers and their union, the United Electrical Workers (UE), actively tried to thwart the move. New York *Herald Tribune* editorialists as well as labor columnist Victor Reisel thought this displacement would help make Brooklyn a more progressive place. City officials, who determined in the first place which land would be taken under Title I, carried out their customary drill of lies, evasions, and unctuous expressions of concern. Strikingly for an academic study, Griffin's featured pictures of workers fighting with police guards who had to be brought in to protect the operatives dismantling the plant – which was being shipped off to Virginia.[23]

Griffin concluded his analysis with a long-term assessment of the viability of manufacturing in New York and a series of recommendations that have been repeated over and over by reformers for the last forty years. Gradually, he argued, wage differences between the suburbs and the city; as well as between the northeast and the south were evening out. The real problem for retaining manufacturing in New York City would not be high wages, but lack of space. And the unwillingness of city officials to provide it. Public agencies, he observed,

have not been sufficiently sympathetic to or conscious of manufacturing industry as a vital force in preserving the community as a viable one.

At a minimum, the city had to acknowledge that

manufacturing has been the economic base of the city and that every effort must be expanded to preserve it.

Griffin proposed that the city preserve industrial land; and that it create new industrial space safe from the encroachments of housing development. Why not, he asked, use Title I to clear areas for industrial development? Griffin concluded:

A major effort directed by public officials in this direction would do much to give the lie to the cynical comment, 'factories don't vote.'[24]

Griffin's study helped create a climate of concern that led to a project so radical and yet so sensible, that it's hard to believe it could have emerged in the planning world of New York City. Abe Stark, City Council President proposed a comprehensive re-industrialization plan for Manhattan's lower east side. The city would promote the formation of industrial co-operatives. They in turn would sponsor the industrial and manufacturing redevelopment of the area between St. Marks, and E. Houston, the Bowery and Second Avenue.[25] As part of a complex deal, in which Stark supported urban renewal in Brooklyn, Robert Moses agreed to support the lower east side project. But withdrawal of anticipated union pension funds killed it at an early stage.[26]

Less consequentially, Griffin's study sparked editorial concern in the *New York Times*. This is the ultimate accolade for a foundation research sponsor.[27] But it's hard to imagine a less palatable set of recommendations or analyses for the family.

Besides their concern about manufacturing in midtown, the Rockefellers were, after all, in the 1950s, the leading promoters of urban renewal in America. Nor did they hide behind Robert Moses. John D. Rockefeller III carried out Lincoln Center clearances: 20,000 residents had to leave to make way for opera singers, ballet dancers, the symphony. With David Rockefeller out front, the Downtown Lower Manhattan Association proposed in 1958 even greater and more comprehensive removals – 30,000 alone were forced to leave the electrical district in the clearances required to construct the World Trade Center. David's Morningside Heights, Inc. eliminated nearly 6,000 tenants in its first round of renewal. When Laurance tried and failed to get Title I status for a project around Rockefeller Institute[28] he was the only Rockefeller brother, aside from the non-resident (and largely non-functioning) Winthrop, who left New York for Arkansas as a young man, without first-hand experience in tenant removal.[29]

Griffin had opened up a new dimension of urban renewal criticism. The program bulldozed jobs not just residences.[30] But no one had seemed to notice. Even though the figures were often faked, the Mayor's Committee on Slum Clearance had to provide an accounting for the people they removed from their residences. No such reporting requirement held for the people who lost their jobs through urban renewal of their factory. In Lincoln Center alone, in an area not particularly industrial, orders were given to demolish over 300 factories.

From the family standpoint, there was already too much attention being paid to urban renewal horror stories. John D. Rockefeller III, in his diary, frequently expressed disappointment at Mayor Wagner's notable lack of enthusiasm for Lincoln Center. He confided:

We have never been able to get Mayor Wagner excited about Lincoln Center, or feeling a responsibility towards it.(sic) It does make it difficult from our point of view.[31]

(Eventually, when Wagner's consent was required for city aide to Lincoln Center, the Mayor had to be brought over to Nelson's townhouse at 801 Fifth Avenue and given the treatment by the Governor.) But at times, Rockefeller showed that he was well aware of the simmering resistance to urban renewal that was undermining Wagner's ability to deliver.[32] And here was Griffin promoting more reservations about urban renewal.

Evidently, neither Griffin's demonstration that job loss wasn't simply a result of objective forces that no one controls, nor his identification of city policy as the matrix of job loss, could have pleased many in Room 5600. Then, too, Griffin didn't just wring his hands. He proposed specific ways manufacturing could be saved and strengthened through, in a cold irony, Title I.

Obviously a second opinion on the New York City economy was needed.

## HARVARD MEETS GOTHAM

We tend to make assumptions. Since the RBF insisted that Harvard, not the RPA, prepare the analysis and projections for the Second Regional Plan, and since Harvard did deliver ten volumes worth, and since finally, the RPA gracefully thanked the Harvard professors for their work, we tend to assume that the Second Regional Plan must be based on the Harvard study. Not at all.

Far from serving as the foundation of the Plan, the Harvard study constitutes an utterly dissimilar – even conflicting – set of analyses, projections, and urban outlooks. The Harvard study carried out a kind of industrial ecology: revealing the complex forms of manufacturing interdependence that allowed blue collar workers to survive in the Manhattan CBD. The RPA adopted a global perspective that abstracted from local conditions. The Harvard study predicted that, by 1985, blue collar workers would be about as numerous as they were in 1955. The RPA argued that, in Manhattan, there'd be only half as many. The Harvard study showed the limits of office growth in Manhattan, how it was dependent on the mass transit web, and further constrained by high rents which pushed white collar work to the periphery. The RPA showed how the number of white collar workers could be doubled by urban planning.

The ten volumes of the Harvard Study were published in 1959–1960. And the Second Regional plan came out in 1968. In the meantime, RPA produced new projections and analyses that completely replaced those of the Harvard study. Simply put, the Harvard study was scrapped.

The RPA came close to acknowledging as much in its publication "The Region's Growth" – published in 1967. According to the RPA, the Harvard study simply failed to recognize that white collar growth was occurring so rapidly. And the professors failed further to realize that blue collar jobs would decline, not simply maintain the same level.[33]

Now if the RPA was able to publish these revised projections in 1967, they had to have concluded no later than 1965 that the Harvard study was flawed. And probably much earlier. What was the rush for a new forecast that had been prepared with such care? The Harvard study was a projection of what was going to happen by 1985. And already in just five years, the RPA decided it was obsolete.

The stance which the RPA adopts is that its policy recommendations are shaped not by the interests of those who pay for the studies, but by the disinterested observation of trends. The inarticulate assumption is, "If we discover this trend, you must follow it." But the RPA was notably willing to go against the trend when it came to squeezing more office space into Manhattan. The trend, which the Harvard study predicted accurately, was for Manhattan to receive a declining share of the region's white collar growth. The RPA simply refused to accept the trend.

Trends, history, urban amenity, and the interests of a diverse economy all militated against their recommendations for more office space. In fact, you could argue that the RPA was predisposed to see that the Harvard study was flawed. Their differences went far beyond projection of trends.

The two groups of urbanists expressed opposite outlooks. They contrasted in mood, method and value. It's not surprising that they came up with totally different projections of where the region will be by the year 1985.

## URBAN PANTHEISM

Harvard's urbanists of the 1950s had a naturalist's attitude towards industrial growth. The variety and complexity of its adaptations enthralled them. When Hoover and Vernon exclaim, "Manhattan has 435 times more jobs per acre than anywhere else in the region,"[34] they're expressing the kind of awe that's akin to what biologists sometimes feel when they look at a drop of water under a microscope. They saw the industries that were here, not as obstacles to the implantation of office buildings, but as the products of a long and successful struggle for adaptation. And the city itself, with its immense variety of industries as a marvelous evolutionary product.

Underlying Harvard's quasi-ecological perspective is an acceptance of what's here based on an analysis of its power to adapt over very long periods of time; a sobriety about the possibility of very great changes in the structure of the city that are simply imposed from above. Or that ignore the patterns of adaptation that have enabled firms to survive here for decades. Like any naturalism, it delights in diversity and the demonstration of contrariness in nature.

The Harvard study emphasizes fine-grained analyses of specific industries in the city. In particular, scholars like Robert Lichtenberg's *One Tenth of a Nation*; Edgar Hoover and Ray Vernon's *Anatomy of a Metropolis*; Vernon's *Metropolis 1985*; Benjamin Chinitz' *Freight and the Metropolis*. These works, ultimately based on Hoover's early industrial location research, provided the "theory" of New York's economy of diversity.

Ultimately, the approach derives from Alfred Marshall's portentous distinction between internal and external economies. Marshall is trying to explain why big manufacturers win out over small. They have the advantage of long production runs, buying in quantity, greater capacity to withstand losses. All these constitute what Marshall called "internal" economies – because they derived from the forces of production internal to the firm itself. But Marshall noticed that the big guys didn't always win out. In situations where the market was uncertain, where production was non-standard, where design was decisive and craft production still reigned, little firms thrived. They could survive by co-operation; by sharing space, facilities, key workers, capital facilities. These advantages which accrued to small companies working together he called "external" economies. Later economists devised the ugly term "agglomeration" economies to refer to the same advantages of co-operation.[35]

The Harvard study illustrated how, as the big firms were attracted to the periphery in search of more space to carry out their internal economies, the small firms came together in midtown Manhattan to promote external economies. And so while there were broad techno-logical trends that pushed big firms out of Manhattan – and urban areas towards spatial deconcentration – there were counter-trends that pulled small firms to stay and start up in Manhattan – trends towards spatial concentration. Indeed, a wise city planning policy could re-inforce these existing tendencies to retain and expand manufacturing in the city.

Large manufacturing firms, especially those involved in repetitive, standard operations, leaving for green field plants in the suburbs was an old story. But by the mid-fifties, the selection process had whittled the survivors down to those which were highly adapted to the ecology of the Manhattan CBD. And who needed its peculiar advantages. Small manufacturers were attracted to the CBD by their very smallness and their need for each other. They required a high density area. The suburbs could offer lower costs – but at the sacrifice of participating in Manhattan's rich industrial culture. The small firm's need for sharing capital and labor costs, compounded by the uncertainty it faced producing non-standard products made the 'burbs an alternative to someone who looked at costs in the abstract – who didn't understand the small firm's specific needs.[36]

The Harvard project's tool for probing New York's external economies was history not algebra or econometrics. It was in the fifty years before the Civil War that the unique and accidental confluence of factors emerged, Benjamin Chinitz showed, that produced New York's amazing growth. The Erie Canal led to the channelling of the midwest's foreign trade through the port. The existence of the port promoted small manufacturing – although exports never equalled imports. Unlike elites in other eastern cities, New York's merchant-banker class then turned to ally with southern planters to promote international commerce, giving a powerful impetus to the whole trading–manufacturing complex.[37]

New York had a strong attraction for new and unsettled activities. The city was the scene for the early development of radio, high fidelity and military electronics. The early stage of development in each industry is a non-standard phase. And those involved in non-standard production had a need for the Manhattan CBD's advantages.

In its early stages of production, each industry which located in the Manhattan CBD had a highly unsettled technology and rapidly changing products. Producers worked in small establishments where they avoided committing themselves to fixed costs as much as possible. Rather they preferred to share facilities, pools of labor and materials with other producers.[38] These manufacturers, dependent on short-production runs, and non-standard production didn't want to tie up capital in buildings. They preferred short-term commitments. If their product were more standard it could be produced away from the big city in small towns. But small producers of non-standard goods need to be near pools of readily available skilled labor.

New York produced consumer goods which unlike, say gas or refrigerators, had a highly variable and uncertain demand. This discouraged mechanization. There aren't long production runs for high-priced dresses. The way output is increased is by sub-letting to more contractors. The contractors in turn hire more workers. Output can't be increased by introducing new labor-savings equipment or by running existing equipment at higher capacities. Dresses are different from oil refining. If you need more of a particular petro chemical, you just turn a knob. If you need more dresses, you have to hire more workers.

For anyone who hoped to find ineluctable technological reasons why industry would melt away in Manhattan, the Harvard Study offered cold comfort. Nor did it offer big hopes for those who banked on soaring office growth. The real growth in office workers was going to occur in the suburbs. Not in the Manhattan CBD. Manhattan would be lucky to capture its share of the region's white collar growth. The big reason office development had held as well as it had was that Manhattan was becoming the location for the white collar elite. The elite office workers took up more space – the heavy haunches syndrome. As long as the elite was willing to pay more to endow itself with bigger offices, the outlook was bright. But for non-elite office work, Manhattan's future was dim.[39]

Above all, Hoover and Vernon wrote, the city's cramped transit facilities put a ceiling on the number of people who could be squeezed into Manhattan. In the future development of the central business district of Manhattan, one factor still stands out as the locational determinant, namely, the location of the mass transit facilities. There would be "no requiem for the skyscraper," they observed, but "it must never be forgotten that the future growth of the skyscraper community is tied to the mass transit web which serves it."[40]

Harvard was right to forecast only modest white collar growth in the Manhattan CBD and wrong about the continued blue collar stability. Whereas the RPA was right about declining blue collar industry, even if they didn't predict the sharp collapse that was about to occur – and wrong about a giant upsurge in Manhattan office workers. White collar workers increased only in cyclical bursts, and never at the fruitfly dimensions predicted by the RPA.

But why was the Harvard study so wrong about the blue collar workers? Here was the most exhaustive study ever undertaken on the New York economy by acknowledged industrial experts. None of them thought NYC blue collar industry was poised for protracted decline, much less the total collapse that followed. And yet it did. RPA chief economist Dick Netzer strongly criticized the Harvard Study for a "tone of complacency about the economic future of the city"[41] but no-one predicted – including Netzer – that the city's blue collar economy would fall off a cliff as it did losing half a million manufacturing jobs between the time of the publication of the Harvard study and the peak of the fiscal crisis. But in November 1959 there were 991,000 jobs in manufacturing. And in November 1975, 553,000.[42]

Subsequently, urban analysts have vastly oversimplified the problem of New York City's blue collar collapse. Why didn't anyone see what was about to happen? And why should they have? Not only had New York industry kept a steady share of the national manufacturing employment, the firms that were in the city had been around a long time: 48.9 percent were more 24 years old.[43] At the same, paradoxically, industry was constantly renewing itself. There was a storm of manufacturing innovation going on in Manhattan, with an unprecedented number of industrial births each year. And the city had a healthy share of the area's growing industries.[44]

Although New York's manufacturing decline which begins in the late fifties is highly problematic, it's portrayed nevertheless as largely inevitable and foreordained. First instead of presenting both the technological trends towards deconcentration and the counter-trends, economists simply emphasize the former. Second, they smooth out the numbers so there's nothing to explain. It's been argued for example that New York City manufacturing has been declining for generations. It's simply, writers say, the nature of the post-industrial age that's manifested itself.

But the Harvard project provides strong evidence to show that there was no gentle deliquescence of the city's manufacturing. On the contrary, it documents the amazing continuity of New York's share of the nation's manufacturing employment up to the mid-fifties. Blue collar jobs gyrated with the ups-and-downs of business cycles, crashing to below 700,000 in the Depression, soaring to 1.1 million during World War II.But between 1898 and 1956 New York had maintained an almost eerily steady 13 percent share of the country's manufacturing jobs.[45]

This constant share contrasted dramatically with other cities in the east. Philadelphia, Boston, Pittsburgh all declined slowly. But New York City grew, at least in absolute terms. The only city in the U.S. that markedly outpaced New York was L.A. And New York's performance was all the more striking for two reasons. First, New York City's population was not increasing rapidly like L.A.'s. Second, New York was maintaining its blue collar jobs despite a strong decentralization of manufacturing in the U.S. Metropolitan areas dropped as a share of U.S. manufacturing.[46]

Since New York's population wasn't growing rapidly, like L.A.'s, what explained the city's ability to hold its share of manufacturing while the other cities in the U.S. and particularly in the east gave up industrial employment was the city's powerful external economies. These could flourish only in the type of industrial ecology provided by the Manhattan CBD. Cities based on manufacturing with internal economies saw their work forces shrink: either because they required great amounts of space; or because capital substituted for labor; or because as routine producers, the low-wage labor in the south or overseas could substitute for high-wage labor.

The Harvard writers' explanation of New York's peculiar strengths also illuminated its signal vulnerabilities. Anything that threatened the ability of small firms to share facilities, capital, and labor would undermine local manufacturing.

They were a tough breed, they could adapt to almost any market conditions, but if you pre-empted their space, you could knock them out. The small producers couldn't be simply transported to the suburbs or the outer boroughs any more than the white collar lawyers and bankers who depended on external economies. There was a reason why the Manhattan CBD had 425 times more jobs per acre than anywhere else. Each firm which crowded into the area below 59th Street depended on the existence of innumerable others for their survival. It was precisely this space which the Second Regional Plan would target for office buildings.

## THE SECOND REGIONAL PLAN

Hoover and Vernon had started their inquiry at the tip of Manhattan. They approached the analysis of industry like naturalists, asking "what explains this adaptation in this ecological niche?" Why do we find this particular industry in this specific location? By uncovering layer upon historical layer of economic activity, by analyzing the metabolism between different industries they give us their answer. RPA however, was not interested in carrying out an historical analysis or identifying New York's peculiar adaptations.

The RPA task force started out its inquiry not with the city at all, but with "the planet," a word they clearly savored. What counted in explaining New York City, for the RPA, is the *world* tendency towards population growth. And within that tendency, the global tendency towards urbanization. Towards bigger and bigger urban agglomerations. (Just before U.S. cities began their dramatic shrinkage, RPA committee member William H. Whyte, then an editor at *Time-Life*, had written a best-seller on America's "Exploding Metropolis."[47])

Purely deductively, they reasoned as follows: world population is increasing. Urbanization is increasing. The world's largest urban region, something they called "the Atlantic Urban Region" would increase. And New York, the largest component in the largest urban region, could thus expect very substantial population increase.

New York's population now is about ten percent less than then, but the RPA's question then, was can a city get too big? The answer, the RPA reached almost effortlessly, was "no." The task force acknowledged the complaints of philosophers and sociologists, from Aristotle to Durkheim who criticize megalopolitan effects: the decline of political engagement; the end of citizenship, the growth of *anomie*, pervasive depersonalization. But there is a counter-vailing bright side to bigness. A lot of people feel comfortable with anonymity. It's a great social attraction. The individual can freely select the persons with whom he desires contact and is allowed to "ignore the rest."[48]

True, there was the annoying problem of traffic congestion, but given sufficient investment in mass transit facilities, there was no inherent reason why big cities should be congested. The bigger the city, the faster the mass transit has to be designed to speed the commuter to Park Avenue from Scarsdale and Princeton and beyond.[49]

It turns out, the RPA explains, that the whole notion of "bigness" is an abstraction based on insufficient recognition of the role of urban "submarkets." And neglect of the ineluctable forces that produce giant-sized cities. A city is really a congeries of "overlapping submarkets" – each of which can maintain its own "optimum" scale within a larger framework. The detached, authoritative tone as well as the purely *a priori* character of the argument effectively repel discussion: The RPA observed

The classic urban theoreticians have shown that service areas form an overlapping, hierarchically arranged system in which the city of each size-rank and functional type has its own special role. There can be no optimum size for a metropolis taken in isolation; its size can only be considered in relation to its function and their market areas [sic] in the equilibrium of a continental urban system.[50]

The RPA appears to mean this:

if you think the city you live in has gotten too large, you've just neglected to analyze its position within the continental urban system. Either that or failed to inspect with proper care the appropriate sub-market you're located in. These vectors do inevitably tend towards equilibrium.

The RPA did allow that urban bigness had some diseconomies: air pollution and so forth. But bad air was counterbalanced by a big advantage of size – rising income. There was a general tendency for per capita real income level to rise with metropolitan size. In New York the regional average income, the RPA pointed out, is 30 percent higher than the nation. As the region gets bigger it will get richer. Especially Manhattan. The RPA predicted that by the year 2000, in Manhattan 77 percent of the households will have incomes of $15,000 or more.[51] (Or over $60,000 in 1992 dollars.) Actually, in 1987 in Manhattan, only about one out of six made over $50,000. And the city-wide real income trends were headed south.[52]

Obviously the RPA had come a long way from Windels' rhetoric about the need for small, nearly autonomous, decentralized communities. The RPA argued now

only a center which provides most of the metropolitan activities used by the residents of the area will create a genuine metropolitan *community*, . . . Spread city works against a sense of community.[53]

But having cleared away misconceptions and objections to bigness in the abstract, the RPA got down to its principal task: explaining the necessity of white collar work force growth. And the correspondingly necessary decline of the blue collar industries within the city's core. The RPA's principle projections are dual: first that by 1985, manufacturing jobs in New York metropolitan region will stay the same – and actually fall quite substantially in the Manhattan CBD. And that the number of workers in office buildings will nearly double.[54]

For manufacturing, the RPA explained, there was a natural tendency for jobs to move out to the suburbs, to take advantage of "low priced, uncongested sites outside the Core." Here the task force simply ignored the Harvard study's careful analysis of the way big firms were pushed out of the city by space needs; but small firms were pulled to the CBD by agglomeration economies. High-fashion garment makers would simply die in Monmouth County. How would financial printers check specifications with their Wall Street clients on Long Island?

But regardless, the RPA looked forward to big declines in blue collar work – as much as 60 percent by the Year 2000 in Manhattan. The planners philosophized:

The departure of goods-handling activities from the Core, and particularly from its very high-density inner portions, could go unlamented.

Why? Because

the land thus released could be advantageously reused for offices, institutions, residential development, parks and open space. Especially along the waterfronts.

Workers, the RPA reasoned, completely ignoring its own and other well-known studies on discrimination against blacks in the suburbs, will simply follow the "out-movement" of plants, "effecting a better balance of families by income throughout the region."[55]

The RPA didn't dismiss the Harvard Study totally, it simply filtered the analysis through its own bias towards elite white collar workers. In this way, urban real estate was the beneficiary of the best possible of all worlds. The people and industries they naturally wanted to see go, were eased out by natural forces. And the people and industries that they wanted to stay, were attracted by natural forces. Because it turned out that corporate headquarters wanted to locate just where the RPA wanted them to. In the Manhattan CBD, in downtown Brooklyn, and yes, even Newark.[56] (And to re-inforce these natural economic forces, the RPA lobbied mightily for subsidies to corporations and FIRE industries to locate in these areas.)

In other words, external economies worked. But just for elite office workers:

Clustering those urban activities that can profit from concentration in large centers is a key policy of The Second Regional Plan for the New York Region.

Clustering was for networking lawyers and deal-making bankers. Small manufacturers needed to be out smelling the potato fields in Suffolk County. Only high rent urban activities truly benefited from the external economies of the Manhattan CBD.

Ordinary citizens would benefit from the exodus of the blue collars and the in-gathering of the whites, too. Since, claimed the RPA, it was the incredible synergy derived from packing all those lawyers and bankers in the Manhattan CBD that made the entire region so productive and affluent.[57] And what external economies have joined together, let no man put asunder. The RPA issued this warning;

If the cohesion of this strategic cluster of jobs were to be weakened by poor transportation, increasing internal congestion, inappropriate tax policies and inadequate public and quasi-public services and capital investment, it is unlikely that its separate parts could simply be relocated elsewhere without suffering a diminution in their quality and probably in their numbers as well.

If the Manhattan CBD were to lose its elite tenants, cautioned the RPA, it might "easily have adverse national implications."[58]

## WESTWARD HO!

Just about all RPA planning since the fifties "U-turn" has been designed to promote, either directly or indirectly, the growth and creation of "centers." And no center has more preoccupied the RPA than the Manhattan CBD. The real aim of all the organization's exercises in deductive reasoning and potted forecasting points beyond the mere need for centers and the desire to "plan", i.e., to expand them.

A June 7, 1967 memo identified for

committee use only "background supplement for the meeting of the Second Regional Plan"

read,

For the Manhattan CBD, we propose at least one new office cluster. This would be about the size of three Rockefeller Centers in office jobs, gross office space and total land area. It would include about 150,000 jobs in office buildings.

At this stage, in the plan, the RPA's preferred location for more offices was the area between Eighth Avenue and the Hudson River; between 42nd and 50th.

The structures that make up the RPA's "west midtown business center" of the mid-sixties are the woolly mammoth ancestors of the elephantine office buildings – the million plus square foot babies – that finally got crammed onto Broadway and the West 40s with such devastating effect in the late eighties. Only in this 1967 version, "the west midtown business center" assumed new transit lines between north and south, east and west. As well as a new terminal for high speed inter-city transportation.

A few years later, however, in its *Urban Design Manhattan*, the scope of the RPA's midtown plan had expanded. New projections of office growth suggested the need for even more office space and office districts.

The report insisted

Midtown Manhattan should be prepared for additional office construction equivalent to about 66 Time and Life buildings, eight Rockefeller Centers or eight World Trade Centers. This is about 400,000 office jobs.

And this was just the moderate growth scenario. Really rapid growth would mean an increase of 700,000 office workers.[59] How would they all fit?

The answer was, that as the blue collar workers left, the white collars would take their seats on the subway and in the traffic lanes coming in from the city's bridges and tunnels. In the alternative growth scenarios projected by the RPA, blue collar workers would shrink from 650,000 to 200,000 or from 600,000 to 300,000. But there had to be a minimum decline of 300,000 for the plan to work.

The big gift, however, that departing blue collar workers would deliver to Manhattan office construction is not just their place in a lane on the George Washington bridge or their seat on the Broadway local. It is the land underneath their factories.

The CBD in 1965 had 800,000 office workers. The RPA estimated there'd be 1.3 million by the year 2000. To accommodate them, the city would have to construct 200 million more feet of space.[60] Where would all the towers go? On the face of it three hundred thousand would replace blue collar workers on a one-for-one basis. But there was a bonus. Compared to office work, blue collar density was comparatively low. In the Manhattan CBD, factories had a density of 900 blue collar workers per acre. Whereas new office buildings between 3,000 and 4,000 white collar workers per acre. So the RPA concluded:

Land freed by the projected decline of 300,000 manufacturing and wholesaling jobs would, because of its much lower employment density, be more than ample for all the office growth.[61]

New York City is a place where savvy residents are supposed to read the obits to get a jump on the latest rent stabilized apartments. No sooner than the deceased's body has been whisked away to Glendale, than a line has already formed in front of the super's door. But nowhere in the city are the expectations of early demise sharper or the stakes higher than in those areas where blue collar industry still gasps along. Only when "freed" of its productive enterprise can manufacturing property be made to yield its full harvest of speculative profits.

## THE HARD AND THE SOFT

Once you understand the most edifying principles that govern the city's economic geography, the rest of RPA plan falls easily into place. Q.Where are the new office districts going to be placed? A.In the areas where blue collar industry is about to be "freed up."

The RPA calls these "soft" locations. The softs are simply the land uses easy to push out. The "hards" are tougher. On a map entitled "'Hard' and 'soft' areas in midtown commercial district: permanent places as contrasted with impermanent areas subject to development with office buildings" the entire midtown area is mapped with three colors. "Red" means there's an office building there. Office buildings can't easily be displaced. They're hard. "Orange" means that it's a soft area – it could easily be converted to offices, because the building isn't throwing off a lot of rent. But the land use is "good" – it's a theater or a concert hall. It adds value to the area indirectly. The RPA admits these are "subjective" criteria. The remainder of the midtown area is colored in blue – it's soft – the most vulnerable to office development. But the RPA says that even those these areas are convertible; sound planning criteria suggests that the emphasis in conversion should go to those plots closest to the subway stations.[62]

Given the location of the soft areas, the RPA concentrates on three main Manhattan neighborhoods. There's the west side between 38th and 56th Streets, Sixth and Eighth Avenues. This is all going to be for office buildings. Then there's the area around Penn Station – office buildings for that neighborhood too. And finally the "valley" from 34th to 14th Streets between Fifth and Sixth Avenue. All this will form an office corridor too. Immediately adjoining the office buildings will be a luxury residential area. So for example the entire swath from about 32nd to 18th Street, Sixth Avenue west to the river will be luxury residential.[63]

## LOCATING "REGIONAL SUBCENTERS"

The Harvard study had predicted that as rents rose in the midtown CBD, the area would become an elite office center, not just an office center. Just as those doing routine factory work were pushed to the periphery, those doing routine office work would have to leave too. Where though would they go? Should they be allowed to find locations on their own, just go anywhere, or should planners determine optimum locations?

The First Regional Plan, as part of the overall decentralization strategy, had recommended "regional subcenters" as locations for out-going factories. Blue collar workers, the plan argued, should be encouraged to move to new towns in the meadowlands; and elsewhere in New Jersey. The Second Regional Plan designed regional subcenters as locations for routine white collar office work. But these are not "edge cities" in New Jersey. Rather they were expressly designed to prevent these unplanned agglomerations of office space springing up on cheap land outside central cities.[64]

Here was the reasoning: as office building development proceeds in the Manhattan CBD, land values increase, rents rise, second-tier corporations, and back office operations move to the periphery – the edge cities. But this would hurt the city, the RPA argues. Why not keep the office workers in New York? Put them were they can do some good outside the CBD but still inside the city.

An RPA confidential briefing book on the plan, for directors only, written by William Shore "on the basis of staff analyses" and distributed at a 1968 Princeton meeting suggests that besides the gain in ratables there was another reason for channeling the office developments in sub-centers.

## MAGNETIZING BLACK NEIGHBORHOODS

The RPA picked the following areas for regional sub-centers – Newark; Jamaica; downtown Brooklyn; and Fordham Road in the Bronx. "These centers," the RPA briefing book observed "are all adjacent to or in the center of large Negro–Puerto Rican neighborhoods."[65]

According to the briefing book, the centers will serve the neighborhoods by bringing lots of jobs. But the RPA noted also that the regional sub-centers will be "magnets" that attract people to live as close to them as possible. The briefing book noted too that urban renewal and "sky-high rents in Manhattan" attest to the power of such a magnet.[66]

RPA reasoning seemed to be that locating office buildings in ghetto neighborhoods would help some community residents to find jobs. But the Association also seemed to realize that to the extent office buildings were implanted, their development would attract people from outside the community. And since the incoming people would have higher incomes, they would tend to displace the lower income people.

In fact, although never stated explicitly, it's hard not to conclude that the RPA chose the areas for regional subcenters *because* they offered an opportunity for what planners called "secondary displacement": bulldozers being "primary displacement, the high rents that force people to move, the "secondary" variety of the species.

## ON THE RPA'S WATERFRONT

Uses planned for the waterfronts should be those which *bring people to the River*.
RPA, The Lower Hudson, December 1966.

If there is one thing I want my administration to be identified with, it is that we
brought the harbor back to the City of New York, that we built on the waterfront
our greatest treasure, that we opened the waters to the people of the city.
Mayor Ed Koch, January 18,1979.
speech marking the 40th anniversary of the New York City Planning Commission.[67]

One of the overriding principles of the waterfront plan is to re-establish the public's
connection to the waterfront by creating opportunities for visual, physical and
recreational access.
David N. Dinkins,
New York City Comprehensive Waterfront Plan, Summer 1992.

The rosy-fingered dawn of every post-war real estate boom has been
marked by vast Homeric plans for the exploitation of the city's
waterfront. Even now, when prospects have never been more clouded,
the dream lives on.[68] The waterfront offers itself as real estate's Troy:
its zone of conquest and adventure.

Urban coastal areas assume this role because waterfront land – river
views notwithstanding – are the hardest to develop. First and most
obviously, because historically, the port attracted manufacturers to the
waterfront. And these manufacturing industries as well as the maritime
industries located there received legal protection for their right to
remain. And also because there are few mass transit lines that touch the
edges of the city. The further you get from mass transit, the less value.[69]
But since land values are low, the rewards for converting it are high:
thus, the plans by the Downtown Lower Manhattan Association for the
Second Avenue subway which was actually a *Water Street Subway*, i.e., an
East River subway;[70] as well as the more successful revival by the Port
Authority of the Hudson and Manhattan tubes which opened up
development on the Hudson river (the PATH trains).

And thus, ultimately, too, the profane object of real estate's passion
for "bringing people to the waterfront."

Of course the RPA was knocking down an open door in its report
on "The Lower Hudson" when it insisted on bringing people to the
waterfront. They were already there. But not, perhaps, as Nelson
Rockefeller would say, "the right kind of people." On the lower

Manhattan waterfront prior to the great heroic age of planning that dawns in 1958 with the Downtown Lower Manhattan Plan, there were longshoremen, truckers, fish mongers, coffee processors, electrical district workers and merchants, fruit and vegetable produce workers, etc. To assert then, as the RPA did, in their principal waterfront recommendation: "There is both opportunity and strong interest in turning most of the land on the Lower Hudson – both banks – from goods handling and production uses to activities that primarily serve, engage and house people . . ."[71] is to reduce hundreds of thousands of blue collar workers and small businessmen to the status of people who need not be served; people with whom one need not engage. Nor for that matter house. Since there has there been very little enthusiasm in higher real estate circles for housing working people along the water-front – at least below 96th Street.

Today's waterfront planners continue to insist on the priority of the public amenity dimension, romantic walks around the harbour, fog horns in the mist, winding bike paths, people once again swimming, fishing and boating in clean waters, low income housing, etc.[72] The RPA, however, made it clear in 1966 that it was office buildings not amenities that were primary. The RPA's 2nd Regional Plan argued

From 12th Street to the Battery, housing, parks and related facilities should be built along the River *to complement the growing office developments like the World Trade Center.* This is in accordance with the Lower Manhattan Plan recently submitted to the NYC Planning Commission.[73]

The sixties' sudden frenzy for executing downtown waterfront projects – World Trade Center, The Westside Highway, Battery Park City, Man-hattan Landing, South Street Seaport, The Second Avenue Subway, the revival of the PATH commuter trains, – was interrupted by the long sleep of the seventies. But when real estate revived again in the eighties, the concern for "serving, engaging and housing [rich] people" remained unabated. The RPA's map of the downtown area in "The Lower Hudson" showing the location of railroad yards and docks as likely areas for conversion to office buildings has since proved most prophetic. And its analysis of the obstacles to conversion provides the key to under-standing subsequent development.

Besides the obvious political and legal problems confronting de-velopers there were three principal physical impediments to downtown transformation: the docks, the railroad yards and the Westside Highway.

The 1929 Regional plan had opposed the construction of an elevated Westside Highway all down the Hudson shoreline on the grounds that it would block real estate development – creating a wall between the river and the construction of office buildings. And nearly forty years later, the RPA was still trying to bring it down.

The elevated West Side Highway separates lower Manhattan from the Hudson. Unless the reconstruction of the highway is coordinated with the many waterfront projects . . . it will continue to be a major deterrent to redevelopment of the waterfront.[74]

The Westside Highway promoted during the Koch and Carey years ("Westway") was an even more real estate driven project – by depressing the highway below grade, it could squeeze offices on the banks of the river and on platforms in the river. While citizen activists, led by Marcy Benstock of the Clean Air Campaign helped kill the project on conservation and environmental grounds, Westway has been reincarnated by Governor Cuomo in accordance with basic karmic principles as "The Hudson River Conservancy."[75]

In physical terms, if you looked at the RPA's 1966 Hudson river map, the two remaining obstacles, the railyards and the docks, effectively merged into one giant economic obstacle – the port of New York. Rail yards ran all along the west bank of the Hudson river. But why were they there? For one reason: to transport freight to the Manhattan docks: the world's largest cargo port. The river was the natural break bulk division. Unaccountably there was no way to get cargo from the Jersey side of the river to the Manhattan side except by "lighter" – the boats that carried flatcars back and forth in the absence of the long-planned freight tunnel promised by the Port Authority in 1921.

If there was no lower Manhattan port, however, if, just if, the port could be moved, say, to New Jersey – as the New York Times had urged as far back as 1922 and the First Regional Plan had recommended in 1929 – the railyards could be moved too. Would the railroad's owners mind? It's hard to see why. They claimed they were losing money on their Manhattan freight operations. Certainly they'd been trying to get out of having to operate the car floats for decades. Plus they owned the land.

On the Manhattan Side of the river there were two big railroad yards – at 60th Street and at 30th Street. Both yards were owned by the then Pennsylvania Railroad (subsequently the Penn Central). Conversion of the upper west side yards – now Donald Trump's Riverside South – would obviously be a bonanza,and also for the interests located right next to them, e.g., the *New York Times* which owned property next to 60th Street.

In the late sixties, Lazard Realty bought air rights and land in around and over the 30th Street yards. Olympia & York owns a plot that includes air rights over the railroad tracks between Ninth and Tenth Avenue at 31st Street.[76] At one time, Trump had an option on the 30th Street yards too.[77] It is now being discussed as the locale for George Steinbrenner's proposed new Yankee Stadium. The owners and the options frequently shift. But the point should be obvious: these yards had and continue to have great conversion potential. And they were also critical to the survival of the garment industry. It was the 30th Street yards, for example, where the freight-forwarding firms were located – the firms which Benjamin Chinitz in his Harvard study *Freight and the Metropolis*, had described as absolutely vital to the garment industry.[78]

On the Jersey side, from west New York, through Hoboken and Jersey City, the land was owned by the New York Central – merged into the Penn Central, the Erie and Lackawanna, the Pennsylvania, the Baltimore and Ohio, the Central of New Jersey, Lehigh Valley, New York Susquehanna & Western and the Hoboken Shore railroad. Altogether they owned 1,875 acres of waterfront land – The Pennsylvania, RPA President's George McAneny's old boss, owned the most – 508 acres. Central of New Jersey, of which RPA director and chief funder Robert De Forest had been a director owned the second most at 411 acres.[79]

On the Jersey waterfront today, it's all office development and commercial malls too: Sam Lefrak's Newport Mall, the Merrill Lynch Building, Exchange Place Center, Harborside Financial Center, "home to more than 25 companies" including Bankers Trust and the Bank of Tokyo.[80] Thus has the lonesome whistle's sound been replaced by the faint whine of the laser printer.

## THE 1969 LINDSAY MASTER PLAN

The 1968 Second Regional Plan and the volumes leading up to it provide the template for New York City planning for the next quarter century. Not because the RPA invents all the plans. Or because it has a stable of influential political insiders who drive planning change as in the good old days of the Great Depression when Larry Orton stood on the right hand of La Guardia and Paul Windels on his left.[81] The RPA, greatly diminished in potency and originality, still wins battles here and there. Downtown Brooklyn is its shiniest recent trophy. And they may bring home another in the south Bronx.[82] But the RPA operates less as the fount and force behind plans and more as a kind of clearing house and validator for plans and perspectives that powerful FIRE estate interests already support.[83]

In essence, its publications function increasingly as a kind of ruling class bulletin board that suggest what the higher real estate consciousness is thinking.[84] If you read the Second Regional Plan publications, you could skip most of the 1969 Lindsay Plan and just flip through the pages of notable photographs of the city and absorb some of the very revealing data about manufacturing, race and housing that the Department of City Planning shared with the public.

The Lindsay Plan adopted nearly all the RPA projects – the west midtown plan, Westway, the second avenue subway, just about the whole downtown Lower Manhattan perspective, as well as the over-arching dual emphasis on center expansion and port riddance. The Lindsay Plan contains these similarities however, not because it wants to please the RPA per se – but because the administration's priorities were broadly determined by the same people who promoted the Second Regional Plan. Indeed, the one project most identified with the RPA itself – its idea for regional subcenters – Lindsay completely ignored in the plan itself,[85] a slight which drew RPA criticism of a plan they broadly approved.

But, in rhetorical terms, the Lindsay Plan differs substantially in tone and logic from the Second Regional Plan. The centrist politician adopts the inclusive logic of both/and. Not the disjunctive logic of either/or. The RPA explains how the city cannot serve two masters: it's either the speculative midtown developers or the small manufacturers dependent on CBD space. Lindsay presents what is almost identical to the RPA's west midtown plan as simply unproblematic. Far from suggesting that the lamb must be served up to the lion, he insists that they work together to find makings for a salad that both can enjoy.

An early draft of the plan however – call it "the smoking memo" reveals that Lindsay planners may not have been so naive. It reads:

> In the long run, New York does not want to retain the low skill, low wage segment of its industrial mix . . . The displacement of manufacturing activity in the CBD is the complement to the expansion of office construction which results in more intensive land use, higher investments and more jobs than manufacturing activities they replaced.[86]

There is lots of this kind of thinking, perhaps not phrased quite so baldly, in RPA literature. (In Urban Design Manhattan, and The Lower Hudson, for example.) But this may be the only *city* document which states in such an unqualified way that policy makers aim to be rid of vast amounts of industry so that office buildings can be implanted. That is until the recent Dinkins Administration's Industry Survey which practically celebrates the loss of more than 800,000 industrial jobs.[87] A lot more was at stake in 1968, however, when there were more than 1,000,000 industrial jobs to lose.[88]

In the final draft of the Lindsay Plan, though, the earlier language is not just softened; it's almost reversed. It says,

The white collar sector may be where the main growth is, but industry accounts for one-fifth of the city's jobs and is still one of the greatest strengths of the City.

What Lindsay assumes is that the city can carry out west side expansion of the CBD, get rid of the port, execute the elements of the downtown Lower Manhattan plan and still preserve manufacturing.

The difference between Lindsay's perspective and the RPA's wasn't just rhetoric. The Lindsay Plan not only pledged preservation, it proposed adding two to three million square feet of industrial space annually. There was nothing in the RPA plans of the sixties that talked about preserving industry, or creating new industrial parks. Perhaps too much shouldn't be made of the differences, however, since even Lindsay never talked about saving industrial jobs in the Manhattan CBD: i.e., the most important location, numerically, and functionally for New York manufacturing. Lindsay pledged to create blue collar jobs not in Manhattan, where small firms wanted to be: but on east river along the Brooklyn and Bronx coasts. And much of what seems like passion for creating manufacturing jobs in the outer boroughs derived from a desire to get them out of Manhattan. Such relocation would subsequently become official city policy.[89]

## "THE NATIONAL CENTER"

An urban archeologist from the year 3000, sifting through a pile of old papers from the late second millenium, could date the Lindsay Plan as a document of sixties, purely by its concept of the city's function as "the national center." Just as certain pottery styles appeared and disappeared at very specific times and became bench marks for other seemingly unrelated phenomena, so the national center concept was very specific to sixties planning, but quickly disappeared. This is because the corporate headquarters that were the basis for "the national center" idea disappeared so quickly.

In 1969, however, the corporate flight out of the city hadn't yet taken on the staggering proportions it would in later years. So the rationale for the CBD was still argued in terms of New York as the place where the U.S. corporate headquarters choose to be. Paradoxically, as the city shrank, it began to promote itself in even more grandiose terms: its functions hypertrophied – at least in marketing terms. New York became the global center of intelligence; the information capital of the planet; "the world's economic command post."[90]

But in 1969, the notion of New York as simply the United States' business capital received great prominence. Following the summary of what's in the plan, the first chapter is entitled the "national center". On the page facing the text is a stunning picture of the dawn breaking above Manhattan's CBD: an almost heavenly light streams down from above, bathing the office buildings in a stirring scene of extraordinary power, energy, and even dignity.

The text begins:

Commercial office growth has prospered in New York and has brought New York prosperity. This growth is the reason why New York City has not had to use public funds to subsidize the redevelopment of its business district.[91]

The author goes to exult,

In the last two decades 195 major new office buildings have added 67 million square feet of office space in the city – twice the total office space in the next nine largest American cities combined.

And there were plans to build 55 more office buildings, with 50 million square feet. Of course, every bit of space is needed because

the city is headquarters for a large proportion of the country's most influential firms and they are expanding their headquarters.

The vacancy rate, bragged the author, was "an astonishing one-half of per cent."[92] It would quickly rise by an equally astonishing factor of forty.
Nineteen sixty-nine was New York's annus mirabilis – the year that

30 million square feet of office space were built. The city never truly recovered. The office building industry revived in the eighties only on the basis of heavy subsidies. And throughout the seventies, the city paid heavily in protracted unemployment, liquidations, and ultimately in fiscal crisis, for the illusion that big national headquarters were expanding their space in New York. Manhattan's dynastic developers and the FIRE industries that coddled them refused to accept a diminished role. So like sugar beet farmers or dairy cattlemen, facing glut, they insisted on carrying on as before, demanding city subsidies to do so. So whereas the Lindsay Plan explained how the genius of the city consisted in not subsidizing the construction of office buildings, future planning documents would mouth the same rhetoric, while stuffing the developers' pockets with billions in tax breaks.[93]

At the time, however, future gluts were unimaginable. In 1969, the entire emphasis was on "channeling growth." William H. Whyte, the celebrated urban essayist and RPA committee member who wrote the text, tried to do for the Manhattan CBD what Wordsworth and Coleridge did for the Lake district. In particular he celebrated the possibilities of lower Manhattan and west side development prospects. He writes:

West midtown offers a golden opportunity. . . . It is ripe for redevelopment. Office construction has been moving west, but it has not yet crossed Eighth Avenue. . . . The major redevelopment lies ahead. Intelligently guided, it can be highly profitable and amenable, and can provide expansion room for the midtown area for the next twenty years.

Whyte proposed what would become familiar as the Times Square Two Step. First is "rebirth for the squalid blocks of 42nd street between 6th and 8th." This "renaissance," it was proclaimed, would materialize at any moment. Second, and flowing from the removal of the cheap entertainment district, would come the development of the area between 47th and 49th – from Eighth to the river. Here the city needed to help promote the building of 30 million square feet of office space. The idea, wrote Whyte,

is that the increase in land value alone will produce enough revenue to pay for the public improvements. It will be a lively and exciting place.

Just south of this area, the city needed to execute the Ford Foundation's plan for prestigious office buildings for daytime activity and a lively exciting theater and restaurant area at night.

And to add to the excitement, on the west side, Whyte suggested a convention center, whose costs, far from being a drag on the budget, would generate tremendous revenues for the city.[94]

Finally, the document also pledged the city to complete the Lower Manhattan Plan – the 1966 update of the DLMA's 1963 version – the clearance of the remaining markets, the upbuilding of Battery Park City, The Second Avenue Subway, completion of the World Trade Center, and perhaps most importantly, getting rid of the port:

the Manhattan waterfront is a priceless asset. Instead of being wasted on obsolete functions, it should be opened up to new uses.[95]

In this de-industrial vein, Lindsay's Plan attacked the 1963 blueprint drafted by ports and terminals to redevelop the North River docks for container use as "a grandiose proposal" and congratulated the City Planning Commission on killing it. After all, Whyte exclaimed, reviving the port would have cost upwards of $600 million. Lindsay's own plan however, the proposals for dumping 200 acres of land fill in the Hudson and East rivers and then paving them over with five million square feet of office space and state-supported luxury housing for 100,000 people – this was not "grandiose."[96] And when the DLMA's World Trade Center opened in 1973 the price tag would be over $1 billion.

## NOTES

1. Paul Windels, "The Metropolitan Region at the Crossroads," American Planning and Civic Annual, 1948, p. 64 cited in Mel Scott, *American City Planning* (Berkeley: University of California Press), p. 448. Scott makes the excellent point that Windels' speech is rare in American planning discourse for its evocation of the question of urban structure at all. He writes, "city planners as well as city officials and civic leaders, tended to dodge the whole issue of metropolitan form. Culturally conditioned to problem-solving and socially rewarded for displaying short-term practicality, they felt more at ease adapting to well-recognized trends and working cautiously within the context of a business-dominated economy." Ibid. p. 451.
2. For the mid-forties RPA Weltanschauung, see Regional Plan Association, The Economic Status of the New York Region in 1944 (New York: RPA Inc., 1944).
3. A defender of Windels might argue that although he embraced his awful specter, he never attacked his prized goal, *true* decentralization, because "spread city" didn't resemble the positive ideal the RPA was putting forward, garden cities, like Radburn. It's true that Windels never advocated endless strings of shopping malls and large lot zoning, but RPA methods of the thirties certainly promoted that result.

4. The only faint acknowledgement in the RPA literature that I know of which even suggests that the RPA party line from the twenties to the fifties was *mistaken* comes from an RPA sponsored book by William A. Cauldwell entitled *How to Save Urban America* (New York: New American Library, 1973). "'Decentralization' has been written on the banners of most planners in the twentieth century, and it was the goal of our first Regional Plan prepared between 1922 and 1931," wrote William A. Cauldwell for the Association. "The planners of the twenties did not foresee that Manhattan's population would drop one *third* between 1920 and 1970, or that distant Suffolk County would have six times the population they projected."

5. Paul Windels, "Private Enterprise Plan in Housing Faces First Test," National Municipal Review 22 (June 16, 1943), p. 286. Cited in Joel Schwartz, *The New York Approach* (Columbus, Ohio: Ohio University Press, 1993), p. 97.

6. Gene Setzer to files, November 16, 1954, RAC. Cited in Joel Schwartz, *The New York Approach* (Columbus, Ohio: Ohio State University Press, 1993), p. 256.

7. For Osborne's role see "In Memoriam," in Regional Plan Association, Focus/1987, January 1987, p. 2.

8. A rentier capitalist is one no longer active in the accumulation of real capital. Someone who lives off investments, a "coupon clipper."

9. Dowling debated Windels in planning publications on the question of centralization vs. decentralization. On a purely impressionistic basis, built up on the basis of small pieces of evidence, it seems as though Dowling was the single most politically influential developer in the city from the mid-fifties up to Lindsay's administration. Item: when Wagner came to visit John D. Rockefeller III at his One Beekman Place townhouse, he came accompanied with Dowling. And when Rockefeller complained that it was hard to reach Wagner because he didn't have his private phone number, it turned out that Dowling already had the number. (John D. Rockefeller III, "Meetings with Mayor Wagner regarding Lincoln Center," John D. Rockefeller III, Personal Papers, Box 48, folder 2–48, Rockefeller Archive Center (RAC).)

10. See chapter 5, sect. "The Family Subway."

11. David came out of the Morning Heights Inc. experience a few hundred thousand dollars lighter and with an honorary degree from Columbia – but no renegotiation of the bitterly contested ground lease the Family suffered under since 1928. The Rockefellers sought ten times to get the University to sell them the land underneath Rockefeller Center. Finally, in 1985, the University sold them the land. And the family was finally free to sell their midtown property. See chapter 5, "The Deal of a Dynasty".

12. A Morningside Heights Inc. report evaluating the project reads, "Leaders of the uneasy element found recruits among certain families on the cooperative site who were not familiar with the provisions which the law makes for their re-housing. Their fears of eventual homelessness were encouraged by the leaders." (MHInc, "Relocation: Critical Phase of Redevelopment," p. 7. Rockefeller Brothers Fund, Box 59, Folder no.2 "Morningside Heights Inc", RAC.)

13. Following the appointment in January 1972 of a committee to "re-examine the goals and purposes of MHinc.", the organization re-emerged under another name and never regained its former power and authority. As resistance to MH Inc. grew David relinquished chairmanship in 1965 to Grayson Kirk. Rockefeller's long-time aide, Warren Lindquist served as vice-president. At the height of the student uprising, James Felt, city planning commission chief, bailed out too. (See MH Inc., "The Chronology of Morningside Heights, Inc. for twenty-five years 1947–1972" RBF, Box 185. Folder 1970–1976, RAC.)

14. See Kai Bird, *The Chairman* (New York: Simon & Schuster, 1992), p. 454.

15. Tom Shachtman, *Skyscraper Dreams* (Boston: Little, Brown and Company, 1991), pp. 186–187. In addition, as late as the 1930s, the Astors owned huge chunks of the lower east side.

16. *New York Times*, October 27, 26:7.

17. Carol Herselle Krinsky, *Rockefeller Center* (Oxford: Oxford University Press, 1978), p. 60. Regional Plan Association of New York and its Environs, II, *The Building of the City*, Thomas Adams (ed.) (New York: 1931), passim.

18. Joel Schwartz, *The New York Approach* (Columbus, Ohio: Ohio University Press, 1993), p. 256, see footnote no. 51.
19. Department of City Planning, Midtown Development Review, New York City, July 1987, DCP 87-05, p. 6.
20. *New York Times*, December 20, 1955, p. 26.
21. Joel Schwartz, *The New York Approach* (Colombus, Ohio: Ohio University Press, 1993), p. 235.
22. John I. Griffin, *Industrial Location* (New York: CUNY 1956), p. 3.
23. When ASR left for Virginia, Griffin pointed out that the big difference between Virginia and New York was labor costs. It was land costs. Even taxes were exactly the same *rate* – but the tax burden was ten times higher here because land values are ten times higher. Real estate taxes in New York City were $55,000 per year, in Virginia $5,500. The differential is strictly due to the higher land costs in New York, ibid., p. 92.
24. Ibid., p. 4.
25. *New York Times*, April 10, 1956, p. 33.
26. See Joel Schwartz, *The New York Approach* (Columbus: Ohio University Press, 1993), p. 247.
27. *New York Times*, June 6, 1955, p. 24.
28. Joel Schwartz, *The New York Approach* (Colombus, Ohio: Ohio University Press, 1993), p. 285.
29. John Ensor Harr and Peter J. Johnson, *The Rockefeller Conscience* (New York: Charles Scribner's Sons, 1991). pp. 19–20.
30. The most powerful indictment of urban renewal – surprisingly by the conservative Martin Anderson – *The Federal Bulldozer* (New York: McGraw-Hill Book Company, 1967), p. 4. – attacked just four dimensions of the phenomenon:
    1) The forcible displacement of millions of citizens from their homes.
    2) The seizure of one man's private property for some other man's private use.
    3) The destruction of hundreds of thousands of low-rent homes.
    4) The spending of billions of dollars of the taxpayers' money.
31. John D. Rockefeller III, "Meetings with Mayor Wagner regarding Lincoln Center," March 7, 1961, John D. Rockefeller III, Personal. Box 48, Folder 2–48. This is one of several expressions of annoyance. At their last meeting, called at his request, JDR notes that Wagner kept him waiting downstairs at Gracie Mansion. "I wanted to express to him my concern that he did not seem to have more interest in Lincoln Center or willingness to go to bat for it." Rockefeller furnished Wagner with specific examples of "how little help he had been to us." But what really seems to irk Rockefeller is that Wagner has to be coerced. That he is sullen and silent at meetings. That he doesn't realize the significance of what the family is trying to do (ibid; April 12, 1965).
32. John D. Rockefeller III, "Meetings with Mayor Wagner regarding Lincoln Center," entry for September 13, 1957. John D. Rockefeller III, Personal, Box 48, Folder 2–48.
33. Regional Plan Association, *The Region's Growth*, New York, May 1967, p. 80.
34. Edgar M. Hoover and Raymond Vernon, *Anatomy of a Metropolis* (New York: Doubleday Anchor, 1962), p. 11.
35. Alfred Marshall, *Principles of Economics. 8th Edition* (London: Macmillan Ltd., 1979), pp. 237–9, 378–9.
36. Edgar M. Hoover and Raymond Vernon, *Anatomy of a Metropolis* (Garden City, New York: Doubleday Anchor, 1962), pp. 45–51.
37. Chinitz's port analysis was typical of a study that emphasized not just trends, but counter-trends; not just the forces that pushed manufacturers out of New York, but the counter-vailing forces that pushed them to stay. Everyone knows that trucks were displacing rails as the country's main mode of freight transportation, and that the upshot was decentralization. But there was a counter-trend. Railroads were developing piggy-back facilities (now called "Trailers on Flat Car", TOFC). Cities where railroads invested in TOFC facilities would attract industry. And New York as the nation's largest manufacturing city, stood to gain a big rail investment.
    Chinitz was proven wrong about what the railroads would decide to do with their money. The railroads which served New York used the freedom provided by federal legislation in the late

fifties and sixties to abandon their facilities – not to invest in modernized yards and transport. The unbelievably antiquated Manhattan Transfer – the floatation of railroad cars across the Hudson by ferry from New Jersey to Lower Manhattan – lasted as long as the Penn Central. But it wasn't technological imperatives that explain these investment decisions. It's not that the know-how didn't exist to drive a tunnel under the Hudson. It was rather that the New York transportation companies felt they had better things to do with their capital than to invest it in moving freight around the region. The Penn Central flamed out in a series of wild speculative real estate maneuvers that culminated in what was then America's greatest bankruptcy. The other railroads on both the New Jersey and Manhattan side of the Hudson managed to generate big revenue – sometimes only for their liquidators – with sale of their railroad yards for office development in Hoboken, Jersey City as well as Lower Manhattan.

38. Robert Lichtenberg, *One-tenth of a Nation* (Cambridge: Harvard University Press, 1960), p. 89; see also Hoover and Vernon, p. 47.

39. Edgar M. Hoover and Raymond Vernon, *Anatomy of a Metropolis* (Garden City: Doubleday & Company, 1962), pp. 106–109.

40. Ibid., p. 109.

41. Dick Netzer, "New York City's Mixed Economy: Ten Years Later," *The Public Interest*, no. 16 (Summer 1969), p. 20.

42. New York State Department of Labor (unpublished figures).

43. New York City Planning Commission, Plan for New York City, 1969, vol 1, Critical Issues, pp. 70–71.

44. Hoover and Vernon, *Anatomy of a Metropolis* (Garden City: Doubleday & Company, 1962), p. 26, table 3.

45. See chart 3, p. 73, from Robert Lichtenberg, *One Tenth of a Nation* (Cambridge, Massachusetts: Harvard University Press, 1960).

46. Ibid., p. 74. Lichtenberg shows however, that the city's manufacturing industries didn't maintain their share of value added by manufacturing.

47. After the Second Regional Plan appeared in 1968, Whyte would be tapped to write the 1969 Lindsay Plan.

48. Regional Plan Association. The Region's Growth, a Report of the Second Regional Plan, (New York, May 1967), p. 20.

49. Ibid., p. 21.

50. Ibid., p. 22.

51. Ibid., p. 126

52. New York State Department of Taxation and Finance, Bureau of Tax Data Office of Tax Policy Analysis, "New York Personal Income and Tax Liability for Income Year 1987 By County of Residence," RS-431 (11/90), p. 13. There were about 667,000 households, and approximately 113,000 made over $50,000.

53. Regional Plan Association, the Second Regional Plan, (New York, November 1968), p. 41

54. The Regional Plan Association, The Region's Growth, a Report of the Second Regional Plan (New York, May 1967), p. 10.

55. Ibid., p. 123.

56. Ibid., p. 117.

57. Ibid., p. 114. One of the earliest references to "knowledge workers" comes from a speech by RPA's executive director J.P. Keith at an Arden House conference. on February 14, 1962. "The Region's economy depends very heavily upon 'knowledge workers'," he observes, "and one of the challenges facing the metropolitan area is to preserve the tracts of the region for them." Knowledge workers are defined as financial, legal, advertising men and other top corporate advisers.

58. Ibid., pp. 114–5.

59. Regional Plan Association, Urban Design Manhattan (New York: Viking Press, 1969), p. 15.

60. Regional Plan News Release no.1114, January 11, 1971, p. 6.

61. Regional Plan Association, Urban Design Manhattan (New York: Viking Press, 1969), p. 16.

62. Ibid., p. 73.

63. Ibid., p. 75.

64. For a serene view of these edge cities, written just months before their vacancy rates soared even higher than those in the urban cores, see Joel Garreau, Edge City (New York: Doubleday, 1988). Garreau's book also serves as a treasury of post-industrial bias against urban blue collar workers. For example, he says that industrial space "does not create anything urbane." That "no dense centers can ever evolve" on the basis of blue collar work. This is because factories "usually figure one worker for every forty five hundred square feet" (pp. 30–31). Garreau seems never to have been to New York. In Manhattan, the average is less than one-tenth that figure: 387. (See Department of City Planning, Plan for New York City, vol. 1, pp. 70–71.)

65. The Second Regional Plan: A Draft for Discussion, Background Reading for the Committee on the Second Regional Plan, May 23–24. 1968, Princeton Inn, Princeton, N.J. (note on flyleaf: "This workbook written by William B. Shore. It summarizes the staff's work to date.")

66. Ibid, p. A4:21.

67. Cited in Ann L. Buttenwieser, Manhattan Water-Bound (New York: New York University Press, 1987), pp. 205–26. Buttenwieser's book is a useful guide for waterfront history buffs. Especially those who thrill to the sight of towering office structures and luxury apartment buildings ringing the entire coast line. Her account of Donald Trump's Penn Yard's project however would startle the Donald's most brazen publicists. Trump proposes, she says, "seven apartment buildings, with nearly eight million units" (p. 214). Even the Real Estate Board of New York would have a hard time explaining the need for eight million more apartment units on the west side's waterfront. That's square feet, Ann, not units. Inevitably though, perhaps, Buttenwieser wound up as vice president for waterfront development at the city's Economic Development Corporation.

68. Department of City Planning, New York City Comprehensive Waterfront Plan, "Reclaiming the City's Edge" (New York: Summer 1992), NYC DCP 92-27.

69. Long Island City and downtown Brooklyn being exceptions which illustrate the rule.

70. Office of Lower Manhattan Development, Office of the Mayor, Water Street Access and Development, June 1976. See the map on p. 63 for the "Water Street Subway."

71. Regional Plan Association, The Lower Hudson (New York: December 1966), p. 33.

72. Department of City Planning, New York City Comprehensive Waterfront Plan: Reclaiming the City's Edge, (New York, Summer 1992), NYC DCP 92-27, p. i.

73. Regional Plan Association, The Lower Hudson (New York, December 1966), p. 7.

74. Ibid., p. 29.

75. "The Hudson River Conservancy" is a subsidiary of the Urban Development Corporation – a state agency whose leadership suffers from a malady common among New York elites: the inability to distinguish between real estate development and economic development. This is a state-wide agency, but by far the greatest expenditure of resources for this agency have been lavished on redeveloping a few blocks on the west side of Manhattan – besides the Hudson River Conservancy, UDC has also piloted the failed Times Square project, spending well over $100 million with nothing to show. It also promoted the west side convention center.

76. David W. Dunlap, "A Process of Elimination," New York Times, Section 10, August 1, 1993, p. 1.

77. Wayne Barrett, Trump. The Deals and the Downfall (New York: Harper Collins, 1992), pp. 103–104.

78. It was the small-scale nature of the firms that made them particularly dependent on freight forwarders – who put together freight carloads for small producers who couldn't fill up a full freight car. It was the freight forwarders who distributed the garment products around the country. Benjamin Chinitz, Freight and the Metropolis (Cambridge: Harvard University Press, 1960), pp. 142–3.

79. Regional Plan Association, The Lower Hudson (New York, December 1966), pp. 16–17.

80. Jones, Lang Wootton, "Welcome to Harborside," brochure, n.d.

81. Orton went from the RPA staff to the La Guardia administration as a City Planning Commissioner.

82. See Regional Plan Association, New Directions for The Bronx, Submitted to Fernando Ferrer Bronx Borough President, June 1988.

83. Heads of the RPA from the mid-fifties preparation for the Second Regional Plan included AT&T's Harold Osborne, followed by Amory Bradford, former Davis Polk attorney who was Executive Vice President of the *New York Times*. Then Max Abromowitz, partner of Wallace Harrison, family retainer of Rockefeller family. Prominent directors at the time of publication of the Second Regional Plan included the head of Chemical Bank Donald Platten; John Larsen, head of the Bowery who were on the Executive Committee and Thurgood Marshall, future Supreme Court Justice; James Felt, former City Planning Commission chief and Harry Van Arsdale, head of central labor council who weren't.

The Committee on the Second Regional Plan included such influentials as urbanologist William H. Whyte; Gus Tyler the ILGWU's resident intellectual; Richard Ravitch, the master of subsidized luxury development; Andrew Heiskell – head of *Time-Life*, son-in-law of the *New York Times* chief; black psychologist, Kenneth B. Clark; and Morris B. Crawford of the Bowery – who'd become a RPA Chairman later. Funding for the plan came from Ford no.1 at 750,000; Rockefeller no.2, 375,000; Taconic no.3, 300,000; Avalon, no.4, $150,000.

Figures on financing from RBF Annual Meeting Docket 5/18/67.

84. See New Directions for The Bronx (New York: Regional Plan Association, June 1988), pp. 49–50.

85. Although he was extremely attentive to the promoters of the Jamaica downtown – perhaps in part because David Rockefeller backed the plan so vigorously. And Lindsay couldn't afford a two-front war with *two* Rockefellers.

86. New York City Planning Commission, Comprehensive Plan, draft, n.d., pp. C-2, C-3 (1968) citation on page 219 of Maynard Robinson, "Rebuilding Lower Manhattan: 1955–1974" (Ph.D. diss. City University of New York, 1976).

87. Department of City Planning/New York City, Citywide Industry Study, Labor Force Technical Report, January 1993, p. 37. "The data analyzed here demonstrate, that, while many New Yorkers would most certainly have benefitted from the retention of the more than 800,000 industrial jobs lost since the 1960's, the growing nonindustrial sectors of the economy have managed to provide nearly comparable employment to a substantial segment of unskilled city workers since then." This smug assessment is delivered in a month when the city unemployment rate hit 13.4 percent – higher than all but six of 274 metropolitan areas in the country!

88. "Industrial" is more inclusive than manufacturing – in the present DCP usage it includes transportation, construction, public utilities, and some trade.

89. The Report of the Commission on the Year 2000, *New York Ascendent* (New York, June 1987), p. 41.

90. New York City Planning Commission, Shaping the City's Future (New York, Spring 1993), pp. 1–2

91. New York City Planning Commission, Plan for New York City 1969, *Critical Issues*, v. 1, p. 31.

92. Ibid.

93. The Commission on the Year 2000, *New York Ascendent* (New York: June 1987), p. 27. In the flood of praise for laissez-faire and free market forces ("the city's most constructive role is to stay out of the way") you would never suppose the city was granting literally billions of tax exemptions every year through programs like ICIP, J-51, 421-a., etc.

94. New York City Planning Commission, Plan for New York City 1969, *Critical Issues*, v. 1, p. 34.

95. Ibid., p. 51.

96. Ibid., p. 46.

*CHAPTER FIVE*

# DOWNTOWN IRREDENTISM: THE LOWER MANHATTAN PLAN

"He just liked to build. He was a frustrated architect."
Charles J. Urstadt, Sr. former Chairman, Battery Park City Authority,
on his former boss, Nelson Rockefeller.[1]

The Romans used to say, "nature makes no leaps."[2] Neither as we've seen, do New York planners. Anytime they announce a plan, it's likely to be an inbred descendant of some previous plan, one temporarily shelved because the business cycle turned, and mortgage money dried up.

The basic ideas for the downtown waterfront planning, in terms of what should go where, and who really belongs downtown, as we saw in chapter 3, go back at least as far as the First Regional Plan. In 1929, directors – many who served as railroad directors like De Forest and Dwight Morrow or former railroad lobbyists like George McAneny – sought to shift the port to New Jersey – quite prophetically, to Elizabeth. They drafted zoning maps which largely eliminated Manhattan's industry below 14th Street.

But with the Depression, and with the importance of the port for the war effort, plans to demolish the docks had to be dropped. Interest in converting them naturally revived after World War II. And in 1948, a "World Trade Corporation" bill passed the state legislature. This enabling legislation provided for a World Trade Corporation to be headed by Chase Bank chief Winthrop Aldrich. And it envisioned a big office building to house the World Trade Corporation, the shifting of the Washington produce market and the take-over of the city's piers by the Port Authority. So when David Rockefeller of the Chase announced his 1958 plan, ten years later, it has to be understood that we're not dealing with some new urban vision. It's just the same institutions plugging away at the same object. What changes is their reasons, not their goals.

To claim, then, as many do, that the waterfront was "neglected" is like saying the Treasure of the Sierra Madre was neglected. Concern with converting the docks to prime real estate didn't start with the invention of the container and the discovery that there was more room in New Jersey to put them than in downtown Manhattan. Evidently, there were formidable legal, political, economic problems on the waterfront. Not the least of which was that everyone wanted to grab it.

This was next to impossible, however, as long as the Democratic machine – tied to waterfront wise guys – dominated city politics. Tammany Hall protected the Irish-dominated Manhattan ILA locals on the Hudson waterfront. On the East river side, the Brooklyn county organization stood behind the Italian ILA locals led by Anthony Anastasia, head of Murder Incorporated. (The union hall on Court Street in Brooklyn is still named after Anastasia.) All stood for the waterfront/criminal status quo. And as long as the county democratic organizations kept their clout, and the wise guys could keep from going to the mattresses against each other, the docks stayed decrepit, barely serviceable, and starved of capital improvements – since even the county leaders couldn't simply pump up the capital budget for what they wanted – but still in place.

An abrupt shift in the city's politics took place, however, between 1956 and 1958. The kleptocratic Democratic machine suddenly gave way at the highest official levels to newly empowered plutocratic forces. First, and most obviously, Nelson replaced the comparably wealthy, but Tammany-dependent Democrat, W. Averill Harriman, as Governor. From Albany, Nelson was able to influence who got on the Port Authority. He was also in a position to bully the mayor, who can't make a major fiscal move without the governor's say-so. Second, for whatever reason, Mayor Robert Wagner grew increasingly independent of the county leaders[3] – signalized by the 1957 election primary when he ran on an "independent" slate, i.e., one not endorsed by the Democratic county leaders. Finally, in 1956, there was the fusion of the disparate and discordant downtown real estate and financial interests in a single lobbying and planning group – the Downtown Lower Manhattan Association (DLMA).

The DLMA was the Dream Team of U.S. Finance Capital. If there had been Olympic contests in moneylending, stock speculation, arbitrage, land assemblage, these were the guys we'd have sent: S. Sloan Colt of Banker's Trust – soon to be appointed by Nelson to the Port Authority; Fred Ecker of the Metropolitan Life – perhaps the only New Yorker Junior didn't dare patronize – he held the mortgage on Rockefeller Center and Rockefeller came downtown frequently to pay his respects. There was G. Keith Funston, head of the Stock Exchange; J. Victor Herd of Continental Insurance; Bobby Lehman of Lehman Bros., Henry S. Morgan of Morgan Stanley; John H. Schiff, descendant of Jacob, who had elevated Kuhn Loeb to near mythic status; Henry Alexander of Morgan Guaranty Trust . . . the list went on and on. Under David Rockefeller's leadership the DLMA produced very quickly a comprehensive plan in 1958, for the area between Canal Street and the Battery. But the real focus was even smaller – between Chambers Street and the Battery.

It's hard sometimes to remember that this entire area – which contains the financial district, city hall, the old port – is only about one square mile. It's no longer the world's most valuable real estate – but its history may be the world's most complex – chiefly because you have so many different governmental units involved in planning it. There was an incredibly thick nexus of narrow interests.

In the decade following the 1958 DLMA plan, the institutional politics grew so intertwined and frayed that even David and Nelson wound up on different sides on the Battery Park City housing issue. Each brother advocated a different mix of housing, offices, middle, high and low-income occupants.[4] There are dozens of plans which appear, each qualifying the previous one. They are authored by at least a dozen different city, county, state, private, agencies. To say nothing of the "authorities" which are creatures of the city and the state. And the mayor's Committee on Slum Clearance, headed by Bob Moses, who stuck his hand into the downtown planning mixmaster, and got it cut off.

(Perhaps it was a coincidence, but within 13 months of telling David Rockefeller that he, Moses, wouldn't help with the East river clearances for the DLM Plan, the combined weight of New York's true establishment fell on him. Moses found himself stripped of his Title I powers, and exiled to Flushing, where he ran another World's Fair. Given Wagner's delicate position, none of his appointees, even Moses, could simply tell David Rockefeller to take a walk and survive.)[5]

It's unlikely that the larger political questions that the battle for downtown raises can be resolved now. Who first decided to bell Moses? Why precisely did the World Trade Center go from the East river side of Manhattan to the Hudson river side? What ever happened to the Second Avenue subway? What incentives/pressures were put on the city's labor movement to abandon the cause of the longshoremen? How did the alliance between Lindsay and Nelson – the family provided about half of Lindsay's funds for the first mayoral race – proceed to unravel. Historians won't begin to have a clearer fix until Nelson's papers become available in another decade.

In the meantime, until finer details are available, we have to be satisfied with blocking out some of the main historical forces and motives. At least we can try to figure out what some of the main actors were aiming at, and how well they succeeded.

## THE THEORY OF LOWER MANHATTAN

The first principle of CBDs is that they are places that adjoin or are convenient to rich people's residences.

Most elite commuters who come to the city come by mass transit arriving via Grand Central station, or Penn station. The creation of the two big commuter train terminals sealed the fate of downtown. After you've driven to the train, parked, got on the train, and got off, you don't want to take another. Especially not one that's part of the New York subway system. Even though it's now air-conditioned and fairly dependable, like the one-stop express ride on the Lexington line between Grand Central and City Hall. (Of course the cooler the cars, the hotter the platforms, with temperatures rising to 110 degrees and above, in the absence of fans to carry the hot air out of the tunnels.[6]) All other things equal, the choice between the two locations, downtown and midtown, is hardly equal. Downtown has been losing its elite tenants to midtown since 1913. The idea that downtown could regain its former pre-Grand Central glory was an illusion.

Call it, perhaps, "Rockefeller Irredentism." Lower Manhattan's ruling powers never accepted the shift of the CBD's boundaries. Maria Theresa, empress of Austria-Hungary wouldn't acknowledge the take-over of Silesia by Prussia. "Give me back my Silesia," she shouted at Frederick II. All her efforts to get it back just destroyed Austria's power. Similarly, David Rockefeller, in the late fifties, was in effect shouting at midtown, "give me back my tenants."

The irredentist refusal to accept a diminished status, the unwilling-ness to accept downtown for what it was, a mixed-use commercial-industrial-shipping area, led to hypertrophic plans that succeeded in killing off the port and industry without recapturing the area's old primacy. Jane Jacobs predicted this: of the DLMA's numerous schemes she said,

The plans . . . will foreclose the chance of reasonably adequate services ever being developed, because no room, at economical rents for the incubation of new enterprise, will exist for them.[7]

The downtown planners understood the area's limitations. They just refused to accept them. When they exclaimed that "around-the-clock living will bring new light and life to this tip of the island" they were conceding that downtown was largely dead.[8] Their whole dis-cussion presupposed that downtown would be remade into a lively 24-hour community for rich residents who'd work in the expanded financial districts. The plan was to reverse time's arrow by bringing the right kind of people downtown, and getting rid of those who were there. The tools were zoning, mass transit, Title I, urban renewal, subsidized housing, and just building millions of square feet of office space at state expense to house state office workers.

*Re-zoning.* In 1961 the city was completely re-zoned. If you had the 1928 map of the way New York City should be zoned, put out by the RPA in its First Regional Plan, you would have a pretty good idea of how the zoning would come out. Especially given the leaders of the re-zoning campaign. They called themselves "The Committee for Modern Zoning" It was headed by City Investing Chairman, Bob Dowling, and it included such Manhattan-oriented real estate figures as RPA chairman, Max Abramowitz; RPA director and *Time-Life* exec., Andrew Heiskell; Citizen's Housing and Planning Committee executive director, Roger

Starr; Paul Windels, the former RPA chief; Manhattan developers Bill Zeckendorf and David Tishman; and John Butts, who stood just one rung below David Rockefeller in the hierarchy of the Downtown Lower Manhattan Association.

The 1961 zoning law vastly shrunk the area in which manufacturing was allowed, matching the specifications drawn by the RPA's First Regional Plan. Very broad-based resistance arose from small manufacturing, that can hardly be appreciated unless you sift through the hundreds of protest letters the Mayor received from manufacturers and outer borough chamber of commerce types. The successful zoning battle led by the Committee for Modern Zoning represented a post-industrial shift *avant la lettre*. This, plus an institutional shift. Power to obtain very substantial changes in zoning was transferred from the machine-dominated Board of Standards and Appeals to the mayorally appointed City Planning Commission.

The 1961 Zoning Act narrowed the ring on manufacturing all over the city,[9] but Manhattan suffered most. Manufacturing was made illegal on Manhattan's East river side. The Hudson river side was initially affected much less. This was in accordance with zoning recommendations in the 1958 DLMA plan which initially foresaw the location of the World Trade Center on the *East river* – where, coincidently, the project would add value to the Chase Manhattan Bank. (Chase Manhattan Plaza is so huge that even after accommodating its own work force, it still has 1,000,000 square feet to rent.) In the light of these concerns, perhaps, the DLMA focused its demands for de-industrialization on that side of the island:

the East River waterfront between Old Slip and Brooklyn Bridge is in the logical path of expansion for the Financial District,

David noted in the 1958 Plan. The whole area north from Courtlandt Street to Canal, the area that contained the Washington Street Produce Market would have to go eventually, too. But David left the area south of Courtlandt Street largely intact. At least until the plan changed.[10]

*Urban renewal.* What was so revolutionary about post-war urban renewal? Before Title I, prior to 1949, city governments got rid of poor people – at least thinned out their numbers – by building roads, highways, very long approaches to bridges through poor neighborhoods.[11] The disadvantage, however, with these blunt tools is that, for the propertied interests, at least, they were left with a bridge approach instead of a ghetto. And the bridge didn't even pay taxes. At the same time, under capitalism, you can't just take people's land away without compensation. And lots of the ghetto property was owned by the city's richest families. Title I vastly alleviated both the problems of changing the land use to something higher and the compensation problem as well. It provided federal subsidies – up to 90 percent – to compensate property holders for their confiscated property. And it expanded the reasons you could use to take it. The legal reasons for getting rid of the poor could be stretched far beyond housing – even Lincoln Center somehow fitted. But politically, there had to be some uplifting social purpose politicians could point to. (At the very least you had to call the shopping mall a "Museum" as with South Street Seaport.) Moses couldn't just be brought in to say,

All you poor people out! out! out! We're building a rich people's shopping center here.

But this is exactly what David Rockefeller and the DLMA proposed: they wanted the city in the form of the mayor's Committee on Slum Clearance (Moses) to provide Title I subsidies on behalf of ordinary commercial projects – luxury housing, commercial stores – the whole 24-hour community idea. Now, for the whole downtown area, especially as you got close to the financial district, it's clear that there was a big battle over who would do the dirty work, what kind of projects would get built with whose money, and who would take the political weight. And that ultimately Moses lost.

But because Moses lost didn't mean that the Rockefellers got to proceed as they wished. Moses had cleared out some of the area below Brooklyn bridge. But he had his limits. When he was approached by David Rockefeller to get rid of everyone from Old Slip to Fulton Street along the East river he refused. This goes against the stereotype of "Bob Moses, the Human Bulldozer." You would have thought he would have loved the chance to knock down a truly large area of the city. But he turned David down flat:

We [Moses naturally preferred the royal "we"] have carefully considered the proposal to redevelop the area between the upper and lower housing projects along the East River below Brooklyn Bridge by commercial sponsors, he said, and he recommended that Rockefeller go find someone in the Mayor's office to help him.[12] David's project couldn't fit under the big Title I tent, Moses observed. Try another law, he suggested to Rockefeller. On the other hand, Rockefeller might just need to pass new legislation. And finally, Moses advised, if he wanted to get the benefits of urban renewal, he'd have to take some of the public responsibility:

We believe it also would be feasible to have one or two members of your downtown group work with the [Mayor's] committee. These should be designated by you.[13]

Three days later Moses wrote to the mayor, informing him that he'd dumped Rockefeller's proposal in his lap. Moses said his urban renewal plate was full – he had three downtown projects already. Wagner should appoint a committee to work with David and the DLMA.

I recommend that you appoint such a committee immediately so that it can begin to function. . . . We shall, of course, be glad to help all we can. . .[14]

In the next few months, highly influential real estate – figures like Roger Starr, then executive director of the Citizen's Housing and Planning Council; and New York Life Insurance's Otto Nelson, head of Governor Nelson Rockefeller's Task Force on Housing – began to attack Moses publicly – and, indirectly, Wagner himself. Wagner replied with lengthy self-exculpating memos.[15] But pressure to fire Moses must have become intolerable. Of course there were more reasons for getting rid of Moses than just his downtown refusal to co-operate in David's downtown clearances. There was the general feeling in the higher real estate circles (you'd never guess this from his biographers) that Moses was *slowing urban renewal down*. He took too long to get rid of people. He spent too much time, money and effort on housing low-income groups. And he was insensitive to the greater priority of the Mitchell-Lama (middle-income) housing program.

The mayor threw Moses over the side, replacing him with a troika which included Milton Mollen, future deputy mayor under Dinkins; Herman Badillo, who supervised clearances on Manhattan's west side; and Hortense Gabel, a Wagner aide who would later serve as the judge in the famous Bess Meyerson divorce case ("The Bess Mess").[16] But Wagner, no more than Moses, would yield on the issue of giving David Rockefeller Title I subsidies for purely commercial projects just north of Battery Park.

Moses' own plan to build $50 per room per month housing projects got replaced by 1 New York Plaza (1969) and 4 New York Plaza (1968). So right next to Battery Park (not to be confused with Battery Park City to the north-west) there were more office buildings. No upscale housing or commercial stores to enliven the area. Clearly this whole battle over getting city permission to clear out residents and factories for downtown luxury housing set the stage for intervention at a higher level, more ingenious planning to get around the need for permissions, and – the plans for Battery Park City and Manhattan Landing landfill projects. If it's too hard to bulldoze the people, pave over the rivers.

*Housing.* Battery Park City (BPC) sits on the north-west of Battery Park: 21,000 units of luxury housing nestled next to six million square feet of office space. Construction still continues intermittently on the publicly supported marina that enables arbitrageurs to yacht in from Westport, and avoid the train altogether. BPC residents will have docking privileges too. And to relieve BPC condo owners, concerned about a good neighborhood school, the city moved the elite Stuyvesant High School down from 15th Street and First Avenue. Funds were found in the capital budget for a new $300 million edifice for the kids. David Rockefeller called Battery Park City

the largest and most complex single urban real estate development ever undertaken in this country.[17]

It is also quite possibly the largest single example in this country of what John Kenneth Galbraith used to call "socialism for the rich." Governor Mario Cuomo confessed he couldn't reply to the question of visiting Soviet officials, who asked him

Why are you so proud of a state-subsidized housing program for rich people?

Cuomo explained that it was that rebuke that stimulated him to insist that the state get upwards of $30 million a year from BPC which is turned over to a fund for low and middle-income housing:

From the wealth we derive from wealthy people who live there, we will rip off as much as we can and put it into affordable housing. . . . It's the theory of the progressive income tax. It's a theory as old as civilization.[18]

Even older is political sleight of hand. For the same year the BPC bourgeoisie coughed up $37 million to the state, they got back from the city in the form of tax abatements $126.3 million.[19]

*Water Street subway.* Every new mass transit facility produces a redistribution of real estate values – from the areas served by the old transit lines to the new. New lines only get built when one set of interests wins or some sort of accommodation is reached. The plan for the Water Street subway seems like an example of the latter. It represents an extension of the Second Avenue subway – on the drawing boards since 1924 – which would have helped east midtown by taking the congestion off the Lexington. What made it all possible was the demolition of the Pearl Street El. in 1951 which like Westside Highway had created a barrier between the waterfront and office development.[20]

The plan for new sub-surface transit, however, first emerged in the DLMA's 1963 report. It would have extended the Second Avenue subway below Houston Street, widened Water Street, and ran the subway underneath Water Street – along the waterfront. The Association's consultants had established the need for a subway:

Approximately 80 percent of the people who work in the area come by subway. If that ratio holds and the working force expands by an estimated 75,000 by 1975, it will mean attempting to cram an additional 60,000 passengers into the downtown area's already over-taxed subway facilities.

By 1969, in the tenth annual report, the DLMA insisted that it was

exerting every possible effort to advance the lower Manhattan subway link to the Phase One priority stage.

*Conclusion.* The tenth annual report of the DLMA was by far the most hypertrophic and self-congratulatory yet produced, bordering almost on delirium. Most of its 23 pages were just filled with pictures of office buildings and office buildings being erected: a kind of real estate porn. The rest was devoted to exaggerated claims of downtown employment growth. All this of course, just before the city's collapse. In three years, David predicted, the downtown job total would be 580,000: up 120,000 in four years. In fact, his totals were calculated by simply taking the total amount of existing office space, adding the amount planned, and dividing by a fixed amount per worker. David's method didn't take into account that the buildings might not fill up. By 1972, the DLMA was negotiating with Cities Service Company not to simply wreck its three buildings just off Wall Street – because it harmed downtown's international prestige. But David's exaggerations were not entirely self-delusory.

The idea seems to have been to persuade city officials that the crush of office workers was so great that more mass transit was needed. "Now that a Second Avenue subway is in definite prospect," David wrote, the MTA would have to re-map the area to extend it to "lower Manhattan within the optimal immediacy of the MTA's Phase One." (Read: run the subway to the front door of Chase Manhattan Plaza immediately.)

The Port Authority first argued for the World Trade Center on the grounds that it would help the port. In fact, the twin towers were the wedge which led to the creation of Battery Park City and the physical elimination of the docks. The docks were effectively buried under the landfill created by the World Trade Center. When the Manhattan port finally died, and when the Manhattan Transfer between Jersey and the city was cut off, there was no way for many of the city's industries to operate. The food industry was particularly hard hit. Within a year of the elimination of lighter service, three breweries shut down in Brooklyn. Whatever other problems beer makers had to struggle with in New York, beer can't be made without hops. And the hops came from the west coast, by freight car on the lighters.

Some would dispute the reasons for the industrial deaths and exodus following the shut down of the port. Others would say that the estimate of 400,000 jobs dependent on the port – which comes from a Port Authority brochure – is too high (Chinitz). What is incontestible is that the clearances for the World Trade Center alone swept out 30,000 jobs.

How many is that? In one of the most eloquent chapters of *The Powerbroker*, "One Mile," Robert Caro immortalized the victims of the Cross Bronx expressway. There were 1,530 households affected.[21] Thirty thousand jobs was close to 1 percent of all the jobs in the city. But it's striking how shallow a ripple the clearances made in the media.

In summer 1962, the *Times* ran a story on page 23: "Small Business men Assail Center." It was accompanied by a photo of workers and small store operators marching along Greenwich Street. Some are carrying a coffin with a placard, "Here lies McSmall Businessman. Don't let the

P.A. bury him." Others are carrying signs, comparing the P.A. to the Kremlin. As the marchers pass down the street, they shouted out to passersby to sign a petition aimed at fighting "the forces of injustice to working people of this area."

Something had gone seriously wrong with the priorities and politics of a city where 30,000 people can be made to disappear from their jobs and stores for a state office building. And the news of their protests turned up on page 23. Of course Pravda rarely provided any news at all about forced relocations. But were the workers and small business people so wrong to compare Rockefeller and the Port Authority to Stalin and the Kremlin?

## CONCLUSION: REAL ESTATE STALINISM

The entire period, from 1949 when Title I was enacted to Lindsay's last term, in the mid-sixties, when massive rioting and fear of urban anarchy brought it to an end, constitute a distinct mode of urban development in New York – call it "real estate stalinism."

Nearly every large city had urban renewal. But no city had a program so vast and intrusive: With about 4 percent of the nation's population, the city had 32 percent of all the urban renewal construction.[22] Admittedly, however, as destructive as it was in U.S. terms, it was tame compared to the Soviet model – city governments in our system lacking the power to erect gulags, confiscate leaflets, shoot strikers etc. Stalin killed millions, our urban planners merely drove hundreds of thousands from their homes, factories and small stores without real compensation. And the goals were ultimately different – David, Nelson and the FIRE elite weren't ideologues trying to bring about a new society; they were simply trying to earn more speculative profits in this one. Still, there were some striking similarities.

*Methods.* Our urban planners, like theirs, were engaged in top down economic planning. In the high period of real estate stalinism, planners were almost completely unaccountable. No neighborhood ever voted to be "renewed." Planners operated through commissions, authorities, public corporations that frequently didn't even issue annual reports or hold public meetings. Entities such as the mayor's Committee on Slum Clearance were dominated by unelected officials like Moses who could only be dismissed by a purge. When it became necessary to get rid of Moses, the higher real estate forces did, substituting other officials who were nearly as unaccountable.

When facts suggested that history was turning into a nightmare, the planners cooked the facts, or suppressed them altogether. Even in Moses' political obituary, the 1959 Panuch Report, designed to find out how many people had been cleared away, the city's many programs came up with a composite figure of 75,000 *households*. But how many people were in a household? And there is still no reckoning of all the industrial jobs lost by urban renewal and its successor programs.

*Ideology.* Because what they were doing was widely unpopular, both New York's real estate Stalinists and the Soviet variety stressed historical necessity and inevitability of progress. Both avoided ultimate responsibility by insisting that in the use of force against the weak, they were only obeying history's inevitable course. Trends must be followed.

For each elite, there was an historically defunct class. For the Soviets it was the "kulaks" – the small farmer. There was no point in arguing with the kulak, history had doomed him. The future was clearly with the giant collective farms.

For New York planners, history had doomed the blue collar worker. He would be replaced in the city by the elite white collar worker. Gradually, as the ideology fed upon its own illusions, the scope of blue collar replacement grew. The post-industrialists would claim that, throughout the advanced world, manufacturing everywhere was being replaced by a higher, worker-less mode. The Cravath lawyer, billing 2500 hours-a-year, emerged as the equivalent, in economic development terms, of the Soviet's Stakhanovite worker.

*Consequences.* One plan irrationally promoted heavy industry. The other destroyed industry and promoted office buildings at the expense of everything else. But perhaps the most important result of these plans is that both forms of top-down forms of modernization have failed. Both promoted terrible social disintegration in the name of a one-sided doctrinaire mode of development that benefits a narrow elite at the expense of the vast majority.

Both ended in ruin because no matter how badly off-course they steered, it was impossible to change direction. There was no system of responsible political parties. Bad policy results could be hidden or explained away. Scapegoats were found. The people who thought up, promoted and executed the policies escaped paying the consequences.

Ultimately then, the failure of planning in both cases was political: no democracy. Of course the Soviet model is a limiting case. But New York, may be, as Saul Alinksy argued, the most undemocratic city in the U.S. Journalists have been cataloging and describing its strikingly anti-popular features for a generation. But here are seven important ones:

1.   An emasculated legislature – where, because of its essentially one-party character, no issues ever emerge; the scrapping of proportional representation, which re-enforces the absence of political alternatives.

2.   Over-centralization of executive authority in the mayor and the "covered" agencies. This was actually re-enforced by the new charter which abolished not just the board of estimate, but borough government.

3.   New York's famous electoral culture which specializes in keeping independents off the ballot. Half of all the U.S. lawyers who specialize in ballot law, it is said, live in New York.

4.   The comprehensive system of economic development authorities, linked with the independent and thus unaccountable planning commission: the Community Planning boards are appointive, their decisions are non-binding and their presence purely decorative. To grasp their true function, try the German verb for "decorate" ("schmucken").

5.   The concentration of communications media ownership and the lack of separation between business interests and editorial focus.

6.   The vast growth of foundation-dependent community organizations which muffle rather than amplify grass roots energies.

7.   The grotesque role of political "contributions" which gradually renders even the politicians with true civic concerns into little more than mules for the real estate and financial industries.

All this has helped produce political stagnation that has lasted for nearly two decades – a kind of Brezhnev era which followed the high tide of real estate Stalinism which began under Wagner and lasted through the Lindsay years. While the forms of real estate Stalinism disappeared – viz. Title I – the goals did not. New forms evolved: private–public partnerships, "planned shrinkage," "community self-help." It is the planning of this "Brezhnev era" we must now examine.

# NOTES

1. Cited in Jeff Plungis, "The Building of Battery Park City," Empire State Report, May 1992, p. 21.
2. "Natura non facit salta," Lucretius.
3. Wallace S. Sayre and Herbert Kaufman, Governing New York (New York: W.W. Norton & Co., 1965), p. 689.
4. Henry Raymont, "Split on Planning Looms Downtown," New York Times, September 12, 1966.
5. While both biographies of Moses, Robert Caro's The Powerbroker, as well as Joel Schwartz' The New York Approach, are splendid books, absolutely fundamental reading, neither deals passably well with Moses' overthrow in 1960. This should be Caro's set piece, how Moses is destroyed by those he helped, but he blows off what may be the most fundamental change in New York politics of the post-war period, in a couple of paragraphs, even claiming that Moses was tired of Slum Clearance and that getting publicly fired after a scathing report damning, in effect, his whole post-war career, was a "victory." (Robert Caro, The Powerbroker (New York: Random House, 1974), p. 1063. Schwartz, as far as I can determine, doesn't even mention Moses' firing.
6. Why there are no fans, is hotly debated.
7. Jane Jacobs, The Death and Life of Great American Cities (New York: Vintage Books, 1961), p. 157.
8. Downtown Lower Manhattan Association (New York: 1963), p. 5.
9. To take only one of hundreds of examples, which elicited massive protest, in the Bronx, at Hunt's Point, then known as "Little Pittsburgh" which was upzoned from unrestricted to M1-restricted. See for example Robert Ross of Ace Spray Finishing Corp. to James Felt, November 18, 1960.
10. Downtown Lower Manhattan Association (New York: 1958). See maps pp. 6-7. entitled "land use" and "redevelopment areas." The focus for Hudson river redevelopment was north of Courtlandt Street.
11. For the London variant of early capitalist clearances, see Gareth Stedman Jones, Outcast London (London: Penguin, 1971), ch. 10.
12. Robert Moses to David Rockefeller, January 27, 1959, Robert Wagner Papers.
13. Ibid.
14. Robert Moses to Robert F. Wagner, January 30, 1959, Wagner Papers.
15. Mayor Robert Wagner to General Otto L. Nelson January 18, 1960; Mayor Robert F. Wagner to William F.R. Ballard, n.d. (October 1959). Ballard was Chairman of Citizen's Housing and Planning Council. See also Otto Nelson to Nelson Rockefeller, May 27, 1959: a thirty-page proposal for housing reform that criticizes city inaction, Wagner Papers.
16. Jack Newfield and Wayne Barrett, City for Sale (New York: Harper & Row, 1988), pp. 396–404.
17. DLMA, 10-Year Progress Report (New York: June 10, 1968), p. 5.
18. Jeff Plungis, "The Building of Battery Park City," Empire State Report, May 1992, p. 23.
19. Message of the mayor, Fiscal year 1993, p. 84.
20. Office of Lower Manhattan Development, Water Street Access and Development (New York: June 1976), p. 4.
21. Robert Caro, The Powerbroker (New York: Vintage Books, 1975), p. 850; 1530 units would amount to some 5000 persons, but Caro says the figures are "almost certainly far too low."
22. Martin Anderson, The Federal Bulldozer (New York: McGraw-Hill Book Company, 1967), p. 102.

# THE LAST PLAY? PLANNING IN THE KOCH/DINKINS ERA (1977 – 1993)

## LESS THAN ZERO

Since World War I, New York City has been shaped and battered by three great speculative office building booms – the roaring twenties, the go-go sixties and the debt-propelled, subsidy-driven years of the eighties. Of the three, the most recent, the expansion of the Koch years, proved in many respects the weakest. Paradoxically though, it may have created the most long-term economic damage.

Whereas the twenties boom (1925–1933) produced 32 million square feet of prime office space; and the sixties, (1967–1973) 68 million; the entire decade of the eighties (1981–1990) generated just 53 million square feet. While this wasn't the smallest in absolute terms, it was the slightest in terms of the percent added to the total stock of office space. In the twenties the space inventory more than doubled; it the sixties, there was a 33 percent jump. In the most recent boom office space increased less than 20 percent.[1] Still, in the aftermath, New York's vacancy rate stands nearly twice as high as in the downturn of the seventies – very close to the 30 percent level reached at the peak of the Great Depression.

In the wake of a boom, developers always discover that they have built more space than tenants want to rent. The most striking feature of the eighties upsurge, however, is how extraordinarily little of the space built was actually absorbed. Less than zero.

Not only is all 53 million square feet of space built during the boom empty. The downturn, with its inevitable bankruptcies, forced mergers and consolidations (Drexel, Burnham, Manufacturers Hanover, etc.) has thrown another 10–12 million square feet onto the market. The total inventory of empty space has remained stuck throughout the nineties at somewhere between 62–65 million square feet. There is simply no net absorption. The total number of years it will take to absorb the inventory – a better measure of over-capacity than the vacancy rate – stands at over 50 years. This sounds completely farfetched until you recall that after the five-year binge of the twenties it was nearly two decades before another major office building rose in the city.

In other words, it not only turns out that the city didn't need the space it built. It didn't need all the space it had.[2]

Unlike the office booms of the twenties and sixties, the present expansion was heavily subsidized.[3] So the buildings pay taxes at a vastly reduced rate. The generosity of the Koch years to the office developers has produced billions in exempt property values. Add the luxury residentials and the result is a structural budget deficit of over a billion dollars a year.[4]

Unemployment in the construction industry stands at over 50 percent.[5] But private construction won't start until it becomes cheaper to build than to buy. And since many buildings are available for anyone who can afford to pay the taxes where does that leave the economy of a city of which it was often said, "New York is to real estate what oil is to Houston"?

To grasp simple dynamics of the disaster, think of New York's recurrent SOB problem as if the residents lived in a flood-prone city – like inhabitants of the Mississippi delta. The reason New York is still bailing out in the nineties from the flood of the eighties is not that the city experienced the greatest deluge in its history. It's rather that the rivers were already high and soil was over-saturated when the downpour started.

The difference between the natural disaster and our man-made variety is that while no one can stop the rain, the office buildings didn't fall from the sky. It was human beings who decided to build office space that no one needed, or to put it somewhat more generously, it turned out that the space built – at a cost that can be estimated at nearly $20 billion – was needed only briefly, if then.[6]

To permanently occupy the 65 million square feet of prime office space that's empty, New York's FIRE economy would have had to have produced 370,000 new office jobs.[7] The boom never came close to generating that many. Between 1980 and 1987 the *total* number of jobs of all kinds added in all five boroughs was less than 300,000. Of the total in industries likely to rent office space, FIRE jobs increased by almost exactly 100,000.[8] But most of the FIRE jobs – 73,000 – were highly cyclical positions as brokers. These had to be seen essentially as temporary jobs: Wall Street uses and discards brokers during a boom like a hayfever sufferer uses kleenex. If you throw in another 50,000 added by elite business services, that still adds up to only 26 million square feet. Half of what was built.

How was it possible? The greatest minds of world finance, the legendary dynastic families of north American real estate. The top of the Forbes 400 list – couldn't these guys count?

At the end of the boom it got pretty sloppy, but a lot of the players at the outset were legendary for their acumen. You had the Reichmans of Toronto, whose real estate wisdom was so universally respected, that proud U.S. bankers dared not even ask to see their balance sheets when humbly offering to lend them billions. There were Citibank's financial statesmen. Walter Wriston and his highly touted successor John Reed. The savvy institutional investors from the Equitable and the Pru provided permanent capital. And then there was the good, gray, civic-minded *New York Times*, regularly chiming in – sometimes several times a year – demanding more subsidized real estate development, especially on the west side. How could these giant figures and respected institutions have all combined to so misjudge the office space market?

None seemed to be able to read the most elementary market signals. When prices go up, that's green. Invest. When they stay the same, that's yellow. And while no one would expect developers to show the appropriate degree of caution, since their own money is rarely at stake, at least institutional investors might think twice before committing the $250–$500 million dollar loans that the west side behemoths typically required. But during the eighties, the lights were actually flashing red. Real rents for Manhattan office space were steadily declining – when inflation and landlord's concessions were taken into account. And yet the SOBs kept rising.

Strikingly, the more rents fell, the more developers feverishly outbid each other for land on the west side. In 1986, for one plot, 1544 Broadway, Bruce Eichner paid $2,800 per square foot. That's almost twenty dollars a square *inch*. Eventually, Bruce's building was sold to German publishers, Bertelsmann, for less than twenty dollars a square *foot*.[9]

As intimations of the over-building disaster became clearer, developers madly reconfigured their structures from SOBs to luxury hotels.[10] In five years, they added 6,000 new rooms. But selling temporary residential space to visiting businessmen and conventioners hasn't proved any more lucrative than selling permanent space to the local businessmen. The economics aren't that much different. Occupancy rates which exceeded 80 percent in 1979, have fallen into the 60 percent range. Like office developers, hotel developers paid too much for the land and now have to charge paying guests too much. The Four Seasons, located on E. 57th Street has to charge room rates of between $250 and $3,000 a night. Each room at the Four Seasons cost $1,000,000 to build.[11]

What was created, in the name of "economic development", particularly on the west side and on landfill downtown where the city was channeling construction, was a kind of highrise Potemkin village. The office space and hotels erected there bore no more relation to actual economic needs than the fake villages put up by Prime Minister Potemkin to impress the easily fooled Czar of all the Russias that his peasant subjects were thriving and enterprising. Unfortunately, our sham economic development wasn't made of wood and papier-mâché. And after it was built, no one knew what to do with it. Should it be a park? Luxury housing? A home for non-profits?

No doubt the same urbanologists who got foundation grants and city contracts to explain how the city would be saved by unlimited office expansion, and then insisted that the problems of overdevelopment would soon pass, are now addressing the empty space problem. Even as the city's job totals sink, new city planning initiatives call for clearing out the remaining manufacturing sites along the waterfront.[12] Predictably, critics will be blown off as "gloom and doomers." They will be reminded that New York has weathered many crises before. Efforts to show how past commercial development and anti-industrial planning has failed will be dismissed as "20/20 hindsight."

Besides, FIRE's defenders will argue, it was the eighties. What could you expect? The whole country – indeed the whole capitalist world from Tokyo to Helsinki – was caught up in a speculative real estate mania. New York City isn't the only city around with lots of empty office buildings. Why pick on New York?

Because, for one reason, while commercial real estate speculation ran rampant in other cities too, it was in New York where a unique set of political circumstances and high level wire pulling seem to have produced the most gigantic pig out. Arguably, New York has the world's biggest office space glut. Not just in terms of total space where it's no contest, but as a share of the total stock. In the Bank for International Settlements 15-city world-wide survey of commercial real estate fallout, New York ranked first in office space vacancy rates – beating out Tokyo, Berlin, Frankfurt, Paris, Milan, London, Toronto et al.[13] Within the U.S., a survey of secondary office space did show Dallas with 39 percent vacancy as No.1. But New York was a strong second, and sections of the city – the Wall Street area with 35 percent vacancy rates – were producing wide-open spaces almost at the Texas rate.[14]

For the city's FIRE establishment, it's convenient that there be no debate and no questions asked about past economic development priorities. This way they can continue to set the development agenda and frame the debate. People should just forget about the past. We should move on, holding no one accountable for previous plans. Unless, perhaps, a perfect scapegoat can be found like Robert Moses. (In retrospect it will turn out that Moses' greatest civic accomplishment was not the Coliseum or Jones Beach but taking the rap for two generations of New York City planning failures.) But, unless another Moses can be discovered or invented, at least from the establishmentarian point of view, it's best to treat the eighties collapse as a kind of natural disaster, for which no one need account – or what is tantamount to the same thing – a simple product of impersonal market forces.

It's precisely to avoid this outcome that those who want to re-frame the debate about the direction and character of the city need to examine what actually happened: who did what to whom to get the office buildings built? How was it possible, given the shattering experience with the over-building of the sixties, that – given continuing and even notorious poverty and unemployment, in places like the south Bronx – government decided that its highest economic development priority should not only be office buildings, but office buildings precisely where experience had shown that no one wanted to rent them – downtown and on the west side?

Two specific questions need to be raised. First, given what now seem to be rather flimsy foundations for the office boom, what started the momentum to the west side? In 1982, there were nine office buildings constructed in Manhattan with a total of 5.6 million square feet. All on the east side. In 1989, six buildings were completed with 4.5 million square feet – all on the west side.[15]

Broadway in the forties and fifties was lined with newly built SOBs, and hotels. Early in the boom the fortress-like Marriott Marquis was built right near Times Square over the wreckage of three legitimate theaters. It was soon joined by a new Holiday Inn at 48th and Broadway and a new Renaissance Hotel at 47th and Seventh. Sheraton ITT liked the prospects on the west side; it's got two hotels there, right next to each other. One on Seventh Avenue and 51st, the other at Seventh Avenue and 53rd. In an altogether different price bracket is the city-subsidized Righa Royale just off Broadway 54th Street, where nightly rents for an ordinary double – not a suite – run $750 per night.[16] Then there are the Solomon's three west side buildings – with a total of 2.5 million square feet. Built in 1988, *Crain's* reported in 1992 that 1.8 million were still vacant.

No more than in the rest of the city, can over-building on the west side be explained in terms of the usual mechanism of tightening supply and rising rents. The *Institutional Investor*, in an article about the collapse of Citibank's credit culture – how it wound up financing the west side boom and barely skirting collapse as a result – points out rents didn't rise there after 1982. Yet on Friday May 13,1988, a little more than six months *after* the crash, construction began simultaneously on eleven new office buildings and four new hotels. On that Friday the 13th, between Sixth and Eighth Avenues, Columbus Circle to the north and 31st to the south, more office space was being built than was available in the entire city of Pittsburgh.[17] It was the last day to get the 20 percent bonuses given out by city planning's midtown plan. Development wasn't price-led. It was subsidy-led.

The same incentives and pressures were felt in that other branch of real estate hell, lower Manhattan. Construction there was also promoted by the government. And the centripetal pattern of development was similar to midtown west. Development was pried away from traditional locations to new zones in the periphery. When the recovery began in the early eighties, downtown developers sought to build along the traditional core of downtown – on both sides of lower Broadway. But Port Authority and Battery Park City planners, dangling giant subsidies, pulled development into the new landfill areas, and into the areas around South Street Seaport – the original location planned for the World Trade Center – behind the Chase Manhattan Bank.

On the Hudson river side of lower Manhattan, Larry Silverstein built millions of square feet in two giant deals with the Port Authority. These buildings never filled up at economic rents. And Silverstein, who vaulted from obscurity with the two megadeals to chairmanship of the mighty Real Estate Board of New York, has returned to obscurity. He seems never to have recovered from Drexel Burnham's cancellation of a $3 billion deal for 2 million square feet of space at 7 World Trade Center.

Perhaps even more decisive for the future of downtown, though, Olympia & York, run by the Reichman brothers, got the Battery Park City Authority to give them more than $20 million a year in abatements to build six giant towers with more than 6 million square feet. In return, Olympia & York promised to guarantee Battery Park City Authority bonds. Author Tom Schachtman quotes Battery Park City chief Richard Kahan as exclaiming

I really wanted to . . . jump up from behind my desk and kiss the man on both checks . . . he was the only one in the procession of developers who understood my primary worry – paying off the bonds.[18]

Now of course, the authority has to worry about how bankrupt Olympia & York will make good on its pledge.[19]

At the time, real estate people predicted the Olympia & York project would kill downtown. It has. But there was no way to stop the deals. The World Trade Center and Battery Park City projects, both logical outgrowths of the 1958 Lower Manhattan plan, were being driven by the least accountable institutions in the post-Communist world – the government "authority." The modern authority answers to neither voters nor stockholders; it is accountable only to God and the bond market. (Not necessarily in that order.)

Generally speaking, the over-production of office buildings can be explained in terms of the old vaudevillian Jimmy Durante's complaint, "too many people getting into the act." But in the eighties it was public officials – from City Planning, the Public Development Corporation, the Port Authority, the Urban Development Corporation, Battery Park City Authority – all jostling each other in an effort to stuff builders' pockets with subsidies, pushing not quite ready for prime-time developers like Bruce Eichner and the Solomons onto the overcrowded stage. It was City Planning that devised the real borough buster, midtown development plan. Or, more accurately, it was City Planning that re-tooled, amplified and carried out the Second Regional Plan's goal of swinging development from the east to the west side.

New York's City Planning Commission bears no resemblance to

Tokyo's MITI. It has none of Daniel Burnham's soaring spirit. City Planning makes no plans – big or little. The master plan for New York that was the stated reason for creating the Commission has never materialized. Its role is to validate and legalize the plans and initiatives conceived by the city's private real estate interests. So if the Commission decides to move the city's CBD westward, it's not because the Bronx Borough President's appointee on the Commission agrees with the Brooklyn beep's appointee that it's a good idea. Still less because some staff professional makes a persuasive case. The $300 billion Manhattan property market doesn't allow itself to be shaped by arguments.

If a planned shift occurs it is reasonably certain the initiative came from within FIRE, not within a government agency. The top bureaucrats are appointed by politicians, and the politicians themselves have no independent electoral base or city-wide organization.[20] A single thunderbolt from the *New York Times* is generally enough to cow all but the pitifully few independent-minded ones. Big changes in planning policy, which is to say big changes in real estate values, are initiated by those who own real estate. In this case specifically from families and institutions with formidable land interests on the west side – like the Rockefellers, the Tisch family, the Dursts, financial institutions like the Equitable and Mutual of New York, and media institutions like ABC/Capital Cities, Time Warner, the *New York Times* and CBS through the Tisch's controlling interest.

It turns out specifically that the Rockefellers, operating through the Rockefeller Brothers Fund, shaped the contours of the west side plan and actually paid for City Planning to produce its midtown plan. It was also the Rockefellers, together with Ford and the financial community which funded the 42nd Street Development Corp. – which was the precursor to the Urban Development Corporation's failed efforts at Times Square development. Using taxpayer money, instead of their own, they got UDC to spring for $241 million in site acquisitions in the Times Square area.

UDC's dollars did more than enrich triple XXX lease holders. They temporarily propped up the west side land market – conveniently, just when the Rockefellers, Tischs, et al. wanted to sell. UDC's activity helped convey the impression that the blight around Rockefeller Center's southern boundary was going away. Similarly aided were the institutions like the Equitable which owned property on the east side of Seventh Avenue behind Rockefeller Center. The timing was perfect. Time

Square redevelopment helped the family achieve its principal dynastic objective of the last two generations – getting rid of Rockefeller Center. And not a moment too soon, as the erstwhile family jewel turns to real estate paste. So while the real estate development of the eighties was city-led, the FIRE elite led the city, micro-managing development locations, zoning incentives, tax abatements.

Second question. If the rate and placement of office development can't be explained as a simple response to market forces, can the same be said of New York's continued manufacturing decline? Can planned outcomes – or more accurately, the throttling of planned manufacturing initiatives – contribute anything to an understanding of the failure of industry to revive or even bottom out in the eighties?

If there was less heft to the eighties boom than its predecessors, it also distinguished itself by the rapid *decline* of manufacturing. This was an unpleasant New York novelty. In the twenties boom, manufacturing expanded smartly. The women's clothing industry grew nearly at the rate of office construction, even faster than finance. The sixties boom saw manufacturing at least holding its own. In January 1964, manufacturing stood at 830,300 jobs. By November 1969 there were still 830,700 jobs.

But in the eighties – from the beginning of the decade to the October 1987 Crash – manufacturing shrank from nearly 500,000 jobs to 380,000 – a loss of nearly 25 percent.

In other words, manufacturing declined almost as fast during the eighties boom as in the seventies decline.[21] Meanwhile, in the U.S. as a whole, during the same period, manufacturing also declined – but at a fraction of the New York rate – 6.5 percent. No other large city in the U.S. declined as fast as New York. Several other large cities actually gained manufacturing jobs – L.A., Phoenix, San Jose, Seattle – and even Boston experienced a revival before manufacturing was killed off, in large part, it has been argued, by *its* real estate boom.[22]

So just as New York's real estate boom turns out to be problematic, so too does its rapid and counter-cyclical manufacturing decline. Market forces by themselves simply don't explain all of what's happening. After previous downturns, New York manufacturing always snapped back. Costs got cut, the weak firms disappeared. The survivors came back stronger. New firms entered the market with the revival of demand. This time, there was no recovery. Why not?

By the eighties the city's manufacturing economy had lost its resilience for reasons that are rarely emphasized in the public policy debate. The two principal conditions of manufacturing had disappeared. First of all, at the simplest level, there wasn't room any more for manufacturing. No space. Not just in Manhattan, where the 1961 had illegalized manufacturing throughout much of the borough. But also in the outer boroughs. In 1967, the most comprehensive study ever made of the Bronx economy, by a team of Fordham University economists, argued that the single greatest economic problem facing the borough was the constriction of manufacturing space. The Bronx had nearly 6,800 acres of parks, but with the new 1961 zoning there were now less than 450 acres of industrial space. Hudson County, across the river, with a comparable population and size, had 10,000 industrial acres.[23]

Just about as basic to the survival of industry besides lack of space was the destruction of the second precondition for manufacturing: an industrial infrastructure. With the transfer of the port and the severing of rail freight connections there were a lot of products you just couldn't make here anymore. There were a lot of reasons given to explain why three breweries pulled out of Brooklyn in the same year. One, rarely heard, had to be decisive: the cut-off of rail freight connections from Jersey made it impossible to get hops. No hops, no brew.

True, the city's unique industrial mix, based on external economies and flexible production was less dependent on water-borne shipments and rail freight than cities with a heavier industrial component like Milwaukee or L.A. But if New York was to retain manufacturing for the local market – which was what outer borough manufacturing had been all about – the city would have to re-attach the severed structures.

In physical terms the space and infrastructural problems could have been overcome. The city had thousands of acres of outer borough land – there were even lots of empty land for manufacturing below 14th Street – on the lower east side. There was room for millions of square feet of factory space along Broome Street, near the Williamsburgh Bridge where the grass grows high around the 7th precinct station and tumble weeds roll. The city had railyards that could have been used to anchor a container port – the immediate problem was that Trump backed by Chase, held options on both yards. There was a comprehensive container port plan circulating through the state legislature, being pushed by west side Assemblyman, now Congressman Jerry Nadler supported by the unions. But most significant were the comprehensive re-industrialization plans being pushed by the Port Authority.

The Port Authority's plans were serious stuff: the agency had the resources and the know-how to bring them off. But it didn't. It sunk back into to its now accustomed role of toll-gathering, and de-industrializing waterfront real estate development. Little ever came of the plans. Executive Director Peter Goldmark seemed to lose enthusiasm for big industrial parks just about the time he went on the Board of the Rockefeller Foundation in 1981. He became Chairman in 1989.

All the major re-industrializing initiatives were met head on and decisively defeated. The waterfront plan, first framed by Koch, now published under Dinkins, actually targets the remaining industrial areas of the city for conversion. It represents nothing less than FIRE's end game against manufacturing. Instead of a $2.1 billion program for rebuilding and re-industrializing the Bronx, proposed by Deputy Mayor Herman Badillo, the Koch Administration, under pressure from Wall Street, scrapped the plans.[24] And today we have the RPA's Bronx Center plan – which uses police, jails and court house facilities to nucleate a new commercial complex just south of their failed Fordham Center project. Instead of the re-industrialization initiatives put forward by the South Bronx Overall Economic Development group in the mid-seventies, we have the Rockefeller-funded Partnership's $130 million project to build low-density, ranch-style homes throughout the south Bronx – the site of Jimmy Carter's famous pledge and visitation.

The re-industrialization efforts were met by a co-ordinated campaign orchestrated by the city's most influential foundations, the key foundations – Rockefeller Brothers Fund, Ford, J.M. Kaplan Fund for the City of New York, 20th century – united around the strategy of "self-help community development."

"Self-help" was a step backward even from the priorities established in the First Regional Plan which permitted manufacturing in the outer boroughs. The Foundation elite's insistence on bootstrap industrialization in desperately poor places like East New York and the South Bronx had less plausibility than Chairman Mao's ill-conceived backyard steel-making campaign of the "Great Leap Forward" era. At least in China, the backyard steel-makers didn't have to compete with world-class manufacturers. It's hard to imagine a strategy for industrialization less likely to succeed. By funding neighborhood economic development, however, the foundations could argue that they weren't against manufacturing per se, just the Port Authority's "too costly" plans for industrialization. (Few of the Port Authority's critics could be found among those who questioned much larger subsidies for real estate development.) More important, the foundations and their free standing offspring like LISC and the Housing Partnership, could set neighborhood economic agendas by their funding priorities. They would decide what constituted economic development.

The FIRE/foundation visions easily won out over plans for re-industrialization. Given the lack of any compelling economic strategy, popular mobilization, or inspired leadership from organized labor, the outcome was foreordained. FIRE folk not only had the money, the experience, the influence and the media visibility, they also won the battle of ideas about what belongs in the city. First, manufacturing lost the presumptive right to be in Manhattan at all. Then office buildings gained the right to locate in the middle of thriving outer-borough manufacturing districts – like Long Island City, Flushing, and Greenpoint, Queens. Even in the Bronx, where job loss was the greatest, with the lowest employment population ratio of any borough in the city, and one of the lowest employment population ratios in the U.S., it became possible to argue that the real planning priority should be middle-class housing.

It can't be emphasized enough that planning outcomes in the eighties were determined only partly by money and power politics. There was also a battle of concepts. Both theaters of urban conflict need to be understood: the battle for political influence and the far-less examined battle of ideas.

When David Rockefeller tried to run the Lower Manhattan Expressway through Washington Square Park, you didn't have to have a degree in planning from MIT to know it was destructive. Jane Jacobs led the charge and miraculously sent the establishmentarians back to their Westchester redoubts. But land-use choices involving housing vs. jobs; the mix of income in a housing project; the question of which jobs are really viable in an urban setting; what's the best location for manufacturing – these issues don't lend themselves to such clear-cut resistance. Everyone grasps that it is people who decide where highways go. But the notion that strictly objective forces, like technology and markets, the "logic of capital", determine factory and office locations is disarming. Ideas count. Theories, by explaining what's possible, frame agendas and determine how wide the debate on alternatives will be. In the eighties, the Manhattan office building rose again in New York not just from a hole in the ground, but from a carefully prepared intellectual infrastructure that needs to be probed and investigated.

## SELLING THE SIZZLE:
## GLOBAL CITY/INFO CITY

In the late seventies, New York's economy had fallen into a well. In 1977, employment had plummeted to 3.177 million – the all-time post-war low. The yearly budget process had become an excruciating exercise in service cuts and lay-offs. The South Bronx had not even begun to cool from its arson wave. The year before, not a single Manhattan office building was completed. There was very small output in 1977 and 1978. And in 1979, again, no construction at all. Yet as early as 1977, the Rockefeller Brothers Fund saw prospects for an upturn. Leasing, the Excom noted, was picking up in midtown. And a pickup in leases is always a sign of general improvement.

It might take a long time, however, to turn lease activity into booming construction activity. And even if development began, it might not do anything for the owners of property on the long dormant west side, which builders were treating as if it had all the development potential of greater Matabeleland. For the construction cranes to return to their midtown habitat, loan officers needed a new reason to make mortgages. Something to wipe away the sense of terminal economic disease that hung over the area. More was needed than another order of the omnipresent "I Love New York" buttons, which Governor Hugh Carey, pediatrician-style, was passing out like lollipops. Boosters couldn't simply repeat the old reasons that had been discredited by the "see-through's" like the long-empty 1166 Sixth Avenue, which served as a kind of sepulcher for its dynastic promoters, the Tishman family, and whose years of emptiness just a minute's walk from Rockefeller Center seemed to doom the long-run prospects for the long-heralded west side revival.

In the aftermath of New York's fiscal crisis, even sympathetic economists, some of the intellectual pillars of the post-industrial Establishment, were beginning to have second thoughts. Wilbur Thompson, the dean of urban economists asked:

What ever happened to the post-industrial age that was supposed to strengthen our aging central cities? . . . We meant this time to be a professional-service age. What happened to this new force what was supposed to come in and rebuild the cores of our aging metropolises?

Thompson conceded,

I have no quick explanation for this delay in the second coming of downtown.

All that was clear to Professor Thompson was the need to get poor people out of town.[25]

Two gloomy Rutgers economists wrote:

It had been assumed that New York City could compensate for the gradual loss of standardized production by exporting higher valued administration functions..[sic]. During the sixties, efforts were made to increase New York's white collar, corporate headquarters image

by various efforts which resulted in severe overbuilding. Now there was simply too much office space in New York and no need to build any more. The "unexpected vulnerability of New York's white collar employment," they attributed to journey-to-work difficulties, high rents, congestion, competition from the suburbs, regional competition. All of this led them to an ominous conclusion:

the central city will face the problem of dealing with an increased proportion of unemployed and underemployed citizens with reduced revenues, . . . we are left to conclude that *emigration from the New York region will have to be encouraged.* (authors' emphasis)[26]

To be clear, in the mid- and late seventies urbanologists certainly weren't saying that New York should try to re-industrialize; nor were they questioning the absolute primacy of white collar work. They were just skeptical that New York's white collar corp would increase fast enough to warrant new investment in Manhattan's seemingly exhausted land. The sixties seemed to have been the last big play. The emerging academic consensus counseled slow growth and getting the poor out of town through national urban policy incentives.[27]

Given the skeptical environment for further office development, what Wilbur Thompson called downtown's "Second Coming" would require more than just money. It would need a new discourse. Even the machine politician needs a reason he can give in public. Even real state people like to think they are operating on the right side of the *zeitgeist*. Some answer had to be devised to the question, "Why build more office buildings?" New York, according to the Real Estate Board of New York, had nine times as much office space as Tokyo, twice as much as London.[28] Wasn't that enough? Why knock out industry on the west side to erect more office space? Why clear out whole neighborhoods that had served poor and working-class people as communities, albeit very tough ones, like Hell's Kitchen? Compelling answers required going beyond the simple industrial–post-industrial dichotomy of Daniel Bell.

There's an old saying that if you've got lemons, make lemonade. New York City boosters looked around and discovered that since the 1969 Lindsay Plan had declared New York the *national* center for corporate headquarters, half of them had moved out. What was left? Mainly the money center banks, the dealers and brokers, the financial institutions and the lawyers, accountants, public relations people who fed in their wake.

Instead of looking at these FIRE folk as the residue of the exodus, they could be portrayed as the gathering nucleus of a new *global* center – as the vanguard of a vast inflowing of more internationally-oriented institutions who would locate here to take advantage of New York's unrivalled position within the new *world* economy. In other words, forget Lindsay's *National Center*. You're looking at New York City, the new *Global City*.

"We have a vision for New York City," intoned a 1979 Twentieth Century Fund Task Force composed of the usual real estate lawyers, foundation executives and financial institution types.

It is a vision of a city increasingly oriented toward white-collar employment while maintaining a variety of essentially small-scale manufacturing enterprises; and it is a vision of New York as the true world capital, the principle marketplace and cultural center for the world.[29]

Like the Rockefellers, the members of the Twentieth Century Fund Task Force saw that there had been a pickup in leasing. And the reason why leasing had revived – the reason why the city's banks, boutiques, real estate and auction houses were crowded again, they argued, was the new global economy. It was an intoxicating prospect: tourists, dancing to disco rhythms. Asian immigrants thronging into Queens turning the No.7 to Flushing into the "Orient Express", new capital streaming in from Saudi sheiks, leaders of Japanese *keiretsus*, Mexican millionaires, French business magnates fleeing the Mitterand socialists – the investors were all thronging to New York to buy just what New York's families and institutions had lots to sell – office space. While the immigrants were coming to work for next to nothing.

Left to itself, New York's problems were probably insoluble. The tide seemed to be going out for New York's corporate headquarters complex. But luckily, help was at hand. Increasingly, "Global City" argued, New York will be the corporate and financial base for foreign firms. And what better place in the U.S.? There are 1400 firms here already , the men of the Twentieth Century observed,

> because we have the country's largest port; the busiest airport; the headquarters of the big banks; the stock exchanges; the international lawyers, architectural firms, advertising – are all here.

New York would become "*the* future World Capital."[30]

New York, the report seemed to be saying, would be rescued by the kindness and vitality of strangers. Foreign capital would descend upon us like the mysterious wafer-like bread that fell from the sky on the Israelites in the desert. Immigrants would bring their "vitality" – and a low reservation wage – to provide cheap personal services for the rich. Consumers across the oceans would buy our producer services.

Of course the new New York, the Twentieth Century people explained, wouldn't be for everyone. The vast expansion of the local economy entailed by becoming the capital of the world wouldn't be sufficient to save manufacturing. "Blue collar jobs will inevitably become fewer," they observed. Nor would World City status and wealth mean a larger public sector: government must continue to cut services. It wouldn't even mean a turnaround in the regional economy – the entire northeast quadrant, the report predicted, will continue to lag in jobs.

> But there is no doubt that the city today is throbbing with the vitality of life and renewal. It is already a more important financial center than London; a richer cultural center than Paris, Rome or London; and the headquarters of more major corporations than Chicago. New York's vitality is simply inexhaustible; what it loses in one field it will gain in another. What's lost in manufacturing, will simply be gained in tourism.

The Twentieth Century Task Force had a three-point plan for achieving the Global City. It's worth reviewing not because all the points were adopted. In fact the most important points were all things *not* to do – like revive industry or spend much money on anything but reviving real estate. Its significance is rather that it reflected so accurately the priorities and reasoning of the establishment that was now promoting New York as the Global City.

*Point one.* "Strengthen the neighborhoods". You can't have a strong global city, unless you have strong neighborhoods, the Task Force pointed out. In fact, the Twentieth Century's idea of "strengthening" the neighborhoods was a lot like Lenin's idea of "supporting the bourgeoisie" – as the rope supports the neck. What "saving" meant essentially was planned shrinkage." It is unwise to attempt to rebuild *all* of the city as if its population were still intact," the report said. "At this late date, we believe that it makes more sense to accept the verdict of the residents themselves that certain areas are unsalvageable." Money should be spent on the areas adjacent to the unsalvageable neighborhoods. "It is our view that the city administration must be willing to close facilities or reduce services if they are in excess of the needs of the remaining population."[31]

Above all, and the Task Force put this in bold face:

This task force does not believe that, with the city's population still falling, the effects of the last decade of abandonment can be totally reversed.

## Don't rebuild the South Bronx, the Commission insisted.

Massive rebuilding in an attempt to restore the South Bronx to its earlier population levels would invite a repetition of the abandonment process in other areas of the city.

No reason was given for this judgement. It seemed to be pitched on the same level as the thinking of parents who decide not to buy a naughty child any more toys, since he'll only break them again.

*Point two.* No industrial parks.

Instead of a massive industrial park development or a costly and risky campaign to induce companies to return or to locate here we strongly favor measures to retain and promote the expansion of manufacturing enterprises that are already located in and employ residents of the city.

The task force specifically rejected the Port Authority's re-industrialization plan as too vast and costly. Vest pocket parks are what's needed.

*Point three.* Promote the international sector. Along with the by-now almost ritual calls for an end to midtown congestion and for a mass transit link to Kennedy Airport, the Twentieth Century Task Force was surprisingly bereft of ideas of how to accomplish globalism. About all they could think of was tax breaks for banks and bringing the IMF and World Bank to Manhattan. Of course if you were going to be the world's financial capital, it would be appropriate to have the World Bank here.

Within the task force, support for Global City analysis and strategy split sharply along FIRE/non-FIRE lines. The affirmatives were all people like Gaylord Freeman of First Chicago; John Petty, President of Marine Midland; Julian J. Studley, the real estate man; Charles Breitel of Proskauer Rose, Goetze, Mendelson – one of the U.S. top 50 law firms; Theodore Jackson of the Bowery Savings Bank. Dissenting were the academics – Robert Lekachman of CUNY, Jose Canbranes of Yale, and the retired chief lobbyist for the American Federation of Labor–Congress of Influential Organizations, Andrew Biemiller. Lekachman and Cabranes' reservations remained with bounds of task force propriety. But Biemiller exceeded these limits, producing what may have been the most damning dissent in Blue Ribbon history. Unlike other opponents, he refused to endorse the report at all. Even more startlingly, he stated his objection in class terms.

The treatment of blue collar workers is cavalier, to say the least. . . .The Report fails to emphasize the need for blue-collar and rank-and-file white collar jobs for people. It concerns itself primarily with the problems of bankers and financiers.

Biemiller didn't see the wisdom or equity of tax breaks for bankers and overseas investors which formed the basis of the Commission's strategy for attracting foreign capital. What was the point, he asked, in turning the city into a Big Apple version of the Bahamas or the Netherlands Antilles? We need to condemn, not praise multi-national corporations and banks for exporting capital, Biemiller insisted. It may be possible for the U.S. like Great Britain to live off invisibles for a short period of time, but eventually, the commission's strategy of positioning the New York as the capital of a country that exports capital would undermine the country. Biemiller wrote:

I must conclude that the Report does not pay proper attention to the concerns of human beings because it is concerned primarily with the problems of effete financial groups.

To Freeman of First Chicago, Jackson of the Bowery or Petty of Marine Midland, Biemiller's concerns and imprecations must have sounded like echoes from the paleo-industrial era. Bring back the blue collar worker? You could just as well clone dinosaurs from leftover Jurassic DNA. Even the notion of financial effeteness must have seemed more quaint than offensive. It was the "effete" who were leading the city's charge into the information age. Today's bankers and real estate men were innovative manufacturers of producer services. They produced financial products: securitization, wrap-around mortgages and annuities, mortgage-backed securities. These were the FIRE equivalents of the transistor and the internal combustion engine. And in any case, no one talked about "invisibles" any more. These had been transformed into service "exports". A whole new discourse and vocabulary had emerged of which poor Biemiller, the former boilermaker, was totally unaware.

## GLOBAL CITY OR GLOBALONEY?

Besides dramatically increasing the number of potential tenants in the CBD by several billion, the global city trope proved tremendously prescient. For almost a decade – before chaotic currency speculation forced the destruction of the European monetary system; and before trade and immigration jitters forced postponement of the Maastricht Treaty – global trade, investment and interdependence went steadily forward.

New York City got its share of foreign investment as the leaders of the great Japanese trading companies like Mitsui and Mitsubishi overwhelmed by the growing U.S. trade surplus, their pockets bulging with a supply of steadily depreciating dollars, looked around for something the Yankees had to sell that didn't fall apart almost immediately. Rockefeller Center and other signature buildings in New York City seemed like good buys. Mitsui paid $610 million for the Exxon building. Dai-ichi Life snapped up a share of the Citicorp building for $670 million. Sumitomo paid out half a billion for 666 Fifth Avenue.[32] Soon even a bumbling novice like Brooklyn's Bruce ("Too Tall") Eichner, developer of the whistling Cityspire tower,[33] was able to find Japanese capital for his first – and last – Manhattan office building.

Very quickly those concerned with Manhattan's economic status learned to insist on the city's unique global status. From Donald Trump's promotion of his $10 million a pop penthouse condos at 57th Street and Fifth Avenue to city planners seeking to reframe old proposals in new rationales, the global lingo seemed to move the urban merchandise.

Just about the same time Twentieth Century Task Force was promoting the idea of New York as the capital of the world, Donald Trump was articulating his own more free-wheeling brand of globalism. The customer Trump had in mind for his Tower on 57th Street was not

the sort of person who inherited money 175 years ago and lives on 84th and Park Avenue. . . . I'm talking about the wealthy Italian with the beautiful wife and the red Ferrari.

Trump explained he filled up his condos so fast with Europeans, South Americans, Arabs, and Asians, anxious to avoid being vetted by snooty co-op boards that he was able to double the offering prices.

Trump Tower's global dimensions were genuine, if not exactly those emphasized by Mr. Trump himself. It was built with the help of illegal Polish aliens hired off the books to remove asbestos at a fraction of union scale. Naturally, Trump said he liked their work ethic. On some days hundreds, even thousands, of workers from Poland and elsewhere around the globe "stood in lines down the street, waiting, begging" for jobs at Trump Tower. And, shades of Zoe Baird, Trump would later testify he didn't even know what "off-the-books" meant.[34] Welcome to what academics called the Global City's "informal sector."[35]

Trump Tower's globalism was also manifested in the disproportionate number of its residents who belonged to international crime syndicates. There was David Bogatin – the Russian émigré crime family member who bought five condos. And Roberto Polo who bought half a dozen while he faced charges, "in more countries than most people have visited."[36] They joined Luchese and other crime family associates, who, while they have been in New York a while, still retain a certain international *panache*.

What was important in selling the space, Trump confided, in the *Art of the Deal*, was the promo campaign that emphasized international glamour. What was the difference between Trump Tower and the slow-to-move condos in Museum Tower, located just a chip shot away on top of the Museum of Modern Art? Location? Not really. Glitzy architecture, perhaps. The most substantial reason, though according to Trump was, "we positioned ourselves as the only place for a certain kind of very wealthy person to live." Says, Trump, "We were selling fantasy."

## THE GLOBAL CITY EXUBERANT

While Trump and Ed Koch squabbled about everything, from how best to freeze water at Wollman Rink to the zoning at the 60th Street Yards, one thing they seemed to agree on was the need to sell New York as a kind of global fantasy. The 1987 report of Koch's Commission on the Year 2000, which predicted the city would have a total of nearly 4,000,000 jobs by the millennium, did so on the basis of New York's emerging global strengths.

Hard-working Asian immigrants and incoming foreign capital had created what the Commission called, an "exuberant" city. "Ours is a time of New York ascendent" the Commission headed by Robert Wagner wrote, the summer before the Crash,

New York City is once again crowded, energetic, and exciting. Its economy is booming. Everyday brings new businesses and new customers to a wide variety of neighborhoods – from the European *panache* of upper Madison Avenue to the Asian vitality of Flushing.

Just a few years ago, the Commissioners recalled, nay-sayers were raising questions about the city's future.

Very few observers in the 1970s foresaw that foreign capital would come to New York in such large amounts, transforming the real estate market and fueling new businesses throughout the city.[37]

Now New York, with its European panache, its Asian vitality, its thriving information industries and international banking was poised to become nothing less than the next century's "unrivalled world city."

Of course there were many claimants for the title. Global competition was fierce. But if the city continued to respond to the international economic forces, as it has, the authors insisted, the title was in our grasp. Assuming of course, that their recommendations for global greatness were followed.

Here are the main things we had to do: First, of all, expand the CBD. Spread it across the east river into industrial Long Island City and downtown Brooklyn. Second, revise the city's antiquated zoning laws – acknowledge the post-industrial change – it makes no sense to retain manufacturing zones in neighborhoods that have become residential. Third, develop regional centers – bring office buildings and commercial development to places like Jamaica, Queens, Harlem and 161st Street in the Bronx. Fourth, develop the waterfront. There was still a lot of industry located on the waterfront that didn't need to be there. It could be replaced with various public recreational uses and "perhaps office buildings." Finally, create a strategic planning office whose first assignment should be the waterfront.

You might think, given the global transformation, that the city's development program might have changed in some of its essentials from the sixties when the RPA and the Lindsay Plan made nearly identical recommendations. Or for that matter from the 1920s, when the RPA took up the same stance on the waterfront, the role of industry, the need to reduce the amount of industrially zoned land. In the 1920s the watchword was regionalism. The sixties development was supposed to be driven by the idea of New York as a national center. Now everything is justified in terms of globalism. But the program is always the same.

Increasingly, modern New York was becoming as set in its ways as ancient Egypt. Who was mayor made as little difference as who was pharaoh. The same institutions had the same interests, and the same interests and institutions seemed to always turn up.

## KLEPTOCRATS AND PLUTOCRATS

Jack Newfield and Wayne Barrett in *City for Sale*, their illuminating account of the underside of the Koch years, show how in the non-visible bureaus and agencies, such as the Parking Violations Bureau, Department of General Services, and the Taxi and Limousine Commission where rich opportunities flourished to steal in the dark, the mayor chose the nominees of the kleptocratic county leaders. Brooklyn's Meade Esposito, Queen's Donald Manes and Bronx leader Stanley Friedman appointed crooks like Geoffrey Lindenauer, Herb Ryan, and Alex Lieberman. The appointed and the appointees all wound up sentenced to jail. (Or committing suicide, as in the case of Donald Manes.) But then each of the *predecessors* of the three county leaders had also gone to jail.[38] There is probably some inherited genetic trait at work here.

In the more visible jobs, it is generally argued, however, Koch appointed highly competent, well-qualified public servants. Planning, economic development, human resources, the blue ribbon commissions were staffed with representatives of the city's plutocracy – the prestigious foundations, the white shoe banks and law firms. These institutions provided the men and women who crafted multi-billion dollar giveaways like the Industrial and Commercial Incentives Program and J-51; who decided it would be too costly to rebuild the Bronx; and who promoted the overbuilding of SOBs which essentially condemned a generation of youth to joblessness. Did these establishmentarians really damage the city less than people like Stanley Friedman who sold the Parking Violations Bureau computers that didn't work or Alex Lieberman who shook down landlords who wanted the city to rent their buildings?

Like his predecessors, Koch appointed the usual banker types like Ken Lipper and Peter Solomon. But he broke new ground in the systematic favoritism he showed towards non-profit appointees from the Ford Foundation. Just as Catherine the Great pursued the economic modernization of Russia with the help of the ascetic, but highly militant Jesuit order, Koch carried out his de-industrial revolution through the militantly anti-manufacturing, non-profit Fordies, the veritable inventors of workfare.[39] Stanley Brezenoff became his first deputy mayor; former Ford lawyer and Ford-created Fund for the City of New York chief Fritz Schwartz served as his corp counsel. Then Koch appointed him head of the potent Charter Revision Commission after Richard Ravitch quit.[40] William Grinker was made head of the $7 billion welfare department. Herb Sturz, also from Ford became head of City Planning. And at a somewhat lower level, Ron Gault – who would later turn up as head of First Boston – was brought in from Ford by Brezenoff to run the Department of Employment.

Blue ribbon outfits like the Commission on the Year 2000 were very much plutocratic affairs. Bankers, foundation bureaucrats, favorite intellectuals of the foundations. Serving were people like Peter Goldmark, director of the Rockefeller Foundation; The Rev. Joe Sullivan of the Fund for the City of New York; Herb Sturz, who'd left City Planning and was now writing editorials for the *New York Times*; Donald Platten head of the Chemical Bank, Dick Netzer, former chief economist at the RPA; Alex Cooper, architect, former planning commissioner, who'd worked out the highly praised waterfront plan at Battery Park City, was a favorite at the Rockefeller Brothers Fund for his pro-SOB emphasis in seminars funded at the Columbia Planning school.

Did the Commissioners really think the city's global economy would add another 300,000 jobs just by emphasizing elite occupations in the CBD? Netzer, probably the only commissioner capable of forming an independent opinion, raised serious concerns.[41] He cited some forecasts – those of the New York State Department of Labor and the National Planning Association – that suggested the city's employment would shrink. The most optimistic projection came from the RPA which predicted the city would add a couple of hundred thousand jobs by 1990 – reaching 3.7 million. But Netzer had a problem with this.

All the projections assumed that population would stay constant. Yet somehow the RPA was saying there would be hundreds of thousands of new jobs. Evidently the only way the increase could take place was through big changes in the employment/population ratios. In the Bronx and Brooklyn the ratios were notoriously low – only about one in three in the Bronx was working, and not many more in Brooklyn, whereas in the rest of the region about half the population was working. Netzer didn't put it this bluntly, but if, as even the optimistic RPA projections suggested, there would be a loss of 50,000 jobs in the outer boroughs, how could Brooklynites and Bronx workers raise their employment rates? Especially if the development focus was going to be on elite jobs?

In the end, the Commission ignored Netzer's concerns and simply added another 100,000 jobs to the RPA's optimistic projections for 1990. Something would surely turn up in another ten years. After all, if the world was going global, and New York was poised to become the "unrivalled world city", an estimate of nearly 4,000,000 jobs might just turn out to be conservative.

## "WE'RE BETTER THAN BUFFALO"

By 1993, instead of nearly 4,000,000 jobs, New York's total stood closer to 3,200,000 – and falling. Still, little had changed in the global rhetoric of the planning community. To read the Planning Commission's "Shaping the City's Future," you'd think Leona Helmsley was still reigning as New York's Hotel Queen.

The authors of "Shaping the City's Future" hewed so closely to Koch's *New York Ascendent*, they even reproduced the same quote from

Saul Bellow about the global city's endless fecundity. "What is barely hinted in other American cities," the Koch plan had said on page twenty-one, "is condensed and enlarged in New York." Dinkins' people valued this line so much they moved it up to page one.[42]

Like fraternity brothers recycling old term papers from the upstairs "frat. library", the Dinkins planners not only came up with the same quotes, they duplicated the same analysis, the same conclusions and the same recommendations.

*Analysis.* Because we have the world's largest concentration of FIRE people we're the capital of the planet.

*Conclusion.* FIRE is our engine of growth:

The city's best prospect for expanding opportunity and combatting poverty is to maintain its position as a global leader in finance and advanced business services, communications, and the arts – the industries that drive the city's economy. The global cities of opportunity in the next century will be those that dominate international finance, trade and culture, just as New York prospered by serving these roles nationally during the last century.

All these industries are chiefly located in the CBD.

*Recommendations.* So – just as day follows night – it also follows that the way to expand the city's economy is to expand its CBD. In Dinkins five-point program for economic development, every point involved the CBD. The No.1 priority – just as Koch had insisted in 1987 – was to revive the waterfront; No.2, upgrade the environment of the CBD; No.3, improve CBD accessibility; No.4, spread the CBD to outer boroughs. Only the single recommendation that Koch didn't make – "Re-use and retro fit buildings in the CBD " – suggested that the planners saw any difference between the nineties and the eighties.

But if the analysis, conclusions and program were almost identical, the mood was edgily different. The exuberant tone of the Year 2000 was replaced by the obsessive assertion of New York's global dominance. It was almost as if the planners were trying to convince themselves that New York hadn't lost it. The continued repetition of New York's global hegemony, however, clashed sharply with the authors' review of the city's economic performance in which they were reduced to arguing that the city hadn't yet shrunk as much as Buffalo or Detroit.[43]

## ACADEMIC GLOBALONEY

In the natural sciences, the filiation of ideas operates through a kind of trickle-down process. The general ideas and discoveries of experimenters and theoreticians get simplified and applied by businessmen.[44] In the social sciences, the process often seems to work the other way. The basic ideas – especially in the more policy-oriented sciences like economics and sociology – bubble up to the elevated university precincts from the notions of practical businessmen. Social scientists simply formalize, provide evidence and academic ballast for received business opinion. They attach terminological bells and whistles, making simple ideas more complex. The global city concept developed in this tried-and-true bubble-up fashion.

A paradigm originated in the seventies by bankers and real estate men; by the early nineties Britain's urbanologist Peter Hall could speak of

the early 1990s neo-structuralist litany – the replacement of Fordism by flexible specialization, the shift to the informational mode of production, the globalization of the economy, command and control centers.[45]

Was there really a new global economy? The chief economist of the World Bank, Larry Summers had important reservations. In a December 12, 1991, internal memo Summers wrote:

What's new? Throughout the struggle with the evidence showing what exactly the proclaimed revolution has revolutionized. . . many of the worlds' large firms have been transnational from birth . . . the globalization of production has happened sure, but has the telecommunications revolution had a major impact? I guess the invention of relatively simple things, like steamship transport, did more for world trade, than digitalized data transmission through fiber optic cables; how exactly has the nature of manufacturing been "fundamentally altered"? Aren't people just incrementally better at doing things they've always done: like locate production in the lowest costs for delivery to markets (now globalization of production, now) like manage inventories in a least cost way (now just in time inventory management), like choose the appropriate level of vertical integration depending on the . . . production process (now critical buy-seller links) like match production to demand (now short product cycles). Is a "revolution" really an appropriate metaphor for these changes? I think the detailed evidence from the U.S. about the very small impact on productivity from the large investment in information technology should convince us to hold off on the breathless tone about technology.[46]

The new academic globaloney consisted of three parts. And Summers had nailed two of them. First was "the breathless tone about technology." He got that right. Second was explaining the present extent of global interdependence as something revolutionary when a great deal represented merely incremental changes.

A vital third dimension of the new global discourse confused cyclical tendencies with secular movements, i.e, up-and-down vs. steady change in the same direction. The degree of global interdependence is no constant tendency. It goes through jagged peaks and valleys driven by long waves of investment – twenty-five years up and twenty-five down approximates the pattern. The investment waves go back to the beginning of the industrial revolution in the eighteenth century.[47]

A century later, under-thirty revolutionaries Marx and Engels pointed to the emergence of a new global economy: "The need of a constantly expanding market for its products chases the bourgeoisie over the whole surface of the globe," they wrote in 1848.

It must nestle everywhere, settle everywhere, establish connections everywhere . . . . The bourgeoisie has through its exploitation of the world market given a cosmopolitan character to production and consumption in every country. . . . It has drawn from under the feet of industry the national ground on which it stood. All old-established national industries have been destroyed or are daily being destroyed. They are dislodged by new industries, whose introduction becomes a life and death question for all civilized nations, by industries that no longer work up indigenous raw material but raw material drawn from the remotest zones; industries whose productions are consumed, not only at home, but in every quarter of the globe.[48]

White out the class struggle, focus simply on how markets and technology are creating a global society, paint the whole scenario in roseate hues and you have our modern academic globalonists. Naturally, many of them tend to be former Marxist radicals, but to get the picture right, it's not enough to push the bourgeoisie back into the foreground and paint everything black instead of rose color.

There is no steady, secular tendency towards a global economy – any more than there is a steady tendency towards economic growth. The periods of global interdependence generally coincide with long economic expansions. Interdependence breaks up however in the downturns – as in the 1930s, when each nation seeks to repel the commodities and immigrants of the other. "Beggar thy neighbor" replaces international comity. The falling of trade barriers gives way to the erection of protectionist measures like the famous Smoot–Hawley tariff.

The upshot of all this back-and-forth movement is that while the world is more global than it was a couple of decades ago, it's no more global than it was a century ago, if anything, less so. In trade and financial terms, the international economy is simply not as integrated and as interdependent as it was before World War I in the age of the Gold Standard when travelers didn't need passports.

David Rockefeller's Trilateral Conference seems like a boy scout jamboree compared to the supervening role of late nineteenth century-early twentieth century international *haute banque* dominated by the Rothschilds.[49] As émigré Columbia professor Karl Polyani wrote in *The Great Transformation*, his penetrating but premature autopsy of the global economy in 1944:

> The Rothschilds were subject to no *one* government; as a family they embodied the abstract principle of internationalism; their loyalty was to a firm, the credit of which had become the only supranational link between political government and industrial effort in a swiftly growing world economy. . . . By the logic of facts it fell to them to maintain the requisites of general peace in the midst of the revolutionary transformation to which the peoples of the planet were subject.[50]

Changes in technology since the age of the Rothschilds, along with shrinking travel distances, haven't been substantial enough to offset the power of national states when they choose to use it. Even the *laissez-faire* proclivities of the major trading powers are checked in times of economic crisis by a more broadly enfranchised electorate. What determines the rate of immigration is not the speed of trans-oceanic travel, therefore, but the business cycle and the political fall out from mass unemployment.

Governments today, just as in the thirties, find that the plans conceived during relatively high employment periods for currency integration, elimination of trade barriers, and open borders for immigrants can't be sustained when the jobless rates hit double digits. The Kismet of big capital, unrestricted free competition on a global scale, begins to resound with the screams of labor. The icy logic of comparative advantage again gives way to fire-breathing protectionism.

Considerations of this kind help explain why although planes may be speedier than ships, immigration – including immigration to New York City – is still just a fraction of what it was in the late nineteenth and early twentieth century, during the Gold Standard years. In 1907, the last year of unrestricted immigration, 1,285,349 immigrants came to the U.S. More than half of them arrived in New York City. In 1992, total legal immigration amounted to a little over 1,000,000, and New York received about 10 percent of the nation's total: 100,000 legal immigrants and about 10 percent more counting illegals. In other words, at the turn of the century, with a lower population, New York was receiving five times more immigrants.

Similarly, the present share of foreign trade in GDP isn't as high as it was in the free-trading nineteenth century, and the share of foreign investment in total investment has not risen. While there was more overseas investment in the 1980s than the 1930s, it didn't reach the levels of the 1880s.[51]

But so what? What difference does it make if globalism is a cyclical or a secular tendency? The economy's still going global isn't it? There are two main differences.

First, as already suggested, the global future may be receding. So to pin the city's future to expanded foreign trade, investment may be a strategy for further immiseration. Second, given that global interdependence is cyclical, and we've been down that road before, we can see that increasing global interdependence doesn't really speak to the question of urban outcomes.

Yes, globalism is a force – even a mighty one – but interdependence by itself doesn't by itself explain the spatial or industrial structure of cities. New York became a great manufacturing city during a period of global interdependence. Now, during another global phase, it's become the country's biggest FIRE city, shaking off its manufacturing industries. Evidently, it's not global interdependence that's explanatory. It's something else.[52]

What's different about the penultimate globalistic age and the present waning period of globalism, is not so much the share of foreign investment, or the mobility of capital, but simply the identity of the capital exporting and importing countries. Great Britain no longer serves as the mature capital exporter. That role has been transferred first to the U.S. and then Japan. While the place of the up-and-coming industrializers of the nineteenth century who imported capital – U.S., Germany, Japan – has been taken by the South Chinese tigers, Korea and more recently by China herself.

In other words, an open economy will allow countries and cities to change their spatial and industrial structure faster. But the direction of the change isn't given by the degree of openness. In periods of global integration, the countries which have gotten rich play the role of capital exporters. Others, the up-and-coming peripheral countries, get rich by applying the capital and expanding their manufacturing base. Rapid manufacturing growth enables the capital importing/commodity exporters to displace the mature capital exporting/commodity importing countries.

The unprecedented rate of growth of the newly industrializing countries has exposed the plodding, Panglossian schema of the global thinkers. Supposedly, the world was becoming one giant global shop floor. The "logic" of capital dictated that the cheap labor jobs would go to the poor Asian city states like Hong Kong and Singapore, and New York would become the high paid command center. But a funny thing happened on the way to global hegemony. Singapore and Hong Kong industrialized faster than any countries in history. Government policy in Singapore deliberately aimed at restricting foreign manufacturing investment requiring cheap labor. Hong Kong got rich enough to export capital itself to China and all over. And the upshot is that per capita GDP in Hong Kong and Singapore stand higher than in the Bronx and Brooklyn. And according to *Business Week*, these Asian tigers are actually exporting capital to the sweatshops of Chinatown, where in some cases, Joanne Lum of Chinese Staff and Restaurant Workers Union reports, piece rates in *unionized* shops have fallen to as low as $2.00.[53]

Finally, the biggest problem with the insistence on a simple global rationalization of production, investment and spatial organization is not just the lack of historical perspective, but a failure to think clearly about fundamental premises. Above all, the failure to consider the relation between markets and business organization. Do freer markets mean more concentrated command centers?

In fact, a moment's thought suggests the opposite. The growth of freer markets and the development of "command centers" are not complementary. They are actually inversely related. The giant transnational corporation is a creature of two distinct historical periods when world market restrictions reigned: the mercantilist 18th century which featured what Adam Smith called the "oppressive and domineering" East India Company with its monopoly of Bengal trade,[54] and the post-World War I twentieth, i.e., the vanished age of modern monopoly capitalism. The nineteenth century didn't develop giant industrial corporations until market conditions began to change at the end of the century.

This is because, as Ronald Coase showed in the 1930s, the more barriers to trade and investment, the more it pays to carry out transactions within a corporate shell.[55] The fewer, the more arms-length transactions make sense. The very real fall in barriers to entry and exchange in the 1970s and 1980s helps to explain why giant corporations began to shrink in their share of U.S. economic activity from 21 percent to about 10 percent.

New York has more corporate headquarters today than anywhere else not because they have been attracted here by global forces, but because of past history – especially late nineteenth and early twentieth century history. First railroads and then the industrial trusts moved here during the springtime of monopoly capitalism to be near the highly monopolized markets of capital distribution. The advertising offices chose Madison Avenue in preference to Jersey City's Journal Square because the corporations had chosen to locate around Grand Central. Finance located downtown because the port was there.[56] What keeps the dwindling band in town is not global dominance, but inertia.

This is probably not enough. All over the world, as the *Wall Street Journal* noted, "going global means 'move 'em out' – by transferring world headquarters of important business units abroad."[57] Not only New York firms like IBM and AT&T, but Du Pont, Hewlett-Packard, Siemens and even South Korea's Hyundai Electronics Industries have moved headquarters operations overseas for the usual reasons: to take advantage of lower labor costs and to be nearer local markets. IBM's office decentralization has been the most intense: driven by pressures to cut costs has folded sales offices, put its world headquarters up for sale as part of an effort to shed five million square feet of real estate.[58] The trend towards removal of back-office operations has been underway for sometime. It began in the early eighties with the movement of New York securities firms out of expensive Manhattan offices.[59] What's new is that even heretofore poor countries are participating – in addition to Hyundai's movement to the U.S., Singapore Airlines has relocated jobs and equipment to Sydney. Hong Kong's Cathay Pacific has relocated headquarters jobs to Canton.[60] While the RPA and its academic chorus continue to insist that New York along with Tokyo and London represent "new forms of centralization required by the new forms of decentralization"[61] the lights are going out all over the global city.

When all the arguments against the coherence and explanatory power of globalism are made, however, there's still a final concern that goes beyond trend analysis. Even if freer markets, against the claims of logic and history, did mean more need for command and control centers, it's hard to see how being a global command center would help more than a narrow band of landlords, traders and elite professionals. Unlike commodities, producer services are hard to export.

Because, as Adam Smith pointed out long ago, they vanish immediately upon delivery, services have to be consumed locally. As opposed to commodity production, this vastly limits their employment effect. New York does seem to be the elite hospice of choice, where stricken despots, like the Shah of Iran and Ferdinand Marcos prefer to live out their dying days, but few jobs are generated by caring for them this way.

The same is true of the fastest growing component of U.S. service exports – license and royalty fees. Whereas the export of goods produces U.S. jobs, service exports generate jobs overseas. When Walt Disney franchises another European amusement park, it provides jobs for Europeans. When Texas Instruments licenses its technology to the Singaporeans, they then became the world's largest exporters of disk-drives. Here in the city, as the *Wall Street Journal* reports,

at American International Group, Inc., most of the huge insurance company's policies are devised by experts at its New York headquarters, but AIG has 16,000 foreign employees, amounting to half its total work force, selling and processing policies in 130 countries.[62]

As for foreign investment, the kind of capital New York receives isn't rich in job opportunities either. David Rockefeller insists that foreign investment is the "key to New York City's growth."[63] Certainly foreign investment was the key to the astounding reversal of the Rockefeller family fortunes in the 1980s, when foreign, mainly Japanese, investors poured nearly three billion dollars into Rockefeller Center just before the city's real estate collapse. But for those of us New Yorkers whose name is not Rockefeller, how does foreign investment make us better off? In employment terms, what difference does it make who owns Rockefeller Center?

Canadian real estate developer Robert Campeau turned out to be New York City's largest individual foreign investor in the eighties. And with his $4.3 billion takeover of Allied Stores and his $4.2 billion leveraged buy-out of Federated, there was no one who had a bigger impact on the local economy.[64] In employment terms, however, the effects of his takeovers (with capital raised locally by First Boston and

Citibank) were spectacular but not exemplary. Campeau's LBOs greatly weakened or bankrupted Bloomies, Brooks Brothers, Ann Taylor, Bonwits, along with the factors that provided garment makers with capital, and dozens of garment makers themselves.[65] Of course the problem was the nature of LBOs, not Campeau's Canadianness. But still, the Campeau collapse puts the bloated claims of foreign investment in clearer perspective.

As it happened, New York as the star of international investment, lasted only a bit longer than the celebrity of an Andy Warhol superstar. Foreign direct investment in New York, pumped up by Campeau and the Japanese acquisitions shot up from about zero in 1984 to $12 billion a year in 1987. Then it fell to below $4 billion. It's still falling. Perhaps even more significant in terms of New York as the global capital model, the city's U.S. share of foreign investment has fallen from just below 25 percent in 1976 to about 10 percent today.[66]

## INFO CITY

Forget Manufacturing – New York is now the Information Capital of the World.
Caption, New York Magazine. "Info City" February 8,1981

In 1815, in an immortal information coup, Rothschild's London office, capitalism's original global command center, received by carrier pigeon the news of Napoleon's defeat at Waterloo. The Rothschilds immediately began to buy British and Allied securities. In the years after Napoleon's downfall, the telegraph replaced the pigeon, and the telephone triumphed over the telegraph and the fax now reigns supreme. But the Rothschilds are still selling bonds in London. And the point of processing information in financial capitals is still to gain a competitive advantage in securities sales.

The remarketing of New York as a burgeoning global center, the refurbishment of its image as a failed national center, required that something new, vital and technologically advanced be found for people to do here. Yes, we were all global now. But precisely what would global people do to add up to more employment and more office space?

The major discovery of the early seventies, made by the RPA, was that New Yorkers weren't engaged in the same old trading, lawyering, and huckstering. There was more to old Manhattan than just transferring and storing money, buying and selling stocks. Manhattanites were now "processing information."

In the new urban discourse that expanded from an RPA press release, "information" developed more occult properties than new age crystallography. "Information" became both a kind of wealth and the prime channel for increasing wealth. The Rothschilds would have been laughed out of town if they had tried to promote City of London real estate on the grounds that they had vastly increased the number or speed of their pigeons. This is because everyone understands what a pigeon is, and few are intimidated by them. The same can hardly be said of computers.

The intimidation factor makes plausible the most grandiose claims for computers and information. Prophets of the information age now claim that it constitutes wealth in itself; that information has replaced profits as the aim of capitalism. Information, we are told, has replaced land, labor and capital as the basis for creating wealth.

The earliest example I have been able to find of the effort to sell Manhattan on the basis that it was the capital of the information age comes from a 1971 press release put out by the RPA. The claim arose in the context of a plea for more luxury housing to promote more office building construction. To save New York's economy, the RPA's chief publicist William Shore argued, it was necessary to build more office buildings, and the lack of affordable luxury housing was a big problem. (Since without satisfactory housing, execs wouldn't locate here and thus no more office construction.)

But, you might ask, what was the basis for anticipating more office space? There was rapid growth of office workers, and even more rapid growth of computers. Why wouldn't the computers start replacing the office workers? Wasn't that what technology did? Why wasn't the upshot of all the information technology a need for fewer workers and thus less space? The answer, Shore explained, was that a new economic force had emerged – information. Information was an economic end in itself as well as a means. This was a tonic for the Manhattan office space market since what really went on in offices was information processing. So the centrality of information meant the centrality and indispensability of Manhattan's central business district.[67]

William Shore, the author of the RPA press release, deserves to be hailed as the Norman Turing of Info City. His argument would constitute the intellectual core of more elaborate academic efforts that surfaced later. But in order for the Info City trope to filter down intellectually to social science academics, it had to percolate a while in journalistic precincts.

In February 1981, when *New York* magazine made "Info City" a cover story, the RPA's ideas and data featured prominently in what was probably the most representative piece of local establishmentarian urbanism of the period. It rang all the ideological bells, giving the clearest, most exciting rationale for converting to informationalism, and at the same time for sinking more billions into Manhattan real estate. After reading the article, you wanted to grab a hard hat and start tearing down factories yourself, realizing the new Jerusalem.

Manhattan *was* Info City. It was vibrating with *data*, a new kind of wealth for the eighties which would be for New Yorkers what oil had been for the Saudis in the seventies. Author Desmond Smith wrote

The RPA estimates that more than half of New York City's 100 billion gross city product (the total value of goods and services) produced is generated by people who process information.

Information revolution. Information has become as never before a major form of wealth. A dramatic power shift had taken place in factors of production. Labor's value was sinking fast. And capital was rapidly being transmuted into information. Money was a form of "Mind." You're not really talking about keeping money; you're talking about keeping records. Money isn't tangible anymore it's an idea.

The power of information to create wealth meant a growing "synergism" between downtown finance and midtown communications. *New York* explained

In a very real sense Manhattan has become the Information Society's R&D center, *the* place for experimental ferment . . . Brokers are now getting into financial futures, and bankers are hedging bond portfolios in commodities. Merrill Lynch, the world's biggest brokerage house, has entered merchant banking overseas and de facto commercial banking at home.

All this, explained Rupert Murdoch's *New York*, makes Manhattan too valuable for manufacturing.

An army of lawyers, computer programers and promoters have marched into convert the lofts and factories into living and work spaces.

In a battlefield report from the conversion front, the magazine noted that where manufacturing tenants paid up to $3.75 a square foot in annual rent, the same space earned as a residence was going for up to $12. Sold for co-operative housing, industrial space can go for as high as $100. It was an intoxicating prospect. And, as *New York* pointed out,

more than half the 4,600 loft buildings in New York now house people – the worker bees in the information hive.

In case you might have qualms about the old worker bees, expelled from their industrial hives, Peter Solomon, Koch's Deputy Mayor from Lehman Brothers was interviewed to allay concerns about joblessness in Info City. "Listen," he said,

we added 6,000 new hotel rooms in 1980. Roughly one person is required in the services for every one of those rooms. That adds up to 6000 jobs. Many more than Ford's Mahwah plant in New Jersey.[68]

Forget Ford plants. Think hotels. This is what Ford Foundation vice president Louis Winnick has been arguing for years. "A sacred tradition assigns manufacturing a higher status than the services partly because the former is an 'export' or 'base' industry," he notes, and because it has provided comparatively high-wage jobs for the unskilled. "But economic history has its phases," he observed. And now it's the service sector's turn. Specifically hotels. "The service sector," he points out, "includes the porters, chambermaids and handymen at the big hotels and hospitals;" these jobs pay as well or better than manufacturing.[69]

Mahwah closed in 1985. On the cleared site of the plant rose the Sheraton International Crossroads Hotel. In 1988, a photo of the hotel and the plant were juxtaposed in the RPA's "Region in the Global Economy," a report funded by the Ford Foundation and written by a team of academics and economists including John Mollenkopf of the City University of New York; Mitchell Moss of New York University; Dr. Carol O'Cleireacain then of District Council 37, later David Dinkins' Finance Commissioner; and Saskia Sassen of Columbia.

The photos were placed aside the usual global boilerplate about the emergence of New York, London and Tokyo as the command posts of the new economic system . . . explosive growth in world trade. . . . A burgeoning world market in business, professional and information services. . . . Proliferation of telecommunications . . . internationalization of capital and financial markets.[70]

The caption read,

These pictures illustrate the kinds of changes that have occurred in the regional economy in recent decades. When Ford Motor Company opened its Mahwah plant in 1955, it was the world's largest auto assembly plant, capable of producing 700 cars and 200 trucks a day. The plant was torn down in 1985 and replaced with a large mixed use development which includes offices, a warehouse and a hotel.

In 1992, I called the Mahwah Sheraton. Room attendants are employed by a non-union outside service. The Sheraton supervisor, who asked to be nameless, advised that workers make from $5.25 to $5.75. Benefits, she said, were "minimal." Another worker on the night desk recalled that her father had worked in the plant.

He made more than I do. He raised four children and sent us to college on his wages as a millwright.

## NOTES

1. All figures on Manhattan office space come from the Real Estate Board of New York. See source Appendix 9.
2. This doesn't mean, of course, that all the buildings built in the decade are empty. It means rather that the new "state of the art" Class A SOBs tend to empty out the older buildings.
3. Not just by relaxations in the FARs (floor area ratios) as in the sixties, but by new tax abatement programs like those administered by the Industrial and Commercial Incentives Board (1977) which then became an "as of right" program in 1984, abating taxes for as much as 13 years on a declining scale.
4. To get the total amount of subsidy to luxury and office construction since the sixties boom, add the Industrial and Commercial Incentive Program (ICIP), plus 421a, plus J-51, plus abatements for Battery Park City and World Trade Center construction, and the total exceeds $1.25 billion. See The City of New York, Executive Budget Fiscal Year 1993, Message of the Mayor, p. 84.
5. New York State AFL-CIO, Toward a New Economic Strategy for New York State, May 1993, p. 25.
6. During the eighties, Class A office buildings, depending on the location, cost $350–$400 per square foot to build. Construction costs amounted to about a third of this total.
7. If the amount of office space per worker equals 175 square feet, as estimated by developer Dan Rose, scion of one of the city's premier real estate dynasties (see Tom Schachtman, *Skyscraper* (Boston, Little, Brown), p. 330.
8. For the exact composition of the cohort see chapter 10, The Anaconda and the Cyclone.
9. Jerry Adler, *High Rise* (New York: HarperCollins, 1993), p. 349.
10. Ibid.

11. Claudia B. Deutsch, "New York City Hotels Battling the Blues," *New York Times*, Section 10, June 13, 1993, p. 1.

12. Department of City Planning, New York City Comprehensive Waterfront Plan, Reclaiming the City's Edge, NYC DCP 92–27, Summer 1992.

13. Bank for International Settlements "Asset Prices and the Management of Financial Distress," 63rd Annual Report, Basle, June 14th, 1993, p. 159.

14. Jeane B. Pinder, "Downtown's Empty Feeling," *New York Times*, May 8, 1993, VIII, p. 5. The *Times* source is Cushman & Wakefield.

15. Research Department, The Real Estate Board of New York, "Manhattan New Office Building Construction, Office Building Completions 1978–1990."

16. Actually, the Righa Royale seems like Motel 6 compared to its crosstown luxury rival the Four Seasons where room rates go up to $3,000 a night (Claudia H. Deutsch, "New York City Hotels Battling the Blues," Section 10, June 13, 1993, p. 1.

17. See Department of City Planning, Midtown Development Review, July 1987, NYC-DCP 87–05, p. 2.

18. Tom Schachtman, *Skyscraper Dreams* (Boston: Little, Brown, 1991), p. 318.

19. Olympia & York was bankrupt in Canada and Great Britain. Not yet in the U.S. Doubts about Olympia & York's ability to pay its $125 million yearly New York City tax bill surfaced in 1992. (See David Henry, "O&Y Loses Its Grip on More NY Assets," *New York Newsday*, November 29, 1992, p. 43.

20. There is a Queens Democratic organization, a Bronx Democratic organization, a Brooklyn Democratic Party, etc., but no New York City organization. None of these borough-wide organizations bothers to write a platform or regularize its membership. Each borough party is, in turn, made up of clubhouse organizations, the existence of which is for some reason denied by academic political scientists, but which are still powerful enough to dictate electoral outcomes on a local level, given the abysmal turnout and New York's restrictive election laws which re-inforce each other. The best that could be said of the motives of the participants in these organizations is that they seek "honest graft." But the leaders tend to over-reach, and their fate is usually jail. See Jack Newfield and Paul DuBruhl, *Abuse of Power* (Harmondsworth, Middlesex, England: Penguin, 1977) or Jack Newfield and Wayne Barrett, *City for Sale* (New York: Harper & Row, 1988).

21. Between 1970 and 1977, the all-time job trough, the rate of decline was nearly 29 percent. (All figures from New York State Department of Labor, unpublished data.)

22. Urban Studies Review, 1992.

23. Park figure from James Barron, "Bronx Hears a Slur and Responds with Its Cheer," *New York Times*, June 12, 1993, p. L25. See Table, "New Hampshire vs. the Bronx," (Hudson County figure from Port Authority; Bronx industrial acreage from Fordham study.)

24. Herman Badillo, December 2, 1992, interview. Badillo says Koch told him it was "Wall Street" that wouldn't support ambitious plans for South Bronx revival.

25. See chapter 5.

26. Michael R. Greenberg and Nicholas J. Valente, "Recent Economic Trends in the Major Northeastern Metropolises," in *Post Industrial America*, George Sternlieb and James W. Hughes, (eds) (New Brunswick, New Jersey: The Center for Urban Policy Research Rutgers, 1975), pp. 94–95.

27. See chapter 5.

28. Real Estate Board of New York, Inc., A Foundation to Build On: A Program to Revitalize New York City's Economy, June 1990, p. 12. REBNY's program is a greater New York through greater subsidies for more office buildings. And lower taxes – especially the commercial occupancy tax.

29. Twentieth Century Fund, Report on "The Global City". The official proclamation of the State of New York to post-industrial goals occurred shortly afterwards, see The New York State Economy in the 1980s: A Program for Economic Growth (1981) and Building from Strength: A Program for Economic Growth and Opportunity (1982).

30. Twentieth Century Fund, "Global City", p. 5.

31. Ibid., p. 23. The clue to the Twentieth Century's intent was the use of the catch phrase from planned shrinkage discourse, "bring the people to the jobs, not jobs to the people." This meant incentives and programs to get people out of poor neighborhoods; not neighborhood revitalization. The Carter Commission – composed of a similar mix of blue ribbon types – called for the same thing in exactly the same words the same year. See chapter 5.

32. James Orr, "Foreign Direct Investment in New York City." Final Report, New York City Economic Policy and Marketing Group. February 1, 1993, Appendix B.

33. Cityspire was eleven feet over zoning limits. Authorities made Eichner lop off the excess footage. He insisted that he hadn't been trying to squeeze out more rentable space. He just wanted to make the floors thicker.

34. Wayne Barrett, *Trump: The Deals and the Downfall*, (New York: HarperCollins, 1992), pp. 192–3.

35. Saskia Sassen, *The Global City* (Princeton, New Jersey: Princeton University Press, 1991). Sassen writes of the informal sector, "In this context, one can think of informalization as an emergent, or developing, 'opportunity' structure that avoids or compensates for various types of constraints, from regulations to market prices for inputs," p. 289.

36. Wayne Barrett, *Trump: The Deals and the Downfall* (New York: HarperCollins, 1992), p. 203.

37. The Commission on the Year 2000, New York Ascendent, June 1987, p. 26.

38. Matty Troy, Queens; Pat Cunningham, the Bronx.

39. Through the Manpower Research and Development Corp. For MRDC's work, see Ken Auletta, *The Underclass* (New York: Random House, 1982). For anti-manufacturing bias see Louis Winnick, "New York Unbound," in Peter Salins (ed), *New York Unbound* (Manhattan Institute) (New York: Basil Blackwell, 1988).

40. See Robert Fitch, "Making New York City Safe for Plutocracy," *Nation*, December 11, 1989, pp. 709–714. And "Exchange" Frederick A.O. Schwarz, Jr., and Robert Fitch, *Nation*, February 5, 1990.

41. Dick Netzer, "The Location of People and Jobs within New York City," Report from the Urban Research Center to the New York City Commission on the Year 2000, February 1986.

42. New York City Planning Commission, Shaping the City's Future, New York City Planning and Zoning Report, For Public Discussion, Spring 1993, p. 1. The same quote can be found on page 21 in *New York Ascendent*.

43. New York City Planning Commission, "Shaping the City's Future," New York City Planning and Zoning Report, Spring 1993, p. 11.

44. It's also true that specific technological discoveries bubble up from the best practice of industry.

45. Peter Hall, "Three systems, Three Separate Paths," American Planning Association Journal, Winter 1991, p. 16.

46. Doug Henwood supplied me with this memo, p. 3 sect. 2a.

47. The locus classicus of long wave theory is N.V. Kondratieff, "The Long waves in economic life," Review of Economic Statistics," November 1935.

48. Dirk J. Struik (ed), *Birth of the Communist Manifesto* with Full Text of the *Manifesto* . . . (New York: International Publishers, 1971), p. 93. Nationalism, explained Marx and Engels was a spent force.

49. The classic introduction to the decline and fall of globalism is written in 1944 by Karl Polyani, *The Great Transformation* (Boston: Beacon Hill, 1944).

50. Ibid., p. 10.

51. Long-wave theorist, Michael Beenstock, estimates that Great Britain, the largest exporter of capital, sent funds overseas beginning in the 1870s, at the rate of 7 percent of GDP. For the U.S. to have reached that level would mean capital export on the order of 420 billion a year. In fact U.S. levels are less than a third of this rate. Michael Beenstock, *The World Economy in Transition*, 2nd ed. (London: George Allen & Unwin, 1984), ch.6.

52. Similarly, the German economy is a lot more dependent on world trade than America's. Why don't German cities look anything like American? Where are their command and control centers? Their stock exchanges? Their giant office cores? Office vacancies in Berlin and Frankfurt in December 1992 were 1 percent and 7 percent respectively. (See Bank for International Settlements, 63rd Annual Report, p. 159.)

53. *Business Week*, "Why Made-in-America Is Back in Style," November 7, 1988. Cited in Elizabeth McLean Petras, "The Shirt on Your Back: Immigrant Workers and the Reorganization of the Garment Industry" in *Social Justice*, vol. 19, no. 1, Spring 1992.

54. Adam Smith, *Wealth of Nations*, Edwin Canaan (ed) (Chicago: University of Chicago Press, 1976), p. 81.

55. Doug Henwood alerted me to this citation.

56. Edgar M. Hoover and Raymond Vernon, *Anatomy of a Metropolis* (New York: Doubleday, 1962), p. 74.

57. Joann S. Lublin, "Firms Ship Unit Headquarters Abroad," December 9, 1991, B1.

58. Laurie Hays," IBM Speeds Drive to Shed Real Estate as Part of Program to Trim Jobs, Costs," *Wall Street Journal*, June 18, 1993, p. A5A.

59. See Susan Carey, "Airlines Seek to Cut Back Office Costs By Establishing Offshore Operations," *Wall Street Journal*, November 30, 1992, p. A5C.

60. Ibid.

61. Saskia Sassen, *Global City*, p. 154. ms. cited approvingly by Manuel Castells, in *The Informational City*, (New York: Basil Blackwell, 1989), p. 343.

62. Ralph T. King, Jr., "U.S. Service Exports Are Growing Rapidly, But Almost Unnoticed," *New York Times*, April 21, 1993, A1.

63. David Rockefeller, "Foreign Investment, Key to New York City's Growth," (letter) *New York Times*, April 28, 1993, A20.

64. Campeau's wresting Bloomies away from Macys for many billions doesn't count as local investment because Bloomies, as part of Federated Department Stores, was officially a subsidiary of the Cincinnati Corp.

65. John Rothschild, *Going for Broke* (New York: Simon and Schuster, 1991).

66. James Orr, "Foreign Direct Investment in New York City, Final Report", New York City Economic Policy and Marketing Group, February 1, 1993. Statistics from "Figure 1" "Foreign Direc Investment in New York City, 1974–1991". Source: U.S. Department of Commerce, also figure 3

67. Regional Plan Association, News Release, January 11, 1971, No.1114.

68. Desmond Smith, "Info City," *New York*, February 9, 1991, p. 29.

69. Louis Winnick, "New York Unbound," in Peter Salins (ed.), *New York Unbound* (Manhattan Institute) (New York: Basil Blackwell, 1988), pp. 19–20. To show that services offer jobs to more than just foundation execs and lawyers, Winnick cites two other low skill occupations available in the services – key punching and messengers on bicycles. Since 1988, however, these occupations have just about disappeared.

70. Regional Plan Association, The Region in the Global Economy, May 1988, p. 5.

*CHAPTER SEVEN*

# THE DEAL OF A DYNASTY

## MORTGAGING OUT

If anyone proved able to extract the cash value from the popular but mysterious eighties catchphrase, "Think globally, act locally," it was the Rockefeller family. Selling off Rockefeller Center at the peak of a soon-to-crash market for three billion dollars may well have constituted the most awesome New York City real estate play ever, but to bring it off required several sure-footed international steps.

First, in 1985, acting through Goldman Sachs and Shearson Lehman, the family transformed Rockefeller Center into a globally-held Real Estate Investment Trust (REIT). Essentially, REIT investors bought shares in a mortgage that was convertible into equity in the year 2000. The sale of the property also featured the heavy marketing of Japanese zero coupon notes and Eurobonds. Altogether, notes, bonds and mortgage brought the family $1.3 billion. Then in 1989, the family sold a majority interest in the Rockefeller Group to Mitsubishi Properties for $846 million. Finally, in 1990 and 1991, they got two more checks from Mitsubishi for $527 million, giving back all but 15 percent of the equity in the family real estate holding company, the Rockefeller Group, Inc.[1] About the same time, the family also got rid of their share in the Exxon building – part of the 1969 extension of Rockefeller Center across Sixth Avenue, netting another approximately $300 million. Altogether, these globe-spanning transactions transferring their local properties yielded the family in excess of three billion dollars.

Unloading Rockefeller Center was more than the deal of a decade. It was the deal of a dynasty: one which after all the layers of complexity were unravelled, emerged simply as the classic developer's dream –

mortgaging out. The difference was that the Rockefeller's dream was played out in billions instead of millions; across decades instead of years.

From the time John D. Rockefeller Jr. had signed the midtown lease on Columbia's midtown properties, in 1928, the dream had taken more than sixty years to realize. Selling Rockefeller Center had been a secret family objective almost from the moment of its opening. But the successful series of transactions came not a moment too soon.

Since the offering, the Rockefeller REIT's stock price has fallen from $22.00 to around $7.00. The appraised value of Rockefeller Center has fallen proportionately, so that it's now below the value of the REIT mortgage. In 1985, the Goldman Sachs brokers, pointing to the prospectus, told Mr. Average Investor that in a decade, rents in Rockefeller Center would exceed $75.00 a square foot. By the year 2000, when the option to convert the mortgage into equity came due, the rents would stand at $100.00. But $28.00 is the going rate now, and this rate is under severe pressure. By a quirk of the lease structure, nearly 40 percent of Rockefeller Center's space comes up for renewal in 1994, causing speculation that Mitsubishi and the Rockefellers – who now held only a sliver of the equity – might simply walk away from the property – a frequent outcome when the value of a mortgage exceeds the value of the equity.[2]

What though, did all the numbers really add up to? Could the significance of the Rockefeller Center transactions really be boiled down to the terms and conditions of another real estate play? Certainly there is a wider sense in which Rockefeller Center has come to symbolize not just Manhattan, or even New York City, but American commercial civilization as a whole.

The noted architectural historian Carol Krinsky compares Rockefeller Center to the religious monuments of the past, arguing that because of its planning and design, the midtown complex deserves to be thought of as the modern architectural equivalent of a medieval cathedral. Rockefeller Center's soaring towers, she says, express the city's essence – not traditional spirituality or philosophical refinement nor respect for established order. But rather its

drive towards the future, its constant experimentation, its attempts to make the best of its physical limitations and its financial problems, its position in international trade, and its international social composition.[3]

Even more broadly, the midtown office buildings, she says, embody the values of a capitalist democracy,

> ambition, flexibility, the idealism possible within enlightened self-interest, astute management – all are important signs of successful commercial cultures, which Rockefeller Center exemplifies.[4]

Krinsky's assessment seems to place a symbolic weight on the structures nearly as insupportable as the present mortgage. But who can argue with her? My own reaction is closer to those formed in the 1930s, when as Douglas Heskall, the editor of *Architectural Form* wrote,

> the association between Rockefeller Center and some giant burial place has suggested itself to a great many people. The mood of the place is gray, unreal, baleful.[5]

Krinsky's interpretation, however, is widely shared now.[6] And there is no way to confirm or disconfirm perceived symbolic values. Medieval people worshipped relics in the form of God's toenails. Modern New Yorkers enthuse over Rockefeller Center's murals. In these hermeneutical matters what counts is conviction.

It was in such symbolic terms that the meaning of the sale first became understood: the transfer of a precious icon of urban America to a former enemy. Later, as the dubious value of the assets conveyed became more evident, the meaning changed. A sense of Yankee pride at getting the better of the over-achieving Japanese began to replace the sense of national loss.

To grasp the meaning of Rockefeller Center's sale, more objectively, however, what would be required is a knowledge of its political terms and historical conditions. We could better appreciate what the actors were aiming at. But up 'till now, there seemed to be no need to analyze a sale which has been seen as well-timed but otherwise thoroughly unproblematic. What needs to be explained? Why investigate the pre-conditions of a sale that seemed to require no more than the willingness of the owners to sell?

Ever since the 1930s, the premise that urban historians have worked from is that Rockefeller Center combines the highest standards of architectural excellence with commercial profitability.[7] None of the histories of the project have come close to conveying just what an incubus Rockefeller Center proved to be for the family up until the final sale. The wealth-destroying dimensions of the 99-year deal they got themselves into have been imperfectly perceived.

Not realizing how deep the hole was, historians didn't recognize the efforts being expanded by the family to dig themselves out. The Rockefeller family may have been credited with transforming the city – Lincoln Center, the U.N., and all that – but these initiatives weren't seen as materially connected to the well-being of Rockefeller Center. The blockage of Zeckendorf's competitive "X" City project, the transfer of 20,000 mainly Puerto Rican people from the borderlands of midtown – these were seen as civic philanthropies.

Then too, there has been little awareness of just how greatly dependent the family was on Rockefeller Center for its economic survival. On the contrary, the legendary wealth of the Rockefellers made it seem as if the midtown estate were just one small component of the family fortune, not the bulk of it. The very material sense in which Rockefeller Center gave the family its identity through the 1934 Trusts has not been grasped. Still less how the Rockefeller Brothers Fund's endowment rested almost entirely on Rockefeller Center, and further, how the actions of the Rockefeller Brothers Fund itself were concerned with efforts to raise the value of Rockefeller Center by mitigating the blight which surrounded it.

Key city-shaping plans of the eighties – the midtown plan which shifted real estate values to the west side, 42nd Street development, the Clinton plan – were not simply the result of Rockefeller Brothers' Fund grants to City Planning. Nor were the Rockefellers the only actors with large land holdings on the west side who supported the plans. But the Rockefellers, operating at the highest policy forming levels defined the issues in terms of preservation, conservation; made sure that RBF grantees were hired as consultants to the Planning Commission; financed Department of City Planning reports; and helped, through negotiation, to ensure the final outcomes.

Thus, because the story of how it came to be built, and what it cost to make it profitable remains largely unknown, the true meaning of the Rockefeller Center, the extent of its city-shaping dimensions remain wrapped in clouds of BOMFOG – Albany reporters' acronym for Nelson's incessantly invoked appeal to "the brotherhood of man under the fatherhood of god."

It was in part because the wealth and power of the Rockefellers had become so inflated and mystified in the popular mind that their actual sphere of local influence in New York City became almost invisible. You would never suppose that a family as rich as the Rockefellers were imagined to be, could be totally absorbed in what happened to a few empty lots on Seventh Avenue. These were people who elevated family retainers like Dean Rusk, Henry Kissinger, and John J. McCloy to cabinet status. They socialized with the Shah of Iran and the Crown Prince of Japan. How could such a family be totally obsessed with such mean endeavors as driving hotdog sellers away from 42nd Street?

My former *Ramparts* editorial colleagues, Peter Collier and David Horowitz, wrote a 700-page bestseller about the Rockefellers without ever grasping precisely what it was that they did for a living. Together they combined the analysis of Anna ("Rulers of America") Rochester with the sensibility of Oprah Winfrey. *The Rockefellers* wove together the political legends that Horowitz had picked up from his progressive parents with Colliers' fast-paced generational saga about the "cousins."[8] The story of rich kids' fumbling search for personal identity against the constraints of fabulous wealth and parental rigidity struck a nerve just about the time the Loud family was exposing itself on Public Television. But where *did* all that Rockefeller money come from?

From the family's GHQ, Room 5600 in the RCA Building, was about as close as the authors came to pinning it down. They seemed not to know what exactly to make of family retainer J. Richardson Dilworth's testimony at Nelson's Vice Presidential confirmation hearing in 1974, revealing that by far the bulk of the family's $1.3 billion wealth came from midtown – the equity in Rockefeller Center. Collier and Horowitz insisted obliquely and without any evidence that the family income still came from international banking and oil.[9]

Dilworth's testimony, nevertheless, revealed not only how the fortune – while obviously still substantial – had nonetheless dwindled spectacularly. From world-wide oil and banking interests on which the sun never set, it had congealed into a few square blocks in midtown. He also exposed the fact that in real terms, the family wealth had gotten considerably smaller in dollar terms.[10] In the 1920s, Junior's wealth had just topped $1 billion – about $5 billion in today's dollars. Thus by the mid-seventies, the family wealth had shrunk by two-thirds. Where had it all gone?

Certainly Junior and his sons had given away a lot of money. But, Senior gave away substantially more, and he still accumulated a fortune estimated recently at $26 billion.[11] Very simply, the reason why the fortune was getting smaller and not larger was because family capital was being absorbed by the Sixth Avenue tar baby.

Despite insistent public claims of financial success and profitability, for most of its existence, the office complex functioned more as the hospice of Rockefeller wealth, than its triumphant incubator. During the entire decade of the thirties, Rockefeller Center lost money at the rate of about $5 million a year. The property just managed to make a small profit in 1940 – the first year the IND was available to bring mass transit to the Center. But then, with the advent of World War II, as John D. Rockefeller III's official biographers Harr and Johnson attest, Rockefeller Center failed to earn income until 1964. Even worse from the family standpoint, when the profits began to come, there could be no payout. Because of the restrictions in the lease, no dividends were paid on Rockefeller Center stock until 1976. As a result, throughout most of the seventies, the Rockefellers found themselves cash poor.[12]

Up until the eighties turnaround, whatever Rockefeller Center may have accomplished in architectural terms, or for the iconography of business civilization, as a bare real estate investment it was bad business. By the family's conservative accounting, it cost $125 million to build Rockefeller Center. In 1952, Junior gave the RBF a note which Rockefeller Center owed him for $57.7 million. This represented additional capital expenditure.[13] So when Rockefeller Center finally turned a profit in the sixties, the earnings on the order of $1–2 millions[14] represented not even a 1 percent return. Indeed, if the establishment of the original Standard Oil Trust by Senior stands as perhaps the most ingenious business arrangement in American business history, his son Junior's creation of Rockefeller Center may ultimately loom as one of the most hare-brained.

Five main reasons stand out. First, Junior, on the bad advice of his real estate experts, committed himself to a long-term ownership of *buildings* – which can't possibly appreciate. And simultaneously, he failed to acquire the *land* underneath them which can. Second, before construction started, the project lacked a plausible tenant for any of the buildings. The Metropolitan Opera, the supposed "anchor" couldn't possibly provide income the way a corporate tenant could. Third, suitable office tenants were reluctant to locate off the beaten track on the west side: Sixth Avenue was too far from serviceable mass transit, too far from Grand Central, too far from Times Square. Fourth, the Sixth Avenue Manhattan Elevated ran right overhead. Who wanted to rent office space underneath the ear-splitting, soot-scattering El? Fifth, Junior simply invested much too late in the business cycle to hope for success. Even better located buildings that beat Rockefeller Center into the ground, like the Chrysler Building, had difficulties.

Some of the problems seemed completely insuperable. Having driven such a lucrative bargain with the Rockefellers, why would Columbia University ever change the terms? (The family did successfully plead poverty in the early thirties, getting a deferment of rent without interest from Columbia during the period when Rockefeller Center was being built and rented, with the proviso that the money be repaid between 1942 and 1952.)[15] Other obstacles seemed insuperable without changing the structure of the city, but this is precisely what the family now proceeded to do. Ultimately, the city officials proved far easier to manipulate than the trustees of Columbia University or the thirties real estate market.

It's highly likely that the inspiration for the Rockefeller Center project came from Chicago. Samuel Insull's Civic Opera House, begun in 1927 and completed just after the 1929 Crash seems to have served as the unacknowledged model. The timing and the similarities are striking. It too was a product of the miscegenation between bogus philanthropy and blind real estate speculation. Utilities mogul Insull's idea was to use Chicago's Lyric Opera to anchor a giant office building – 750,000 square feet. Like Rockefeller Center, the building was poorly located in an out-of-the-way area, poorly served by mass transit. When the Crash came, however, Insull's project fared even worse than Rockefeller Center. His utilities empire collapsed, the building went into receivership, and Insull himself spent a lot of time hiding in Turkey from the Feds. So it is no wonder that his intellectual paternity has not been affirmed. At any rate it seems more than coincidental that Rockefeller's advisors began to show interest in converting Columbia's midtown plot to a home for office buildings and the opera in late 1927, just after news had been made public of the start of Insull's spec office building plus opera project.[16]

Certainly the inspiration for the "Opera Square", as it was originally called, had nothing to do with any family interest in opera. Junior never attended the Metropolitan. Nor did his sons. Junior's advisors' idea, rather, was that the prestige of the Met could somehow be made to rub off on office and commercial tenants, making leases more valuable.[17]

Ivy Lee, Junior's long-time aide, who'd stemmed the adverse public relations tide following the massacre of Colorado Fuel and Iron workers and their families at Ludlow, explained to his best client the way it would work,

> The plan is that half way between Fifth and Sixth Avenues, a square area shall be cut out between 49th and 50th Streets . . . The idea is that the new Opera House will stand between this square and Sixth Avenue and that facing the square on the other three sides shall be buildings developed on land owned by Columbia University which shall contain high grade shops and offices in the buildings above.

Lee advised,

> The thought is that this will make the square and the immediate surroundings [the] most valuable shopping district in the world.[18]

The deal was this: Junior would *buy* a small part of Columbia's midtown estate. He then would *give it away* to the Opera Company – known then as the Metropolitan Opera House and Realty Company. The opera people would then construct a splendid building on the site. Having sown his cultural seed, Junior would then *rent* from Columbia the rest of its midtown plot, the area between Fifth and Sixth Avenues 48th to 51st Streets. But then Junior would turn around and get developers to pay him for the right to develop commercial and office space on the remainder of the Opera-enriched soil.

There were a lot of parties involved, a great deal of swapping and leasing and sub-leasing but after the initial swirl of transactions, the deal seemed to radiate a rich, austere beauty. Junior had a chance to make two or three million a year, just about indefinitely, with an investment of only $3.6 million and little work. Attorney Christy of the Debevoise firm explained the motives in a private memorandum after the deal collapsed,

> Rockefeller Center originated as a limited real estate project with the idea, in the main, of leasing ground areas to others, who would build and finance their own buildings. The management of such an enterprise would have been comparatively simple and would have required comparatively limited financing. The functions of the corporation would have been to prepare a general plan for the whole development and to clear the general area of existing leases in order to assure a harmonious and economic development and to collect the rents.[19]

## WIPING OUT "THE DEAD SPOT"

A small hitch in the deal was discovered just after the big hitch – the Crash – emerged. No one seems to have told Junior that the opera has *seasons*. And that when it's not in season, no one sings, and therefore no one shows up. He discovered this when he finally hired someone who really knew real estate and whose horizon transcended collecting commissions. John R. Todd, who'd developed the successful Greybar Building right next to Grand Central wrote Junior's uncle Winthrop Aldrich a memo just a couple of months after the crash, when it became apparent that "Plan A" – sub-letting wouldn't work. And that "Plan B" – Junior developing the property himself – would have to be put into effect. Todd was delighted that the negotiations with the Opera had struck an impasse. Todd asked Aldrich,

I am wondering, if you realize how much this means in increased income and how important it is to increase the income. The Opera House would be a dead spot and greatly reduce shopping values in all the property facing it . . . I am saying this because I am hoping so keenly that the matter will not be reopened, and am enclosing a copy of this letter and asking if you think well of it to pass it on to Mr. Debevoise.[20]

Junior was faced with the prospect of handing over $3.6 million every year to Columbia for 21 years. Even that sum seems hardly ruinous to someone of Rockefeller's reputed wealth until you begin to consider what the Depression had done to equities. Junior had been worth a billion at the top of the market, but by 1933 stocks had lost five-sixths of their 1929 values. The capitalized value of $3.6 million a year equal at 1930s interest rates amounted to more than half of Junior's entire fortune. It was no wonder that he decided to offset the income loss with the construction of buildings whose rents could defray the ground rent payments to Columbia. The next thing Junior realized, however, is that he not only had a yearly $3.6 million payment due, but a $49 million mortgage and 4 million square feet of empty office space.

It's no wonder that Junior often despaired and secretly searched for a buyer to take the income-gobbling project off his hands. Such buyers proved to be even more scarce than developers, but at one point, in 1931, Junior thought he'd got one. A certain Mr. Greenhouse of Philadelphia. A report on Greenhouse, however, came back unfavorable. "Mr. Stotesbury of Philadelphia who has a summer home here and is a good friend of mine," reported Junior to his friend and Attorney

Tom Debevoise, "telephoned me yesterday to say that a Mr. Greenhouse of Philadelphia had just been to see him, asking an introduction to me." Junior told Debevoise it turned out Greenhouse "is a very shrewd, slippery Jew speculator."[21] Junior would never deal with him.

## BENVENUTO BENITO

The supervening commercial fact the family had to face in the 1930s was the reality of a renter's market. Corporations were shrinking, not expanding, their office staffs. While office space could be sold in such a market, the deals had to be ingenious. Reciprocity ruled. Given the family's stock holdings, and the names on the Rockefeller Center buildings, as well as some of the prime tenants, its tempting to conclude that Junior used his stock holding power to compel corporations like Esso, Chase and Westinghouse to move to Rockefeller Center.

It didn't work that way. Chase rented space, but brother-in-law Winthrop drove so hard a bargain it infuriated Junior. Westinghouse moved in too, but the company negotiators made sure they got a deal to install all of Rockefeller Center's elevators. Morgan interests rented space but they took back contracts for structural steel.

Junior's note to Todd, reflects not only just how stiff a price the family had paid to get tenants, but an almost stupefied sense of shock at the turn of events:

I presume we may regard the first stage of the Rockefeller Center enterprise as drawing to a close. How different the situation is from what we had anticipated it would be at this point is almost incredible. The changes that have taken place since the work began have been kaleidoscopic. What we confidentially expected would be our best tenants, who would pay a full rental under any and all circumstances, have turned out to be businesses in which we find ourselves with large stock holdings and a heavy although indirect responsibility of management. To the extent this is true it is the fault of none of us but is due rather to circumstances which no-one could have dreamed could arise.[22]

So bad were renting conditions in the U.S. it made sense to try to scour the globe for tenants. To fill space in the small buildings along Fifth Avenue, the family propositioned foreign governments. The plan was to have each of the then four great European powers rent a building. If you look south, the buildings in question are the small six-storey structures which face Fifth Avenue. Today they are called from north to south the International Building, the Palazzo d'Italia, La Maison Française and the British building. They have gone through several name changes and tenants. What is now the International Building, was supposed to house commercial space rented by the Third Reich. Junior had fondly hoped that the Palazzo d'Italia would be rented by Mussolini himself.

In 1935, Junior visited Italy with the goal of getting Mussolini to rent space in the "Palazzo d'Italia." In a letter to John R. Todd, he seemed to think he had moved closer to a deal, "We (I) did pretty well, didn't we, at least for Rockefeller Center and Mussolini." Junior enclosed a clip from *Il nuovo cittadino* which had this quote from an interview in the Geneva fascist paper,

I am a sincere friend of Italy and a great admirer of Benito Mussolini whose every effort I have always followed with the keenest interest. Upon this man today rests the eyes of the entire world. He has the marvelous gift of being able to instill real life and zeal in every undertaking with which he is associated as I have been personally able to experience when the plans and details for the Italian palace were being developed in New York. From him, we received keen inspiration for the ultimate triumph of our initiative. I have not yet had the pleasure of meeting with Duce and I would be very happy indeed to shake his hand.[23]

But a deal with Il Duce proved slippery too. It seemed as early as 1933 as if the deal for space at the Palazzo d'Italia was approved. Rockefeller Center officials thought they had a "yes" from the National Fascist Confederation of Industry. And from Mussolini himself. The rents had been worked out: terms involved half the space in the building for $350,000 a year; the second year $450,000; and the third $750,000. The deal fell through, and local Italians wound up renting the space. Even the name had to be changed temporarily from Il Palazzo d'Italia after Mussolini declared war on the U.S.

A lasting trace of Junior's flirtation with the fascist regime can still be found on the walls of what is now the GE building. After using air hammers to remove Diego Rivera's Marxist mural of workers taking over the means of production, with Lenin looking on, Junior decided to commission Jose Maria Sert, Franco's ambassador to Italy. In 1940, Sert was allowed to paint over Rivera's mural, an unmistakable fascist tableau. Sert's work is entitled "American Progress, The Triumph of Man's Accomplishments Through Physical and Mental Labor." It depicts Rockefeller Center's towers looming in the background, symbolizing modern America. In the foreground, the transformation of

American society through the efforts of "the man of Action" is represented by a huge nude figure carrying the wooden bundles of rods and axes of Italian fascist symbolism. The nude, heavily muscled man has the powerful jaw, shaved head, unusually high cheek bones and thin lips that suggest Mussolini. He dwarfs Lincoln and Emerson who are shown helping him deliver the fasces to a grateful American people who reach out to grasp them.[24] Sert's mural still stands.

## NAZIS IN THE NEIGHBORHOOD?

Renting the space in the Palazzo d'Italia to the fascist government had a high priority not just for the obvious commercial reasons, but also because Nazi representatives had said they wouldn't rent space in Rockefeller Center until a deal was consummated with the Italians. Ultimately, the Rockefellers lost both tenants, but apparently not for principled reasons. The Hitlerites appeared to have turned down the Rockefellers rather than vice versa. No available evidence suggests that Jr. himself admired Hitler the way he did Mussolini or thought the prestige of Rockefeller Center would be enhanced by the presence of the Third Reich. But John D. Rockefeller III reported to his father that Uncle Winthrop strongly backed the idea of reserving the building for the Nazis. In 1933, Aldrich had telephoned from Germany, "urging at length the importance of making it a German building."[25]

At least one of Junior's advisors, Ivy Lee, also backed the German option. Lee told John D. Rockefeller III that

> there was no question as to the future of Germany. He felt that the future of the whole of Europe depended on it . . . that if Germany fell, Europe would go under and that if Germany succeeded, the other countries would do likewise. He has complete confidence that Hitler is doing much to bring this about.

Johnny reported that the only cloud in Germany's future, according to Lee, was that Hitler lacked the armaments to save Europe. "He felt very strongly that the fourth International Building must be held for Germany."[26]

Johnny also interviewed influential American Jews to probe their reactions to a place in Rockefeller Center for the Nazis. Future Treasury Secretary Henry Morgenthau predicted war in Europe "soon," and then the dismemberment of Germany would follow. He warned that if the

Rockefellers rented space to Nazis there'd be bad publicity in New York. Banker Felix Warburg, on the other hand, had a more nuanced approach. He appealed to the Rockefellers' conscience, not their fear of bad publicity. Warburg discounted the possibility that Jews would launch a boycott. But at the same time, he felt even without serious economic consequences, renting to the Nazis would tarnish the Rockefeller name, which, he said, had always stood for "liberalism and the like." Johnny reported to his dad:

On the one hand, Warburg said he'd hate to see us have any thing whatever to do with the present German government. On the other hand, he had real confidence in Germany's future and was strongly in favor of holding the 4th international building for Germany.[27]

The strategy Junior opted upon for dealing with the delicate public relations problem of Nazis in Rockefeller Center was to say nothing about the future use of the building either publicly or even privately. But Junior insisted to Johnny, at the same time, how important it was that

we make no statements denying that we are contemplating the rental of this building to German interests; as if this were done, it would put us in an embarrassing position with the Germans with whom we have already been in touch.[28]

## THE FAMILY SUBWAY[29]

Clearly, Junior seemed to find himself in a delicate situation. He didn't know which was worse, embarrassing the Nazis or being embarrassed by them, but this was far from his most serious problem. Put simply, the family had put four million square feet of office space in a bad neighborhood that wasn't served by effective mass transit.

It happens in every office building boom, in every city. Speculation drives developers to ever more implausible locations. Just as Insull's Civic Opera House was built too far from the Loop, and more recently, the Reichmans constructed their Canary Wharf development on the Isle of Dogs development too far from London's mass transit, so too, Rockefeller Center was developed too far from either the Lexington Avenue Line or the Eighth Avenue subway lines.

L. Alfred Jenny, an engineer and transport consultant, was hired to analyze why tenants were so scarce. Jenny explained in a memorandum written in 1933:

Radio City, is placed at a disadvantage with reference to Manhattan's mass-transit facilities on which it will largely depend for its success. Whether a person wishes to go to his office or to a show the distance one is willing to travel on foot from a subway or a railroad station is limited. The limit of this travel is known to be one-fifth of a mile, and in a study of the frequency of rapid-transit stations in Greater New York bears out this connection.

About four blocks was the average trip from a subway station to an office building – about a fifth of a mile. But the distance from Rockefeller Center to Grand Central Station – the nearest train station – was three-fifths of a mile. And the trip to the nearest subway – on the IND Eighth Avenue line – half a mile. The only mass transit that served Rockefeller Center directly was the Sixth Avenue El.

Very few commuters, however, rode the El. anymore. The Lex handled about 77 percent of the traffic in Manhattan; the Eighth Avenue 10 percent. Jenny noted that two-thirds of the buildings on Sixth Avenue were less than seven stories high – a sure sign of low land values in an area not zoned for low rise buildings. He was convinced however that the introduction of mass transit would immediately enhance the value of the Rockefeller's property.[30]

Persuaded that the mass transit question was a profit or perish question, Junior put Nelson, then only 26 years old, to head the Rockefeller Center Subway Committee. Sizing up the situation, young Nelson wrote a precocious memo not only outlining the transit problem faced by the center in 1933, but laying out a strategy for future years.

The question of transportation . . . is of vital importance to Rockefeller Center. If a continuous flow of the right kind of people to the Center can be maintained by rapid and convenient transportation, the future of Rockefeller Center would seem to be answered. If however, the flow of the right kind of people to and fro should be hampered by undue traffic congestion or by the development of greatly improved transportation in other centers in other areas, the future of Rockefeller Center might be very seriously affected. The protection of the interests of Rockefeller Center in this matter requires a continuous vigilance – in keeping in touch with civil and governmental projects which effect transportation in a large way, and also the development of other sectors of the city which might tend to isolate Rockefeller Center.[31]

Here is a yellowing 60-year-old memo written by a 26-year old man. It's important not to use it too like the skeleton of Lucy, to reconstruct an entire historical epoch. But the Rockefeller perspective is an important corrective to the long-suffering, but politically impotent, commuter's.

Straphangers on the legendarily crowded Lexington Avenue line (the east side), naturally tend to see congestion in a different perspective from office building owners on the west side. What may be intolerable from the commuters' standpoint, conditions that cry out for the completion of the Second Avenue Subway – delayed now for seventy years – may, from the perspective of Room 5600, signal not the need for more transit on the east side, but more development on the west. If you promote transit improvements on the east side, it will only encourage developers to build more space. Why make the east side more accessible? Why at any rate, if you were a Rockefeller, would you want to pay taxes to promote well-being of your competitors?

Other features of the New York City transportation landscape that seem so bizarre – the lack of parking garages; the policy which allows owners to charge $50 a day for parking – make more sense when it is understood that the aim of transportation policy is to ensure the "flow of the right kind of people to and fro" while at the same time avoiding congestion of the wrong type of people.

From giving next to no thought about transit, the family swung around to the position where they sought the most ambitious transit policy imaginable. Nelson had a four-point program:

1. The demolition of the Sixth Avenue line.
2. The creation of a Sixth Avenue subway with links to Grand Central Station and Eighth Avenue subways.
3. The creation of a railroad terminal connected to Rockefeller Center.
4. The creation of a subway link to New Jersey at Fort Lee.

The family's desire to wreck the Sixth Avenue Elevated expressed one of modern capitalism's most bizarre conflicts of interest: they owned it. The Manhattan El. had been under family control since before World War I when in a dispute over investment policy, the Gould family withdrew their capital and allowed the Rockefellers to elect five directors to the Gould family's four.[32]

Owning and operating the El. were completely separate. The Rockefellers leased the El. to the Interborough Rapid Transit (IRT) Morgan–Belmont interests which did run it for $4.2 million yearly. The basic relationship was almost exactly like Columbia's arrangement with

Rockefellers. The IRT had to pay whether the El. made money or not. Increasingly, with the building of the subways, it didn't. Commuters preferred the faster subways. And operating the El. was a money losing operation. The refusal of the family to renegotiate the lease helped doom the IRT. Slowly the IRT – which at one time had been the second largest corporation in the world – was sliding into receivership.

Junior was counseled not to worry about the increasingly desperate fate of his tenant and not to sell. But, what if the IRT finally goes bankrupt, wouldn't we then have to run the line, he wondered? His financial advisor Bertram Cutler convinced him to do nothing and hope that the Interboro, "through experience with politicians here will be able to make some deal with the City." Besides, Cutler noted, "certain politicians are buying Interboro and Manhattan stock."[33] Enrichment however would come not from the "tinpot brigade" of Tammany placemen, but from the not altogether clean hands of the Fusion reformers.

In 1940, the Seabury–Berle Commission provided a $400 million plus bonanza for the bankrupt IRT-Manhattan properties. The Morgan and Rockefeller interests would get paid. And the city would pay off bonds till the millennium. Thus, in the words of *New York Times* historian Herbert Mitgang, "the Seabury–Berle plan paved the way for the long-dreamed of municipal ownership."[34]

Meanwhile, Junior had been accumulating property in midtown since 1929 on the strength of rumors that Tammany would take down the El. By 1932, he had accumulated 21 different parcels, ostensibly for protection of the family manse. In addition to the personal holdings, Rockefeller Center had purchased 1265–6 Sixth Avenue, appropriately called "Underel Properties" for $10 million. Other Rockefeller Center properties fronting the Sixth Avenue El. included RKO and Radio City Music Hall. The extensive land holdings, together with the ownership of the El. sometimes made for confusion among middle-level Rockefeller operatives.

## CHRISTY'S QUERY

Lawyer Francis W. Christy, who attended the city's hearings on the demolition of the Sixth Avenue El. for the family, needed guidance. Should he represent the family's transit interests and fight against demolition? Or the real estate interests and side with the wreckers? He observed:

For the present time, I have asked [that] no intimation be made that we are in favor of the removal of the elevated. My reason for this is that I know Mr. R or the Rockefeller Foundation has or had a substantial interest in the elevated which might possibly be inconsistent with a position in favor of the Elevated.[35]

In fact, Christy's worries were groundless. No conflict existed at all. Indeed, the improvement of the "Underel" properties cried out for the government destruction of the Manhattan. The elevated covered 18 blocks from West 53rd Street to West 35th Street. A Real Estate Record inventory of this stretch of Sixth Avenue shows that it contained forty-eight lunch stands of the "open front type" selling soft drinks, frankfurters, cigarettes and candy; twenty-seven employment agencies all on the second storey of their respective building and all dealing in jobs that paid nine to ten dollars a week on the average; twenty-three cigar stores; nineteen barbershops; eighteen shoe stores; sixteen jewelers; twelve haberdashers; twelve hardware stores and eleven second-hand magazine stores; all "attracting a continuous loitering crowd." The entire area carried an assessed valuation of $40 million.[36] Municipal socialism could only be a tonic for the long depressed values beneath the Sixth Avenue El.

But how to proceed? Christy's lawyer-like caution would extend to the manner of how the family should advocate demolition. He argued against open pleading of the cause. The opposition would be able to convince "a certain number of people that they were being imposed up on for the interest of wealthy property owners on Sixth Avenue." The way to advance the cause was to work through RKO. The motion picture company was Rockefeller Center's largest Sixth Avenue tenant, but its independence was only nominal: Rockefeller Center held over half a million shares of its stock. Christy reported,

All of our investigations [sic] have been made through them [i.e., RKO] and we will continue along that line, as they have a lobbyist who appears to be quite efficient.[37]

Thomas Debevoise, senior partner in Christy's firm wrote back,

I think if your investigation of the elevated can be continued through RKO that should be all that is necessary at the present time.[38]

It took five more years and a change in administrations, but Christy's "investigations" finally paid off. On December 20, 1935, radio station WJZ broadcast that the long, tedious, difficult negotiations with property owners conducted by Judge Samuel Seabury and City Chamberlain Adolph A. Berle have resulted in an agreement advantageous to the city.[39]

The tedium would have been quite understandable in Berle's case, because all the while he was essentially negotiating with himself.

For Berle, former Columbia University law professor, and the co-author of the famous Modern Corporation and Private Property, which had announced the disappearance of private property to a startled world, was also the husband of the former Beatrice Bishop, who had inherited the estate of Cortlandt F. Bishop. The Bishop estate controlled a strip of property along the east side of Sixth Avenue – at the corner of West 49th Street and Sixth Avenue. Berle, as trustee of the estate was, along with Columbia University, Rockefeller's landlord. He was leasing 1242, 1244, 1246 and 1248 Sixth Avenue as well as 71 and 73 West 49th Street to Underel properties.

But the conflict of interest didn't stop there. The Bishop estate also controlled frontage along the east and west sides of Sixth Avenue: 1210–1216 Sixth Avenue; 1221–1227 Sixth Avenue; 1242–1248 Sixth Avenue; and 1280–1286 Sixth Avenue. All these plots lay under the elevated. In 1943, Berle sold them all to Rockefeller Center Inc. along with 72–78 William Street for $3,235 million.[40]

Had Mr. Berle held on for just a year more he could have shared in the giant windfall received by other Sixth Avenue property owners. When the El. came down, property owners' assessments rose. But property owners protested the increase on the grounds that the building of the El. had been a taking of their property, and so the elimination of the El. merely restored their rights. In 1944, the city's tax court ruled in their favor. Underel's share was $30 million.[41]

A seemingly unaccountable feature of the Seabury–Berle Commission's plan for Sixth Avenue was the decision to begin wrecking the El. immediately, five years before the scheduled completion of the IND. Commuters who suddenly had no way to get to work, workers who were deprived of a job could protest, the State Transit Commission could try to intervene, but the press unanimously backed the Seabury–Berle Commission and denounced state authorities as former hacks and crooks. The "tin pot brigade" Judge Seabury called its members.[42]

In March 1936, the city held ground breaking ceremonies for the Sixth Avenue IND. John R. Todd wrote to Nelson of the grand opening

The going ahead with this work was a good job on somebody's part and eventually it will be immensely helpful to Rockefeller Center.

"Somebody" appears to have been Lester Abberley, the Rockefeller Center-based lawyer, lobbyist, cash dispenser and family retainer. Abberley is identified in the minutes of the Rockefeller Center Committee on Subway Construction as working to reverse the city's decision to delay subway construction.[43] It was Abberley, at any rate, whom Todd now suggested be delegated to try to bring the railroad terminal to Rockefeller Center and work on the Ft. Lee subway. Nothing however came of these projects. Railroads showed no interest in the family's grandiose plan to rival Grand Central station next to Rockefeller Center. And southern New Jersey real estate interests blocked efforts to promote development in northern New Jersey. But two grandiose plans out of four isn't bad. And the results – vastly increased land values through political action – created a pattern.

# NOTES

1. Barry Vinocur, "The Rock's a Hard Place: Outlook Grows Gloomier for Rockefeller Center REIT," *Barron's*, April 19, 1993, p. 18; Jeanne B. Pinder, "Rockefeller Center With Clay Feet," *New York Times*, June 17, 1993, D1.

2. Barry Vinocur, "The Rock's a Hard Place: Outlook Grows Gloomier for Rockefeller Center REIT, *Barron's*, April 19, 1993, p.18.

3. Carol Herselle Krinsky, *Rockefeller Center* (New York: Oxford University Press, 1978), pp. 2–3.

4. Ibid.

5. Cited in Alan Balfour, *Rockefeller Center* (New York: McGraw-Hill Book Company, 1978), p. 223.

6. See Vincent Scully, *American Architecture and Urbanism* (New York: Praeger Publishers, 1976), p. 154. Scully acknowledges the Center's symbolic significance a little more ambivalently: "Flags snap, high heels tap; a little sex and aggression, the city's delights. Jefferson would have hated it." (Ibid.)

7. For example, the opening line of Alan Balfour's monograph reads, "Rockefeller Center is one of the twentieth century's major architectural achievements and also one of its most successful," *Rockefeller Center* (New York: McGraw-Hill Book Company, 1978), p.vii.

8. Peter Collier and David Horowitz, *The Rockefellers: An American Dynasty* (New York: New American Library, 1976).

9. Ibid., p. 498.

10. Not "slightly more than it had been at its highest point sixty-five years earlier." (Ibid., p. 496) Economists Claudia Goldin and Bradford DeLong at Harvard along with Edward Wolf of New York University estimate that the value of John D. Rockefeller I would have been about $26 billion in today's dollars, *New York Times* August 16, 1992, E3.

11. In 1910, The New York *American* estimated Senior had given $134 million through the Rockefeller Foundation and he'd given the University of Chicago $43 million. (Cited in Collier and Horowitz, pp. 54–55.) Just these two sums taken together amounted to more money in real terms than the entire value of the family fortune as estimated by Dilworth in 1974.

12. John Ensor Harr and Peter J. Johnson, *The Rockefeller Conscience* (New York: Charles Scribner's Sons, 1991), p. 492. The property did pay a "technical dividend" of $281,000 in 1960 by agreement with the University. (Ibid.)

13. Ibid., p. 520.

14. Ibid.

15. See for example Debevoise to Turnbull, October 27, 1942, RAC.

16. See T.M. Debevoise to C.O. Heydt, December 27, 1927, RAC. Heydt is Junior's top real estate advisor. Debevoise, Junior's top attorney and friend asks him to get in contact with Fulton Cutting, the head of the Opera and put him in touch with Junior's brokerage house, William A. White and Sons. This is the earliest instance of interest in the Opera project I have seen in the Rockefeller papers.

17. See T.M. Debevoise to J.R. Todd, 7 May 1945, RAC. Whereas Todd, in his autobiography wrote that Rockefeller first became interested in the Columbia property and then got involved with the Opera, Debevoise suggests the reverse order. First, Junior got interested in moving the Opera and then, "perhaps at Mr. Heydt's suggestion", he decided that if he was going to find a purchaser for the Opera Company, he might find it worthwhile to own the property around it. (Heydt was Junior's real estate expert in the 1920s.)

18. Ivy Lee to John D.Rockefeller, Jr, May 25, 1928, RAC.

19. F.W. Christy Memorandum dated September 17, 1934, RAC.

20. John R. Todd to Winthrop Aldrich, December 4, 1929, RAC. (Tom Debevoise was one of the few people Jr. treated as a peer.)

21. Jr. to Debevoise, August 25, 1931, RAC.

22. John D. Rockefeller Jr. to John R. Todd, September 8, 1933, RAC.

23. John D. Rockefeller II to John R. Todd, April 4, 1935, RAC.

24. The picture can be seen as figure 339 in Alan Balfour, *Rockefeller Center* (New York: McGraw-Hill Book Company, 1978), pp.176–177.

25. John D. Rockefeller II to Arthur Woods, September 6, 1933, RAC.

26. John D. Rockefeller III, interview with Ivy Lee. September 8, 1933. RAC. By "fourth international" Johnny meant the building located up the street from the French, British and Italian buildings.

27. John D. Rockefeller III to John D. Rockefeller II, September 8, 1933, RAC.

28. John D.Rockefeller II to John D. Rockefeller III, September 15, 1934, RAC.

29. The research in this section is drawn from my essay entitled "The Family Subway," "Research in Political Economy," Paul Zarembka and Thomas Ferguson (eds), vol. 8, 1985.

30. L. Alfred Jenny and Co., consulting engineers to John R. Todd, March 14, 1933, RAC.

31. From the Committee on Subway Construction, "Suggestions Regarding Transportation Studies Affecting Rockefeller Center," November 1934, RAC.

32. See T.P. Shonts to John D. Rockefeller Jr., February 8, 1913; John D. Rockefeller to Starr J. Murphy, July 16, 1913, RAC. The family also shared control with the Goulds of Colorado Fuel and Iron.

33. B. Cutler to John D. Rockefeller Jr., March 12, 1926, RAC.

34. Herbert Mitgang, The Man Who Rode the Tiger (New York: W.W. Norton & Company, 1963), p. 346. The deal required an exemption from constitutional limits on city debt. But reformers like Berle and Seabury were relentless in the fight for New York-style municipal socialism, i.e., the socialization of rich people's bad equity. Who else but "municipal socialists" would have bought the bankrupt, depleted properties?

35. F.W. Christy to T.M. Debevoise, September 11, 1930, RAC.

36. Real Estate Record and Guide, October 8, 1938.

37. F.W. Christy to T.M. Debevoise, September 11, 1930, RAC.

38. T.M. Debevoise to F.W. Christy, September 15, 1930, RAC.

39. Transcript in RAC.

40. The principals of the estate were Beatrice Bishop Berle and A.A. Berle Jr., guardian of Alice Bishop Berle and Beatrice Van Cortlandt Berle. The Van Cortlandts name goes back very far in New York City history. There is of course the park in the Bronx. And a Stephanus Cortlandt who served as Mayor of New York in the seventeenth century. At a dinner in his honor at City Hall it was said that "he became so intoxicated and merry that he snatched off his hat and wig and skewered them on the tip of his sword, set fire to them, and waved them happily over the banquet table." Edward Robb Ellis, *The Epic of New York City History* (New York: Old Town Books, 1966), p.102.

41. F.W. Christy, *History of Rockefeller Center*, p. 39, Rockefeller Archive Center.

42. Herbert Mitgang, *The Man Who Rode the Tiger* (New York: W.W. Norton, 1963), p. 345.

43. See minutes of the Committee on the Subway Connection, July 31, 1934, RAC.

CHAPTER EIGHT

# THE WESTIES

It took the Rockefeller family python nearly a quarter century to digest the pig of four million square feet of office space produced between 1930 and 1933. Not until the mid-fifties would hunger pangs be felt again. But before satisfying them, the family carried out a much more thorough series of preparations then those which had preceded their 1928 investment decision. First, the Rockefellers, through the Rockefeller Brothers' Fund and in conjunction with the Ford Foundation financed a nine-volume Harvard-MIT study on New York's economy. Thoroughly analyzed was the need for office space up through 1985.[1]

Assured by the Harvard-MIT experts that they could count on a moderately growing market for office space in the upcoming decades, and reassured by the RPA's more expansive vision the question became not whether to expand but "where"? In the thirties, the Rockefellers had devised plans to expand north and link up with family-owned land. In the mid-fifties,[2] this avenue was checked by the growing post-World War II Puerto Rican presence just north of Columbus Center – clearly a west side story the family wanted to revise. And until John D. Rockefeller III led the Lincoln Center project to clear out the 20,000 mainly Puerto Rican people from the area, a move north may have seemed too risky.[3]

Expansion to the east was blocked by St. Patrick's Cathedral and darkened by the pricey shadows cast by Saks and the rest of the *haute* retail district. South meant movement towards 42nd Street – the baddest of the city's badlands. So westward expansion turned out to be the only plausible course, and even crossing from the east side of Sixth Avenue to the west in the hidebound world of real estate caused a lot of eyes to roll in fear.

As much credit as they received at the time for commercial daring, the Rockefeller venture on the west side of what the family now called

"The Avenue of the Americas", was mounted, however, with due caution. First, unlike the thirties, the Rockefellers were building on land they owned. Second, the family hedged its bets by taking a partner: Time Life Inc. In 1956, they joined to form something called Rock-Time in which the family held 55 percent interest and Time Life the rest. Together they produced a 48-storey building with 27 floors of spec office space. Again, though, the timing was just a bit off. When the space was ready, the tenants weren't, and the usual suspects from the Rockefeller orbit of corporations wound up renting offices.[4]

Nevertheless, as the city's real estate boom gathered force in the late sixties, the brothers prepared again to participate on an even vaster scale – befitting the biggest tax payers, and the largest owners of commercial real estate in the city. This time, however, Rockefeller Center Inc. (RCI) expanded across Sixth Avenue more than just tentatively. Rockefeller Center Inc. built four million square feet of new space – in the McGraw Hill, Celanese, Exxon buildings – which together with Time Life brought the total owned or co-owned in New York City to 17 million square feet of space.

The Sixth Avenue expansion, however, brought neither commercial nor critical success. Vincent Scully dismissed the new buildings as an "incoherent spatter."[5] Historian Alan Balfour termed it an exercise in "bureaucratic imperialism". He observed

Each building is a general-issue product of bureaucracies that differ only in name, unconstrained by history or nature.[6]

Even the kindly Carol Krinsky who has produced what comes closest to the Center's official bio, described the Sixth Avenue procession as "a powerful army of tall but unimpressive soldiers."[7]

In the marketplace, though, the move met with an indifference much more costly than aesthetic disdain. The Celanese building whose corporate partners eventually sold their equity had trouble renting space.[8] Rents sagged throughout the mid-seventies.

The increasingly poor operating results in Rockefeller Center created only one wave in a sea of troubles for the family. In the early seventies, Chase Manhattan's relative decline in size and profitability was accompanied by increasing criticism in the business press of David's stewardship, calling into question how he got the top job in the first place. About the same time, Nelson's extraordinary four-term governorship began to disintegrate.

The first intimations of disaster were the financial problems of the State Urban Development Corporation – which Nelson had founded. He had claimed, just after the assassination of Martin Luther King, that he had created UDC to memorialize the martyred civil rights leader. In fact, one reason for UDC's existence was Nelson's belief that, given an agency with powers of eminent domain and unlimited credit, blacks could be relocated from the city to the suburbs.[9] UDC worked with the family-funded Suburban Action Institute to find suitable locations outside New York City for black residences,[10] but mainly, UDC in its early days operated as a giant piggybank for developers.

UDC made mortgages chiefly to residential developers and raised cash for the mortgages in the short-term money market. (They warn you not to do this in freshman finance. It's called "lending long and borrowing short.") In legislative hearings, housing expert Roger Starr called for a "fairy godmother" to come in and buy up all the bad paper.[11]

In fact, New York needed two fairy godmothers. One for the state, and one for the city which had adopted the UDC model for comprehensive insolvency by borrowing some $5 billions in the short-term money market chiefly for the same purpose: middle-class housing mortgages.[12] When UDC collapsed, the city's position quickly crumbled too. If the state couldn't save UDC – its own agency – markets figured it wouldn't be able to save New York, which had borrowed even more money on the same terms. Nelson was able to escape accountability for having led the two New Yorks over a fiscal cliff only by having already resigned from the governorship in December 1973. His friend Ed Logue – whom Nelson had named to be UDC chief and to whom he had given $250,000 worth of gifts – took the whipping.

Hoping, nevertheless, to be named the nation's first unelected president, Nelson had to settle for becoming the first appointed vice president. This was an office he publicly disparaged ("I wasn't made to be stand-by equipment," he insisted.) But at least the job got him out of New York. Respite, however, was only temporary. On November 3, 1975, Gerald Ford called Nelson at home to tell him he'd been kicked off the 1976 ticket.

According to relatives and associates, Nelson returned from D.C. in a frightful mood.[13] Not only did he have to bear the humiliation of being told he was a drag on Republican re-election prospects. At 67, his own political prospects were clearly over, and while he wasn't about to collect unemployment benefits, his cash flow was surprisingly meager.

The Vice Presidential hearings of 1974 produced testimony by two California professors purporting to show that Nelson sat athwart a financial empire whose assets totalled $70 billion. It turned out, however, that Nelson's true net worth had actually declined to $62 million. And even this total seems to have been pumped up by rather charitable estimates of the value of his art collection. Besides his art, Nelson owned about $11 million worth of real estate and $12 million worth of stocks.

Millions had gone into his favorite charity: re-electing Nelson. In fact, he had little choice if he wanted to continue in New York electoral politics. Who else but a Rockefeller was going to contribute to the campaign of a Rockefeller? But the main reason Nelson was worth comparatively little was that, of all the family members, he had invested most in Rockefeller Center. The terms of the Columbia lease had prohibited public stock sales, so the easiest way of raising capital for expansion was to get it from the family. And of all the family members, Nelson had been the most bullish on RCI's future. In 1955, prior to the Rock-Time development, he received special permission from family members to own a disproportionate amount of RCI stock.[14] So while he would be the greatest beneficiary if Rockefeller Center ever paid real dividends, he was the greatest victim of its poor performance.

Evidently something had to be done about improving the earning power of Rockefeller Center. In 1973, the family had entered into a twelve-month round of negotiations with Columbia for a 97-year lease, and for the tenth time, Columbia turned them down on their request to own the land under Rockefeller Center. But the University did yield on a few points. The amount of cash the family had to hold in escrow was cut; and the family was allowed to reduce their share of the stock from 80 percent to 20 percent.[15] Now the only problem was to create a market for the stock.

This in turn required more capital expenditure and greater personal investment by the family members – so that by the mid-seventies, more than half of the assets from the 1934 trust were tied up in Rockefeller Center stock. This was a stock that paid small dividends, and seems destined not to reward its present owners in this millennium. It would, nevertheless, justify all the faith that its managers expressed, giving the family an ultimate $3 billion pay out.

On the face of it, all that seems to have been involved in the transformation of Rockefeller Center was exquisite timing. A tiny aperture of opportunity opened up, through which the family made their deal and got out. But there was a great deal more. For Rockefeller Center to be able to participate in the eighties boom it had to get "fixed." Fixing Rockefeller Center in the late seventies and eighties required just as much political ingenuity as the family displayed in the thirties.

## THE MIDTOWN MAKEOVER

There were basically two things initially wrong with Rockefeller Center: the terms under which it had been built, and its location. The "family subway" had only mitigated the second problem. Better mass transit couldn't overcome the fact that Rockefeller Center was built on the wrong side of town. If RCI was to pay real dividends, the city's midtown structure would have to be fundamentally altered.

In Chicago, at the turn of the century, to keep the city from choking in its own sewage, civil engineers made the Chicago river run backward. In New York City, in the eighties, planners reversed the flow of real estate development from east to west. Chicago's reversal was accomplished with canals and dredges. In New York, with zoning variances and tax abatements. In the one case, a sickening stench disappeared. In the other, the odor seems to grow more disagreeable as time goes on. To fairly assess the planners' work, however, we have to understand the circumstances they were trying to change.

Ever since 1903 when the Vanderbilt–Morgan interests began building Grand Central station and sunk the New York Central railroad beneath Park Avenue, a residential building boom had shifted the preferred location for office buildings uptown. But strictly to the East side. Everything west of Fifth Avenue was hard to rent.

The power of an office district to attract tenants is determined by its proximity to where rich people live or where they get off the train. Following the construction of Grand Central, Percy Pyne, Henry P. Davison, George F. Baker, Willard Straight, Edward Harkness, Henry Frick, Andrew Carnegie, and James Duke all built mansions on the east side – chiefly along Fifth Avenue. But with few exceptions – Junior on West 54th – rich people didn't live on the west side. Even the Rockefeller brothers, Nelson and David, when they grew up, moved away from the west side. They lived chiefly in Pocantico Hills, but both maintained townhouses on the upper east side.

In some respects, by the late seventies, the discrepancy between the east and west sides was growing worse. In the late sixties, well-known developers had actually tried to build on the west side and gone bust. It didn't seem to matter where – just south of Rockefeller Center – at 1166 Sixth Avenue where the Tishmans went bankrupt; due west of the Center at 1633 Broadway where the Uris failed; or all the way north near Columbus Circle where the WT Grant building bombed.

Then, too, New York City transit riding has undergone a secular decline. Two hundred million fewer passengers rode mass transit in 1982 than in 1976.[16] Rockefeller Center was dependent on this traffic. And while Metro North, New Jersey Transit and Long Island Railroad all increased – none have terminals anywhere near Rockefeller Center.

What Rockefeller Center did have was proximity to world-class blight. There was obviously much more to the west side than blight. Even 42nd Street from Broadway to Eighth Avenue – regularly portrayed as a sewer – can't be dismissed this way. It served mainly as a cheap entertainment district for the city's black working class and poor whose own neighborhoods no longer had movie theaters. You could see a first run movie on Seventh Avenue for half the price of what they cost on the east side, and as scary as they looked, inside, the theaters were a lot safer than their competitors in the boroughs. A lot of the fear and hostility to the area derived from dislike of ordinary blacks who poured in from the city's poorest neighborhoods. But the area can't be romanticized. It was also the locus for city's most famous drug and porno districts: the Eighth Avenue "Minnesota Strip" where in a few weeks after getting off at the Port Authority, teens from Lake Woebegone could be transformed by the alchemy of the area into hardened hookers; the legendary needle parks like Bryant Park. When developers were asked why they wouldn't touch the space on the west side, they would reply that maybe in a boom it would be okay for lawyers, but the type of corporate tenant who would pay rent for class A office space, wouldn't feel comfortable there.

Five big planning interventions of the mid-seventies and eighties changed this assessment, or what was just as good – produced the widespread perception of improvement among developers, banks, insurance companies and above all Japanese investors. The quintet were:

1. The Midtown Development Plan
2. The Clinton Plan
3. The Convention Center
4. Columbus Center
5. Times Square/42nd Street Redevelopment

Of these, two never really came off at all – Times Square and Columbus Center. Despite hundreds of millions in abatements and condemnation costs – more than a billion in the case of Times Square[17] – both projects are "stalled." And one project – the Convention Center – has reduced blue collar employment without replacing it with white collar jobs or construction.[18]

Of the chief west side plans, the Rockefeller Brothers Fund (RBF) played varying roles in three: the Clinton plan; Times Square and the Midtown development plan. RBF seems to have been most influential in shaping the Clinton plan – which in the name of preservation, concentrated development on Eighth Avenue. It was one of three foundations which brokered the terms of the City Planning Commission's Midtown plan. And it played a supporting role in the early 42nd Street development initiatives – Ford led here – which were then taken over by UDC which absorbed the expenses of land acquisition and condemnation costs entailed by the failed project.

## ADVENTURES IN GIVING

It might be reasonably asked, in considering RBF's intervention, however, "Why was there an RBF at all?" Why wasn't one giant foundation, the Rockefeller Foundation, enough? Why does any family need three foundations named after it? Perhaps the same territorial instinct that impels a beaver or a muskrat to urinate all over its home range to show that *"This* is my territory," drives the family to inscribe its name so liberally over New York. For we have not only the numerous buildings of Rockefeller Center; and Rockefeller University; but also the Rockefeller Foundation; Rockefeller Brothers Fund; Rockefeller Family Fund and several others.

The territorial instinct, however, is probably too diffuse a motive. Foundations are not merely namesakes. They distribute wealth. Like the foundations set up by urban landowners in Greek and Roman antiquity the gifts dispersed by modern foundations are not, by and large, doled out to the poor. By far the larger share is bestowed upon political and community groups, other foundations, intellectuals, academics and artists.[19] These gifts, in turn, confer obligation, and the recipients perform useful work to justify the gifts. But for the obligations to accrue specifically to family members, and for the work to serve family interests, there has to be a direct relationship between the giver and recipient.

To some extent, the modern foundation erodes the relationship by interposing an independent layer of professionals between the two. Nelson had claimed it was his brother John's fault that the Rockefeller Foundation had broken loose from family leading strings in the fifties. "You lost the Rockefeller Foundation," he charged, but John's defenders argue that the process of detachment began much earlier.[20]

From the 1920s onward, the Rockefeller Foundation had become professionalized. It had an independent staff, and a self-perpetuating board of directors who were not simply stooges of the family. In 1956–7, when Lincoln Center's financial requirements began to grow, Dean Rusk opposed John D. Rockefeller III's requests for Rockfeller Foundation millions. He said

As an old-fashioned Jeffersonian, I have been skeptical about the propriety of condemnation proceedings for what may in effect, be private purposes.

Rusk confessed that he was "not at all comfortable about the broad policies involved" in slum clearance. What if there is a violent controversy, he asked? What would the foundation's public position be? Rusk desired not to have to give any money to Lincoln Center until its urban renewal phase was over.[21]

That Rusk granted the money anyway illustrates the limits of Rockefeller Foundation autonomy. But that Rusk could make a stand at all shows there was some independent structure to push against. The brothers wanted a vehicle that they could control without having to worry about what the Dean Rusks of the world thought. At the same time, most of the brothers didn't want their children meddling in their affairs, diffusing the power of their gifts. This in essence, was why there was a Rockefeller Family Fund – as a kind of philanthropic sandbox for the cousins; a Rockefeller Foundation – still casting the shadow of Senior's great wealth, but hard to mortgage to today's purposes; and the RBF whose agenda was strictly limited to the goals of the brothers.[22]

In 1952, RBF had become a major foundation with a gift from Jr. of $58 million in RCI stock. And whatever differences between the brothers – which would become quite sharp in the late seventies – they tightly controlled the foundation's agenda to reflect their personal agendas and not those of outside directors or staff. Until fairly recently, with only trifling exceptions – e.g., family architect Wally Harrison – they appointed no non-family members to the board, and unlike many foundations, whose perspectives became broader with age, the RBF's focus seemed to become narrower, more tied to the property which gave it life.

This narrowness became more pronounced with the advent of New York's fiscal crisis. "1971 marked an important change in the Fund's policy of giving in New York City," RBF acknowledged in retrospect. Beginning in the early seventies, the Foundation curtailed citizenship grants and began to focus on "critical problems." Instead of giving to the Community Fund or the Boy Scouts, the Foundation now concentrated more fully on creating what they called "a third force" in community organization, and sought to influence real estate development in particular areas of the city.

New York City, the RBF noted, was experiencing serious "demographic imbalances" (read: too many poor blacks and Puerto Ricans) and "governmental imbalances" (read: too many workers on the city payroll.) Consequently, it was argued, the city becoming a less attractive place, ruining what would otherwise be attractive prospects for renting office space.

RBF noted:

On the one hand, the ongoing transition from blue collar to white collar employment opportunities was expected to accelerate in the 70's and 80's in response to an anticipated increase in office space available for national headquarters operations. On the other, two decades of suburbanization had altered the character of the metropolitan white collar work force.

The whites had left, and the blacks and Puerto Ricans had stayed producing "a cruel mismatch between jobs and people in New York."[23]

To cope with these problems, as the RBF had explained in justifying the narrowing of its philanthropic vision, it was important to focus on specific neighborhoods and areas of the city – rather than give to agencies which operated through the whole city. This shift indicted a desire "to play more of an initiating role in development strategy and encouraging consortia to address the city's problems."[24] This change in outlook would have important effects not only for midtown, but for the outer boroughs.

Simply put, from the mid-seventies through the 1980s, the RBF promoted a policy of heavily-subsidized office building development on the west side, where the family had real estate interests. And it promoted self-help and planned shrinkage in the outer borough ghettos of central Brooklyn and the south Bronx. This "charitable" strategy seems quite consistent with an economic strategy of maximizing family income and minimizing taxes.

The whole evolution of foundation policy from aggressive urban renewal in the late fifties through "Model Cities" in the sixties, to the present focus on community self-help and local development is too vast and consequential to describe here adequately, but it is too important to ignore completely. Suffice to say that the goals have not changed that much – fewer poor people in New York being the constant aim.

The strategies change, depending on the level of community resistance; the cost of implementing them is never terribly great. When Rockefeller, Ford et al. decide to give what for them are trifling sums, a few million dollars, the resultant publicity, front-page coverage in the New York Times, can propel one community group and one set of priorities over all the others in a poor struggling neighborhood. In the battle for funds, the winners, in the long run, seem to be the community groups whose agenda overlaps the most widely with the funding community.

In mid-seventies, joining with Ford, the Fund for the City of New York and J.M. Kaplan Fund, RBF demonstrated the power of philanthropy by successfully promoting their green version of planned shrinkage in the south Bronx. It sounds far-fetched, but working together, and with city, borough, state and federal agencies, the "consortia" initiated and supported projects which aimed, at least temporarily, at turning the south Bronx into a giant vegetable garden. Old newspaper clips bear this out.

"Project to 'Green' 500 South Bronx Acres Begins" headlined the *New York Times* in spring 1978 on its front page. There, in the foreground is a photo of bare-chested compost spreaders, who are seen energetically raking something called "zoo doo". In the background looms a giant windmill, and, just beneath the fold, appeared the story of one woman's vision of an ecologically sound south Bronx. *Times* readers discovered that there were efforts to revive the Bronx. The

South Bronx Frontier Development Corporation, using organic wastes from the Hunt's Point market and the Bronx Zoo was creating top soil and vegetable gardens for 500 devastated acres.[25]

No matter that the whole idea for the community development project seems to have originated with J.M. Kaplan's Joan Davidson; that the group itself had little popular basis in the community; that the city – or at least Deputy Mayor Herman Badillo – had a completely different vision for the Bronx: a $2.1 billion plan for industrial revival and high density housing.[26] The foundations saw their windmills and composting as a mid-course between the Deputy Mayor's proposal for re-industrialization and repopulation on the one hand, and, on the other, to Housing Development Administration chief Roger Starr's call for "planned shrinkage".[27]

"Why not just take this entire area," Joan Davidson said during the height of the planned shrinkage controversy, to Irma Fleck, red-haired diminutive wife of local physician in the south Bronx, sweeping her hand broadly to indicate the scope of the idea, "and make it a garden.[28] Wouldn't this be a fine alternative to Felix Rohatyn's plan to blacktop the entire south Bronx? Ms. Fleck got excited about the suggestion and together with policeman Jack Flannigan was ultimately able to raise millions from the foundations to implement Davidson's vision. The *New York Times* story brought world-wide interest, contributions, federal and state grants. A great vote of confidence was cast when Ford Foundation chief McGeorge Bundy himself showed up in the south Bronx with an entourage.

The direction of development in the Bronx wasn't simply a matter of the Fundies proposing and the government disposing. Evidently, there was a sharp struggle going on. In 1976, during the Beame administration, the *New York Times* had advised that

the accepted thinking of those who now plan and oversee the city's revenues and expenses . . . see New York City . . . return to a concern for pocket neighborhoods as opposed to city wide master planing.[29]

But then Koch displaced Beame and made Badillo his deputy Mayor for south Bronx redevelopment. Badillo announced his plan in April 1978 but little came of it. He says Koch told him that "Wall Street" opposed redevelopment. At any rate, the struggle seems to have been resolved with Badillo's resignation and his effective replacement by Ed Logue. His disastrous tour-of-duty as UDC chief was forgotten, and he re-emerged as the south Bronx development czar. Logue initiated the trend to pre-empt space permanently in the south Bronx by building low-rise homes. The investment in landbanking paid off as Logue's new low-density housing blocked all other development possibilities.

Ford Foundation consultant Janet S. Brown's memo provides a valuable progress report on the conditions in the south Bronx in the mid-seventies at the time of the first funding. She noted that there was "sentiment to make the board and staff more representative of the community." (Nearly all were white and upper middle class.) But what stood out was how the "concept of composting and greening has captured the imagination of the community, public and private groups alike." Brown observed that the program tied in with the goals of the Bronx borough president's "policy of land banking." The City Planning Commission, she indicated, was also co-operating closely. On the other hand, however,

there is a constant struggle within the Department of Real Estate to keep parcels off the auction block as every property is being bought and there are options on all buildings that have the potential for rehabilitation.

In one lengthy conference with city officials, Brown added revealingly,

composting and greening were described as 'welfare instead of jobs' but community land acquisition is at the heart of the movement to prevent rebuilding of ghettos.[30]

Bronx Frontier Development was not the only target for the Manhattan-based foundations. Other groups which received private grants included: the People's Development Corporation; Community Involvement Program; the Trust for Public Land and the D.C.-based Institute for Local Self-Reliance which sent a consultant up to the Bronx to help with the windmill. There was also something called the South Bronx Open Space Task Force whose chairman, Bronx police officer Jack Flanagan, was also co-leader of Bronx Frontier with Irma Fleck.

Open space, windmills, composting, veggie gardens – these were the building blocks of economic development for the south Bronx in the late seventies. The foundations, particularly Ford and RBF, promoted them all as "community self-help development." But what about jobs? How could the poorest community in urban America survive on "zoo doo"? The fundies explicitly opposed broad-scale re-industrialization programs, whether proposed by the city or by the Port Authority. Their real goal, as the Brown memo shows was "land banking" – keeping the land off the market so it couldn't be redeveloped. At least until such time as the Rockefeller Housing Partnership could develop the land given them by the city to create suburban-style white-picket fenced homes at very low densities.

Low densities mean low costs, and low taxes. As one south Bronx activist and opponent of both green and brown versions of planned shrinkage, Harry Derienzo explained,

Developing a home for a household earning $40,000 a year, with a car and kids in a private school is perceived by some as preferential to a household with an income of $8,000 with twice as many children and some level of social service needs. This helps explain why the South Bronx is now being developed by the New York City Partnership with densities of 18 households per acre on land which once housed 120 households per acre.[31]

The same concern for thinning out the numbers of minority people had been evident in the RBF's decision to fund Pratt Institute in the early sixties. RBF responded enthusiastically to a request for funds from George Raymond, of Raymond Parish and Pine – the urban renewal "relocators" – who was teaching at Pratt Institute at the time. Raymond warned that Jane Jacobs who had defeated urban renewal plans in Greenwich Village was agitating now against urban renewal in Brooklyn. He requested funds be provided to create a community development institute which would promote urban renewal and provide "education" and "technical assistance" for central Brooklyn community groups.

The Rockefellers were deeply involved with urban renewal programs all over the city – John D. Rockefeller III at Lincoln Center; David at Morningside Heights and downtown. And the RBF viewed the gathering public reaction against urban renewal as a "very disturbing phenomenon."[32] New urban renewal legislation mandated community involvement, but as Planning Commissioner James Felt, who was working with David on the Morningside Heights urban renewal plan, pointed out, the city couldn't carry out public education itself.[33]

Now if anyone could be relied on to stand up for urban renewal it was George Raymond. The RBF agenda and docket item in approving Raymond's request for an initial $94,000 grant noted that he was the senior partner of a firm that had a contract with the city for relocating residents in 87 urban renewal neighborhoods. Raymond's work and ideas were well known and well-liked. After all, he thought real estate taxes should be simply abolished, and federal funds for urban renewal vastly increased. "What was $5 billion," he would ask before a House committee, "compared to the Defense budget?" Urban renewal hadn't failed. "Its principal failure," he argued, "is that it has not gone far enough." Later RBF grants in 1966 – $133,000 and $60,000 in 1969 were based on the prospects of Pratt's work in promoting urban renewal in Bedford Stuyvesant and Brownsville which RBF felt "show some promise of being amenable to renewal." That the area was prime for renewal was, according to RBF,

> in no small part, the result of the Center's preparatory work, both in the Community and with the City and Federal agencies involved.[34]

Ron Shiffman who was hired with the Rockefeller money together with Raymond wrote of the conditions in Brooklyn just prior to getting funded.

> During the year or two just prior to its (Pratt Institute Center for Community Environmental and Economic Development) founding, the city of New York had experienced some of the most violent upheavals in the history of its controversial urban renewal program. Jane Jacobs published her regrettably slanted 'Death and Life of Great American Cities' and had led embattled bohemians of west Greenwich Village to victories over the prostrate bodies of the city's leading housing and planning bureaucrats. . . . Encouraged by the triumph . . . Jane Jacobs crossed the east river into Brooklyn

and began to agitate against urban renewal in Cobble Hill.[35]

Pratt's work in the subsequent years cannot be easily summarized. The RBF conceived of Pratt as a "third force" in central Brooklyn.[36] It seems to have fulfilled that goal. Basically, Pratt stood for the same agenda RBF supported in the south Bronx: fewer people and no re-industrialization. The Institute helped fight the use of the piers 1–6 in Brooklyn for working commerce; at one point Shiffman sponsored a festival at Pier 1 "to get people exposed to the fact that there is a river in Brooklyn" and promote recreational rather than industrial uses.[37] Pratt organized the opposition to industrial expansion by the S&S Corrugated Box factory; it also supported office uses in industrial buildings at Fulton Ferry.

Opposition to industrialization and planned shrinkage are different sides of a very old coin. Urban industrial development draws people to an area. Pratt was aiming at just the opposite. An editorial in the Pratt Planning Papers read

The first and most important step towards a better future, which the community must insist be taken instantly, is the wholesale re-zoning of its residential neighborhoods from their present R-6 classification [which permits crowding of around 90–100 dwellings per acre] to the next lower 'R-5' District [which permits only about 50–60].

If the R-6 zoning remained, all residents could hope for was "sterile, heartless, monotonous projects."[38]

## HOW THE WEST SIDE WAS WON

If you want to understand the basic elements of the Rockefeller agenda for the west side, simply invert the goals they favored for poor neighborhoods. If poor neighborhoods have to be down-zoned, or risk becoming sterile and monotonous, the west side can only be made lively by up-zoning. Thus high density was bad in the south Bronx and central Brooklyn, an excellent thing on the west side. If poor communities were to be inspired by the vision of self-help, the landed interests of the west side needed massive city subsidies.

"One law for the lion and one for the lamb is tyranny," Blake pointed out. It was precisely this kind of tyranny that the RBF in its struggle for west side development aimed to overthrow. Rockefellers claimed that the city's abatement policies were twisted because they applied across the board. Of course, ever since the abandonment of feudalism, the law has tended in this direction. "Equal protection under the law" and all of that.

The agenda and docket item explaining why the RBF was funding the City Planning Commission's study on midtown is illuminating, not only because it expresses these concerns and feelings so directly, but also because it illustrates how far from genuinely philanthropic concerns RBF had drifted. The executive committee of RBF – with the deaths of Nelson and John, now basically David Rockefeller – sounded not like one of the city's most important charitable institutions, but more and more like the mortgage department of a money center bank. Somehow philanthropy, the love of humanity, had turned into love of real estate.

What seemed to bother David was that there was a real estate boom going on and he wasn't able to participate. A party and no one from the west side was invited.

The recent renewal of development activity in Midtown Manhattan is closely linked to the city's economic recovery. Long vacant office space is now being occupied, and the surge in tourism is putting new demands on hotel and entertainment industries. Thus far, the development has concentrated on East midtown from 40th to 60th and from 3d avenue to 6th. Building is up to the maximum everywhere, cleared sites are increasingly scarce, air rights are being used to "shoehorn" large projects into confined spaces.

What was aggravating the situation as far as RBF was concerned was

recent and sometimes contradictory actions of the city government which provided unco-ordinated, across the board tax and zoning incentives; that have exacerbated the abuse of the most valuable piece of real estate in the world.

But help was at hand. Bobby Wagner Jr., the chairman of Koch's Planning Commission and soon to be deputy mayor for policy and planning, it was noted, was about to undertake a comprehensive review of possible incentives and regulatory actions. The aim of the review, it was noted, was to allow the city to shift new development west toward Eighth Avenue. To achieve the goal, a task force of the commission would be analyzing political alternatives in four areas – zoning; real estate tax incentives; capital investment strategy; co-ordination and management of city services. The task force would be exploring "possible changes in incentives and disincentives," and in order to help the task force, Wagner was asking $98,450 from RBF and other foundations to pay for the work of consultants who would make recommendations. The consultants would be three; RBF wheelhorse William H. Whyte; RBF grantee Alexander Cooper; and James Felt & Co. realty chief Abraham Barkan. RBF concluded

The project would play a major role in the redirection of physical development in Midtown during the years ahead – a key RBF program concern.[39]

Like most New York City planning initiatives, the impetus for the plan seems to have come not from a government agency, but from private parties. It wasn't Bobby Wagner Jr. who called up the Rockefellers to get their support for his plan, it was the Rockefeller Brothers Fund people who called Wagner to lobby for theirs. On June 28, 1979,

RBF staffer Marilyn Levy joined with Joan Davidson of J.M. Kaplan Fund to meet with Chairman Wagner

> to discuss plans being formulated to restructure city incentives and . . . to help preserve what is the key to the area and direct new development where it would strengthen the city's potential for growth.

Levy and Davidson met again with Wagner on September 12. There also followed discussions by phone to work out the details of the plan. On this basis Levy recommended that RBF finance the city's plan.[40]

A year later, the project was still in the pipeline, and Bobby Wagner, who did finally become deputy mayor, reported on his progress, assuring his funders that he was a man of action, not contemplation. He agreed not to produce an analysis of the problem, but a report that will lead to direct action. "There are," he wrote, "on occasion legitimate research or study projects. This is not in that category." Koch, he advised, "expressed his keen interest and I am certain we will have his active support."

As Wagner ascended, he was replaced as head of the City Planning Commission by Herb Sturz. What Sturz, as veteran of Ford Foundation's Vera Institute of Justice had in the way of planning background has never been clear, but Ford functioned as a kind of Triple A farm team for the Koch Administration. (Or was it the other way around?) At any rate, it fell to Sturz to make another interim progress report to RBF on the soon-to-be released midtown plan:

> Our goal was not merely to propose changes but to make sure that they would actually be adapted. Your original support was largely based on this fact. In order to ensure reaching this goal, I directed that a draft report be published and widely circulated.

Essentially, Sturz wanted more money, and he had to apologize for taking so long. The foundation consortia had made clear not only what they wanted in the plan – a set of incentives and disincentives that would shift development – but also that the plan had to be finished by a deadline. Joan Davidson of the Kaplan Fund had this made perfectly clear. She reminded the CPC that the provisions involved not only changes in tax, policy, zoning policy and capital investment strategy, but that the CPC had to "refrain from actions that would render such project recommendations academic." And that "your willingness to accept an offer of a grant signifies your agreement to its terms as set forth in our letter of Oct 15, 1979 and this letter."

The whole premise of the agreement was that the report would be done by April, 1980. Here it was 18 months later, and the planners hadn't finished the job they promised the consortia. What's revealing, is not only that the foundations can demand specific recommendations for a forthcoming government report; that they can dictate who the consultants will be, but they can also insist that the whole package be wrapped up by a deadline that they set. Whose government is this?

From the Rockefeller standpoint the need for timeliness was clear. To be able to take advantage of the shift in values, they had to make sure they didn't miss the boom altogether. It wasn't just a matter of producing a report. Hearings had to be held. Votes had to be rounded up on the Board of Estimate.[41] Only then could the incentives be exploited. Delay would make the whole issue academic.

Throughout the period, there was a strong press campaign on behalf of the shift. The *Times* weighed in many times with editorials. ("A zoning Law in Need of Reform"; "A Building Boom in the Wrong Place.") Architectural critic Paul Goldberger promoted the west side line too ("the Problem of Proportions"). Of course you couldn't blame the *Times* for wanting real estate values to rise on the west side. They owned property there, but the caliber of the arguments they relied on would have made a cat laugh.

You didn't have to be Walter Gropius to figure out that if the city was being ruined by buildings that were too high on the east side, it wouldn't help to transfer them all to the west side. Letting the developers build whatever they wanted, with big zoning and tax abatements would just overdevelop the west side too. Two related themes were developed that helped evade confrontation with this obvious inference.

The first was that the west side was "certain to deteriorate" if the City Planning Commission didn't act. It wasn't developers' fault that they didn't have the proper "incentives". It was the bureaucrats in City Planning. ("The Planning Commissions' most useful act now would be to shift those tax incentives.") The second theme was evoking the mutilation of Manhattan's priceless architectural heritage – on the east side. Developers, whom no one can blame, were being forced to build on top of great buildings like the Metropolitan Club and the Metro-politan Museum of Modern Art (MOMA) – well, that was on the west side but you get the point – using air rights and cantilevering buildings over the low-rise space of these treasures was an urban desecration. Kent Barwick of the Municipal Art Society was given a platform to evoke doomsday for the east side if no zoning change were to come.

We will have an awesome and terrifying city if all of these things happen. If we build to the limits.

Of course the *Times* was knocking down an open door. Bobby Wagner was as concerned with the fine-grained texture of east side development as Paul Goldberger.

I worry about the over concentration, I think it would be better to move the focus of development westward. There is a profound concern that we are over building the core. It is imperative that we find some means of directing development.

Ultimately what the Wagner–Sturz plan did was to divide midtown up into three areas: a development area; a preservation area; and a stabilization area. Rockefeller Center was "preserved." The east side would be the stabilization area – developers there couldn't get any more ICIP; or J-51 tax incentives. No more Trump Towers would be allowed to rise more than 60 stories high. Fifth Avenue was scaled down from nearly 22 to 16 FAR. And mid-blocks reduced to 12.

All the tax incentives were shifted to the west side, and in zoning terms the west side would be able to build to R-21.

Frederick Rose, from another of the city's dynastic families termed the midtown plan "a very imaginative approach" to the problem.

Logic would dictate that if you're hungry and there's no steak on the menu, you will eat chicken. But real estate doesn't always work that way. And I don't know if tenants who want Madison Avenue are going to be so willing to go to Eighth.

Rose used the boom to sell off just about everything he owned in the city.[42]

Brendan Gill of the *New Yorker* wrote

The planning commission lay down like a doormat – a doormat! – on the pretext of luring developers from the east side to the west side when they needed no luring; they up-zoned the west side when it should have been down-zoned. None of this was necessary, it was the product of people eager to become multimillionaires in a few years . . .

Gill was right about the doormat part, but by looking at the most recent footprints, he misunderstood who was laying down for whom. It just seemed like the new money people who were driving the plan. This was because the old money, and the established institutions, the Rockefellers, Tisch's the *New York Times*, et al. had already sold their west side parcels to the new guys in town, the Eichners, the Solomons and the Japanese.

Nor is it true that subsidies weren't needed to suck development across town. In 1986, "the doormat," the CPC, looked back on its record of achievement. They really had achieved something. In 1982, they had predicted that the new legislation would stop chiseling on the east side FARs. In fact, more than 85 percent of the deals were "as of right" (i.e., no deals).

The shift had worked. Whereas before the legislation there was almost no development on the west side, by 1986 there were more square feet being developed on the west side than on the east side. The number of land transactions on the west side was far greater than on the east side – a sign of future development – and most important, the spread between land prices on the east side and the west side was narrowing. Whereas in 1981 land prices on the east side were 300 percent higher than on the west side, by 1986, the difference had narrowed to only 100 percent.[43]

By 1988, the effort to build on the west side to exploit the big FARs and lucrative tax subsidies had reached frenzied proportions. The May 13, 1988 deadline for cashing on zoning bonuses broke a record for developers pouring foundations in a single day for new structures. Unlike other cities, where overbuilding had been driven by the price mechanism, in New York it had been subsidies that did the trick. Up until 1988, the city had largely avoided the real estate excesses of other cities, a fact that planners attributed to the strength of our global economy. But it is fitting that the family who had gotten into the real estate business in 1929 as a result of bad timing and lack of planning, should now escape through very brilliant timing and very well laid plans. The consequences for the city are less sanguine: tens of millions of square feet of useless buildings, billions in tax abatements, and not least, a giant hole on Seventh Avenue and 49th Street where the Rockefeller Group abruptly decided not to leap again. Undoubtedly the hole will be filled before the soup lines in front of the city's churches disappear.

## BEYOND THE ROCKEFELLERS?

If planning is the secret of New York City's transformation, the extraordinary role of the Rockefellers explains a good deal of the shape and impact of planning. Since World War II, and up to quite recently, the private planning establishment has been dominated by a FIRE elite, of whom the Rockefellers exercised the most influence. As urban activists themselves, urban renewalists, as directors of private philanthropy, as public officials, as the city's largest taxpayers, as head of the city's second largest bank, family members have shaped the contours of New York City's development agenda – in particular its focus on the west side.

An explanation relying on the behavior of one family, it must be conceded, seems less than robust. It's not enough to switch villains: Oh I see. Robert Caro thought you could blame all the problems of New York on Robert Moses. He was wrong. It was really the Rockefellers.

On one level, at least, however, this is true. Other cities, seeking to extrude low-rent people and industry and promote high-rent people and industries, had a Bob Moses. Boston had Ed Logue. San Francisco had Justin Herman. It was hard for the urban political establishment in any city to do without a junkyard dog that would menace and bite, and it is important to see who held Moses' leash and who finally had him put in the pound when it suited their purposes.

But there was no city – not even Pittsburgh and the Mellons – where a single family had such a consequential, activist, transformative impact on a city over so long a period. After all, no Mellons ever became governor like Nelson or personally supervised urban renewal projects like David and Johnny, and the Mellons' impact on urban policy through their foundations has been comparatively slight.

Doctrinaire historical determinists will naturally insist that New York would be "just the same" without the Rockefellers. Historical necessity grinds on independently of this or that individual or family. Beware of "great man" theories, they warn.

Let's "bracket" Nelson and his four-term governorship: his creation of the UDC whose fall didn't just signal, but brought on the city's "fiscal crisis." Forget about the family's decades long control of the Republican Party on a state-wide basis, and the financing of Lindsay's first term run for mayor. Ignore also for the sake of argument the influence of the

Rockefeller Brothers Fund, the Rockefeller Foundation, the role of the Ford Foundation under John J. McCloy – how the two foundations transformed the landscape of philanthropy, using the city as their testing ground for social programs in work fare, criminal justice, community development and "self-help." Let's just look at the city in physical terms.

It's simple: without the Rockefellers no Rockefeller Center, and thus probably no Sixth Avenue IND.[44] No United Nations, no Lincoln Center, no Downtown Lower Manhattan Plan. No South Street Seaport. No World Trade Center. No Battery Park City. No Urban Development Corporation. No Harlem UDC. No New York City Partnership with its high-rise towers at Frederick Lewis Douglas Boulevard and its white picket fences at Charlotte Street in the south Bronx. Probably no shift of the port.

No more than Singapore without Lee Guan Yu can we imagine New York without the Rockefellers. If New York would have travelled in the same de-industrial direction as other FIRE cities, without them it wouldn't have arrived there so fast or with such a sure sense that it had arrived in the right place. The Rockefellers provided a leadership at every level that was simply unprecedented. Of course there was the obvious formal leadership – Nelson was governor and the family ran the state Republican Party for the better part of two decades. But even afterwards, in the seventies, following Nelson's resignation, and rise of the state Conservative Party which fractured family control of the party, the Rockefellers and their allies seemed to be better positioned than ever to influence local urban outcomes.

A small example, negligible no doubt in purely economic terms, but the Rockefellers have transformed music in this city. There is still a core of elite musicians making a living at the Metropolitan and the New York Philharmonic; as top club date players and as pianists in the big hotels. But the overall numbers have shrunk drastically. The number of musicians actually able to make a living has shrunk in almost every music field. In 1960 there were about 25,000 professional New York City musicians. In 1993 11,000.[45] The twin rise of musical illiteracy and the growing role of the synthesizer can't be ignored in shrinking the market for live music,[46] but neither can the transformation of the music's space.

Music has been "centered" by the family's creation of Lincoln Center. By the expansion of Rockefeller Center across Sixth Avenue in the late sixties which wiped out the music district. As well as by the

Rockefeller Brothers Fund's sponsorships of Times Square redevelopment and west side rezoning. The mandate of the City Center Opera – La Guardia's effort to bring cheap opera to the people – was repealed by moving it from W. 55th to Lincoln Center.[47] Centralization brought a big increase in capital costs that made musical performance much more expensive. Then Times Square redevelopment, first promoted by the family, and taken over by Cuomo's UDC, killed off practice and rehearsal space. West side re-zoning, also promoted by RBF, has largely finished off what was left of the club scene.[48]

What the Rockefellers did to music exemplifies what centering did to the fabric of the whole city, but "The Assassination of New York" can't be reduced to an Oliver Stone conspiracy. First of all, urban planning carried out by the Rockefellers isn't illegal. Making laws is something different from breaking them. The same goes for zoning. Nor is there anything in the statutes that forbids paying people to write articles that amplify your views.

Second, unlike Stone's conspirators, the Rockefellers didn't even do what they did in secret. They published their plans. They laid out their reasoning. They even opened their archives. It was all there. People could oppose their plans. Many did. And some, like Jane Jacobs, explained with great prescience why the Rockefellers' plans wouldn't work: why the city couldn't absorb two CBDs – a downtown and midtown CBD – the downtown CBD would always be second-rate. David Rockefeller replied to these criticisms. Oliver Stone's conspirators didn't debate.

Moreover, a critique that boils down to the accusation that the Rockefellers killed New York lacks political currency as well as generality. The Rockefellers are gone now. Having struggled for decades to reshape the city in the best interests of Rockefeller Center, they succeeded. And then it was *au revoir*: they bailed out with a $3 billion platinum parachute.

What do we learn from this? Never trust guys named Rockefeller? What do we do with the information? Not vote for David Jr. if he ever runs for mayor? Not eat at the Rainbow Room?

The actions of individuals have made a difference in the shaping of the city. But what's happened here needs to be shaped into a more general explanation of urban development. The most striking dimension of New York's spatial and industrial transformation is that nobody's working. It is one of the handful of cities in the U.S. where less than

50 percent of the population has a job. There are several cities in the country where the rate approaches 70 percent, and in the 1950s, the New York City rate used to be close to 70 percent. Where did the jobs go? Of course it's easy to see that when the bulldozers come, the jobs disappear.

But why didn't the new FIRE-based structure generate jobs? Why didn't the implicit trade off planners always insisted on – more than one job in white collar for every blue collar job snuffed out – why didn't it materialize? And how do we understand the transformation of New York from the richest city in the world to one of the poorest in North America? Besides the notion that the Rockefellers are bad for business, are there any more general principles that explain New York's unprecedented level of stagnation?

# NOTES

1. New York Metropolitan Region Study, directed by Raymond Vernon. Carried out in 1959. All books published by Harvard University Press. See especially Vernon's "Metropolis 1985".
2. Alan Balfour, *Rockefeller Center* (New York: McGraw-Hill Book Company, 1978), p. 229.
3. Robert Moses is often given principal credit, if that's the proper term, for the Lincoln Center urban renewal project. So little leverage did Moses have, he wasn't even invited to the dedication ceremonies, which were presided over by John D. Rockefeller III.
4. Krinsky, Rockefeller Center (New York: Oxford University Press, 1978), p. 124.
5. Vincent Scully, *American Architecture and Urbanism*, (New York: Praeger Publishers, 1976), p. 154.
6. Balfour, p. 232.
7. Krinsky, p. 119.
8. Ibid.
9. For Nelson's view of the impact of blacks on cities, see his testimony, U.S. Cong. Senate, Committee on Finance, Social Security Amendments of 1971 hearings before the Committee on Finance on H.R.1., 92 Cong., February 2, 1972, p. 2149.
10. RBF staffers were embarrassed by Suburban Action Institute's proclivity for arousing white suburban resentment: "Can we quietly and fairly tell Gold and Davidoff (of SAI) to either drop our name as a funding source?" asked William Dietel to his superior Robert Scrivner. "This is one grant we can use a *minimum* of publicity on." (William M. Dietel to Robert Scrivner October 12, 1973, RAC.)
11. *New York Times*, April 25, 1975, p. 39.
12. See Annual Report of the Comptroller, 1975. Cited in Charles Morris, *The Cost of Good Intentions* (New York: Norton, 1980), p. 223.
13. John Ensor Harr and Peter J. Johnson. *The Rockefeller Conscience* (New York: Charles Scribner's Sons, 1991), pp. 483–4. In an interview with the authors, David described brother Nelson's behavior as "appalling." (Ibid.)
14. Harr and Johnson, p. 493.
15. Ibid., p. 492.
16. About a 12 percent decline. See "Regional Traffic Trends," in New York Metropolitan Region 1992–93 Fact Book (New York: New York City Council on Economic Education at Baruch College, 1992), p. 92.

17. Interview Frederick Papert, 42nd Street Development Corp., July 13, 1993.
18. Those who bought up land and air rights as early as the late sixties – like Lazard Realty – have gotten their plans approved for hotels and high rises; comprehensive zoning changes have been introduced – it's okay now to develop over the Long Island Rail yards – but the big developers in the neighborhood, Lazard, Olympia & York and Harry Maclowe, seem to be waiting out the real estate depression.
19. Geoffrey Ste. Croix, *The Class Struggle in the Ancient Greek World* (Ithaca, New York: Cornell University Press, 1981), pp. 196–7. See also Ste. Croix's footnote 35 on p. 579 for numerous references and for English translations of Greek and Latin inscriptions.
20. John Ensor Harr and Peter J. Johnson, *The Rockefeller Conscience* (New York: Charles Scribner's Sons, 1991), p. 535.
21. See Dean Rusk to Chauncey Belknap, August 28, 1956, RAC. For another version of the same events, see Ensor and Johnson, p. 186.
22. Evidently, as in any family, there could be, and frequently were, conflicts over which brother's project would get the most substantial funding; over issues like whether or not to spend the funds which made up the endowment for current projects; even over whether or not to allow the cousins more discretionary power. For these issues, Ensor and Johnson who have access to John D. Rockefeller III's memos and tell the story from his point of view, provide a helpful guide. See *The Rockefeller Conscience* (New York: Charles Scribner's Sons, 1991).
23. Rockefeller Brothers' Fund, Annual Report, 1981, p. 8.
24. RBF, Annual Report, 1973, pp. 5 et seq.
25. *New York Times*, May 5, 1978, p. 1.
26. The South Bronx Plan was announced in April 1978. It involved 27,650 units of housing; 10,000 new manufacturing jobs. Industrial plans were detailed for Charlotte Street; the Bruckner Tier-Port Morris area; the Harlem River Yards; Hunt's Point; the Bronx Terminal Market.
27. Roger Starr, quoted in Charles Kaiser, "Blacks and Puerto Ricans, a Bronx Majority," *New York Times*, April 19, 1976, p. 23. "We should not encourage people to stay where their job possibilities are daily becoming more remote," Starr said, "Stop the Puerto Ricans and the rural blacks from living in the city . . . reverse the role of the city . . . it can no longer be the place of opportunity."
28. Interview with Fleck by Jill Jonnes, We're Still Here.
29. Cited in Harold Derienzo, "Planned Shrinkage: The Final Phase," *City Limits*, April 1989.
30. The Brown memo was attached to a 14 April, 1977 memo from Ford program officer Anita Miller to Marilyn Levy, RBF staff associate.
31. Derienzo, p. 10.
32. Dana Creel and Gene Setzer to David Rockefeller, October 1, 1962, RAC.
33. Ibid.
34. From Agenda and Docket RBF annual Meeting May 15, 1969.
35. Brochure, reprinted from Pratt Planning Papers, 1967, RBF, RAC.
36. Agenda and docket May 15, 1969.
37. See *New York Post* May 30, 1972.
38. Pratt Planning Papers, 1967, p. 5.
39. Agenda for Rockefeller Brothers Fund, Executive Committee Meeting, October 31, 1979.
40. Eventually, Alexander Cooper was replaced by Davis, Brody, see 3/30/81 – Agenda for RBF spring meeting, re: City Planning Department Fund. (The docket states that consultants hired – Whyte and Davis Brody Associates – were "well regarded by RBF.")
41. This turned out to be no problem – the midtown plan passed 10 to 1. Only Borough President Howard Golden opposed it.
42. Tom Shachtman, *Skyscraper Dreams* (Boston: Little, Brown and Company, 1991), p. 16.
43. DCP, New York City, Midtown Development Review, July 1987, NYC DCP 87-05, p. 6.
44. Robert Fitch," Family Subway" in Paul Zaremblea and Thomas Ferguson, eds, *Research in Political Economy*, 1985, v.8.
45. Local 802, American Federation of Musicians. *Allegro*, January 1993

46. If you've never heard live music, you're more likely to find the sounds played on a synthesizer music-like.
47. Even as late as 1960 you could see an opera for 2–3 dollars at City Center. Now the prices at New York State Opera Theater are nearly as high as across the Plaza at the Met – where Pavorotti can be heard for $250.00 for the *cheapest* ticket, *New York Times*, April 11, 1993, Section 2, p. 24.
48. Once there were over 25,000 members of Local 802, the musicians union. Now there are 11,000 about. And a graduate of Juiliard can often be found making less for a performance than what a substitute teacher makes in a day at a local high school.

*PART III*

# WHAT TO DO

# CHAPTER NINE

# AFTER POST-INDUSTRIALISM

Post-industrial New York is a mutation masquerading as a modernization. What is presented as modern is actually, in many respects, deeply archaic, but we are conditioned by our nineteenth century intellectual heritage to think that whatever comes later must be better adapted, more fit, more highly evolved than what it replaces. It's here, therefore it must be fit. There are lots of mutations, however, that don't work. "Throwbacks" they used to be called. Then there are millions of would-be species which putter around for a couple of generations, and never make it on to the phylogenetic charts. Indeed, most fail. Post-industrialism has failed in New York. It displaced manufacturing without replacing it as a basis for truly modern urban life.

Modern cities are different from ancient cities in many ways, but fundamentally by how they earn their living. Ancient cities were primarily places where elites lived, practiced sacred rites, consumed, and gave orders. They were "headquarters, command centers". Non-elites who lived in cities – by far the majority – exchanged labor in the form of services against the surplus that the elites – priests, churchmen, aristocrats, etc. – drew from sucking the agricultural surplus from peasants, estate slaves, and prebends living out in the countryside.

Our FIRE elites imagined they could turn New York into a kind of high-rise command center of this type. There would be no production within city limits. The new urban establishment would live purely off surplus produced elsewhere. An army of retainers, personal servants, guards, office flunkies etc. would be needed to make personal and professional life comfortable and secure. It would be paid out of the rents which modern elites earned from managing the economic surplus, performing legal, accounting, business services, as well as buying and selling securities, speculating in real estate.

There is always a danger in falling to anachronistic thinking, but in purely structural terms, second millennium Babylon was like this – an administrative and commercial center.[1] Commodity production took place in the countryside. Not in the city.[2] There was no social ranking except in terms of income,[3] and at the top of the status hierarchy, the Babylonian merchants and bankers were quite internationally minded. Although they hadn't yet heard of the globe, their government's numerous foreign interventions throughout Asia Minor meant growing amounts of trade and tribute, and high-rise ziggurats crowding the horizon. The ziggurats housed banker-priests who performed the Babylonian equivalent of "higher order services." Babylon worked. Even Jerusalem's elites envied it. Prophets might rail against it, but in its day, there was no place like Babylon.

Modern capitalist cities of which fourteenth century Italian guild cities like Florence and Padua were the prototype – were based on craft production and manufacturing inside the city itself. For all the exploitation, poverty and misery they offered their inhabitants, countries with modern cities thrived, produced more wealth, experienced more technological progress than those countries which retained the archaic urban structure, i.e., elites inside, producers outside.

The reason for the internalization of production was simply that the new economic classes precipitated out of the industrialized manufacturing process needed to be close to their work – the direct exploitation of labor. Cities grew because mass production required masses of people concentrated in one place. As they grew outward, and as the different functions of management became more specialized, the functions which were once housed within a single factory building, were redistributed in specialized districts. These functions – manufacturing, administration, accounting, etc., now had to compete for space in the urban land market. What should go where began to be determined not by what arrangement maximized jobs or welfare, but what paid the most rent.

In political terms, however, the internalization of productive workers in the city made it harder for resident elites to evade their demands. The rise of the urban labor movements, even though they rarely succeeded in gaining power, still shaped the modern political system. Urban manufacturing workers gained rights and status never acquired by unskilled agricultural workers. They became the first subaltern class to achieve full citizenship since fifth century Greece. And their movements wound up changing the value systems of the countries so that greater social solidarity and social cohesion were more possible than in the elite urban model.

Starting in the fifties, especially in U.S. cities, growing physical separation of production from accumulation began to undermine both processes. The rate of accumulation slowed and the rate of productivity fell. Separation took two primary forms: manufacturing capital export and aggressive urban "centering."

The leading fraction of the same class that carried out the centering process also supervised and promoted the overseas redeployment of U.S. capital. David Rockefeller lists his three most important charitable priorities as the Council on Foreign Relations, the Trilateral Conference and the New York City Partnership.[4] His mix of urban and global concerns is typical of his peers. The membership of the Downtown Lower Manhattan Association and the New York City Council on Foreign Relations in the late fifties greatly overlapped.

Thus the "globalism" implied by capital export has to be understood not as some outside force on cities, but together with "centering," as two sides of the same style of accumulation carried out by the same elite stratum. The same people who targeted Third World nations in the late seventies as prime recipients for U.S. capital, in the eighties switched to LBOs and office buildings. For America's elite, busily deploying U.S. surplus capital around the world, the ground under their feet would serve as the global "command center."

By far the greater share of manufacturing capital export – four dollars out of every five – went not to poor underdeveloped countries, but to the advanced capitalist world – especially Europe where U.S. auto, oil, and information industry transplants which had established themselves behind common market trade barriers. The effect of the capital redeployment was first to knock out U.S. producer goods industries like steel, which lost a big share of their market. (The real expansion of steel-using companies like G.M. and Ford was in Europe, not the U.S.) Then the consumer goods industries, like auto, began to decline, as the home market stagnated. They weren't exporting anymore, and they lost the domestic workers in the producer goods industry who had now taken, by and large, lower paid jobs in "services." The falling rate of domestic investment allowed one country after another to pass the U.S. in per capita GDP. "Hollowed out" industries complemented "hollowed out" cities.

Anyone who simply looks around at crumbling U.S. cities, with their potholed streets, and their sidewalks thronging with beggars, can tell that something is going wrong. But social science is put to work – not to solve the problems – but to conceal them. Economists invent new methods of calculating GDP – based on "purchasing power parity" instead of dollars – that perpetuate the fiction that the U.S. is still top nation. Sociologists deploy post-industrial ideology that conceals the damage being done even more profoundly.

Post-industrialism portrayed productive labor as superfluous. Daniel Bell, the Henry Ford II Professor of Social Sciences at Harvard proclaimed the neo-Fordist doctrine: post-modern work would not be a matter of production, but services – "a game between persons." The members of the ancient law, banking, accounting and teaching professions were transformed into "intellectual capitalists" – whose economic function was raised far above that of "routine producers." In political terms, post-industrialism portrayed meritocracy as the new form of democracy. But the unparalleled growth rates of stand-alone cities like Hong Kong and Singapore on the basis of productive labor and the almost equally stunning decline of New York on the basis of the surplus-sucking goes a long way to demonstrate what's fit and what's not.

New York City's urban structure thus represents a "throwback" to the form of archaic elite cities. Its present decision makers are being forced to confront the reality that: (a) a city with no production is not going to have as large a population as was formerly sustainable with production; and (b) (perhaps of more concern to our real estate elites, as well as those who've bankrolled them), it's impossible even to have large armies of surplus absorbers without large numbers of surplus producers.

Dim awareness of these imperatives seems to be growing. It seems to be implicit in the plans being discussed for downtown Manhattan – the proposal to tear down obsolete Class C and some Class B office buildings and replace them with urban plazas. The failure of a whole generation of urban planning is contained in these suggestions. The same recognition of the limitations of the present urban form is also implicit in the renewed discussion of the "mobility options" by Bill Clinton's Secretary of Housing and Urban Development, Henry Cisneros.[5] These policy discussion simply assume the inability of the city to serve as a source of mass employment and concern themselves with how to rid it of its millions of surplus population – the "politics of mobility."

Of course New York can probably survive in its post-industrial form for many more generations hooked up to the kidney machine of state and federal subsidies, more or less gradually losing population, jobs, housing – affording the modern novelistic Juvenals like Tom Wolfe a rich diet of decay on which to feed. What we will see, however, is at best a form of vegetation, not urban life with the possibilities it once had. It will be "New York" only in name.

The obvious question is what are the alternatives?

## "RE-INVENTING NEW YORK"

As awareness sinks in, as more New Yorkers realize that post-industrial cities lack growth and job potential, their immediate reaction takes the form of proposals to "bring back", "re-build", "re-invent" New York. How do we evaluate these proposals? What criteria do we use?

In the case of the "re-invention" plans, a complex methodology isn't required. "Re-invention" seems to be the code word used by those who aim to accelerate existing post-industrial tendencies. Conceived in the eighties, they failed to grasp how severe the downturn which began in late 1989 would turn out, insisting it would cause only short-term damage. New York's elites misunderstood not just its severity but its meaning – that the FIRE city couldn't reproduce itself in its present form. It has to shrink. It can't provide jobs.

Thus the source of the urban problem – our elites are busy absorbing surplus rather than allowing it to be produced – is either evaded or denied altogether. Writers like David Osborne and Ted Gaebler, whose "Re-Inventing Government"[6] was praised by both Bill Clinton and George Bush's deputy assistant, argue that the cities would be better off if they were more like the private sector. The problem of city government lies therefore in bringing the consumer-oriented, entrepreneurial, market-driven character of the private sector to government. And of course as enthusiastic privatizers, they argue for competition between public and private sectors to ensure cheaper, better services. What they fail to realize is that paper entrepreneur in the urban private sector has created the need for a welfare state that is no longer supportable on the basis of a FIRE economy. The urban economy is increasingly incapable of throwing off enough surplus to maintain a decent public sector – much less the corrupt, slothful one we have.

Locally, Hugh O'Neill and Mitchell Moss's idea of "reinvention" – which they articulate in their paper "Re-inventing New York" simply prolongs the eighties illusion that New York can thrive on the basis of its FIRE and business service industries. They dismiss criticism of FIRE's potential to drive the city's economy as "doomsaying". And argue for "prudent realism".[7]

What's novel about their approach is their dichotomization of the whole regional economy into two parts – the bright guys – who they call "intellectual capitalists"; and the dullards – "routine producers". This is not quite the same thing as dividing the region into FIRE and business services on the one hand and manufacturing and distribution on the other, but it comes down to the same thing. They write off the bulk of manufacturing. They urge that officials concentrate on what we do best – elite financial services. They suggest helping the poor and unemployed by providing them with better skills and better mobility – to find those jobs in the growth areas.

What's new here, then, is not the familiar insistence that New York should make more room for the LBO industry, "financial engineering" as they call it; and less for low rent, blue collar types, but the rationale, the notion of "intellectual capital." O'Neill and Moss did not invent this notion. In this respect, they rely a lot on the intellectual capital of Robert Reich.[8] They reproduce his distinction between intellectual capital and routine producers. They also adopt his global *Weltanschauung* in which each individual can no longer rely on the state or the modern corporation, but ultimately has to be understood as a kind of windowless Yuppie monad embodying his intellectual capital.

Intellectual capital theory (ICT) underpins both the economic claim that New York must keep on moving in the same futile direction, and, more ambitiously, it validates the status claims of those benefiting from the futility – the FIRE professionals and the academics who move in their wake. ICT anchors "jobs-skills mismatch" theory – wherein we learn that the problem with the jobless isn't a lack of jobs, but a lack of intellectual capital. ICT justifies the parasitism of the elites, and the strategy of warehousing the poor with welfare and "job training" instead of jobs. So it may be useful to take more than a cursory look at what its saying.

Business professionals, unlike blue collar workers, often have trouble explaining to their kids exactly what it is that they do. Their academic apologists have almost as much difficulty justifying why they should get paid what they do. Here is where the latest version of human capital theory – intellectual capital – comes in.

Considering how important intellectual capital is to urban survival, we might ask how we have gotten along so long without identifying something so vital? What the hell is intellectual capital?

The answer is that intellectual capital consists in the training educated workers receive and the education-enriched work they produce. But how is this 'capital' measured? This is no pedantic question. It's easy to invent imaginary entities and claim that they are responsible for complex processes. Phlogiston was a favorite of chemists for centuries – because it explained the inexplicable – oxidation. Human capital is the economists' phlogiston because it explains what has been for so long inexplicable – economic growth.

The problem is that all efforts to measure human or intellectual capital involve circularity. This is especially true of the effort to treat the salaries as the interest on a capital. And high salaries as a return to highly educated labor. Marshall, the founder of the theory of marginal productivity pointed this danger out quite early, in a section of his *Principles*, vainly warning against this distortion of his method. The marginal productivity theory, he said,

cannot be made into a theory of interest any more than into a theory of wages, without reasoning into a circle.[9]

The implication here is that you can't know if the increased earnings of an educated person are explained by the extra increment of education he received unless you know a great deal more. What's being claimed is that the person is a capital and his salary is the interest on that capital, and that further, the bigger the salary, the more interest he's getting on his educational capital. To identify the extra income with the extra education substitutes assertion for argument.

Is it really useful or illuminating to understand the $127 million income earned in 1992 by Hospital Corporation of America's Thomas Frist Jr., or the $850 million income brought home the same year by currency trader George Soros in terms of the education they received at old Siwash? Is their income really a return to education, or are they simply closer to cash register, i.e., exercise control over the accumulation process? Does it help to explain the steady rise in doctor's incomes over the last two decades in terms of increasing returns to the education they received in med school? Or would we be better off examining the rise of "third party payers?"

The beauty of intellectual capital theory is that it elevates the status of the owner without assigning him definitively to either labor or capital's side – the true mark of a post-industrial theory. Intellectual capital can't be understood as genuine capital. For true capital there is always a market. You can buy and sell bonds, factories, machines, etc., but you can only *buy* education. But try to *sell* the education you've bought. You can sell your labor after you've been educated. But then what you have is not capital, because it is labor being performed *for* capital. And someone who really has capital doesn't have to work for another capitalist.

But intellectual capital isn't labor either. The principle of ICT is that you get paid not for your performance of labor, but for how you've been trained to perform it. This is not the familiar idea from classical economics that a skilled laborer's work costs more to reproduce than an unskilled laborers, so more costly labor is paid more. In this case, the return is not proportionate to the cost. The idea is rather that education creates a special kind of labor. You go to Harvard and get a unique educational training. That training is your capital. It's the capital portion of your labor. But what is "labor" that is really capital?

Some distinctions are useful. For example, between people who are alive and people who are dead. It's possible to invent another category of people who are both alive and dead, e.g., zombies. But this requires a whole series of assumptions, as in the case of voodoo, which winds up clouding the mind. Ultimately it makes no more sense to imagine yourself as a treasury bill than a zombi.

The point of human capital theory is thus to wipe out useful distinctions, e.g., between the returns workers receive for their labor and the returns capitalists receive for their *pro rata* ownership of the means of production. It also helps erode the distinction between productive and unproductive labor – the purpose of which is to distinguish between profits which are derived from mere transfers of income and profits derived from the creation of wealth and value. Finally human capital discourse enables intellectuals to think they're capitalists and capitalists to think they're intellectuals – and allows both to validate the disproportionate income they receive in comparison to workers.

In the case of O'Neill and Moss there is the added effort to justify FIRE's continuing efforts to narrow the ring against manufacturing and manufacturing workers. Since this type of thinking ultimately claims descent from Marshall, and the neo-classical tradition, we should recall his warning:

Every system, which allows the higher faculties of the lower grades of industry to go to waste, is open to grave suspicion.[10]

## REBUILDING NEW YORK

The "rebuilders" are a more promising lot than the "re-inventors." The rebuilders want to do something about the status quo, not simply embalm it. In January, 1993, more than 50,000 construction workers marched across the Brooklyn Bridge with signs demanding "Rebuild New York." They literally seek to rebuild New York's crumbling infrastructure.

Problem is this: you don't need to be George Washington Roebling to recognize that if you don't maintain a bridge it will fall down. Even our city officials recognize this. New York just furnishes an extreme urban example in a country where there's no serious maintenance of bridges – 200 collapse every year and 40 percent are dangerously undermaintained.[11] The problem again is that, locally, not enough surplus is being produced – both to take care of growing numbers of poor and to maintain the bridges. Bridges don't riot, which explains why they get even less attention than the poor.

Assuming, however, you could somehow borrow the money to fix New York's famous wavy-gravy streets, the bridges, tunnels, schools, etc., we still would be left with a city that's unable to maintain the extent of infrastructure it's got. Literal rebuilding of New York – while absolutely necessary – is clearly insufficient. And besides, when New Yorkers saw the marchers on TV that night, they had to notice that not that many looked like them – they were basically white guys from Long Island.

Then there are those who want to rebuild not the present New York, but the New York which once was. The problem here of course is that you can't step twice into the same stream. Because when you try, the water's evaporated. A lot of the industry that disappeared during the period from 1880–1950 shifted out for good reason. It was – in Darwinian terms – selected out. We shouldn't be sad that the animal fat rendering plants got closed down, or that the fume-spewing chemical plants were banished to the countryside.

## RETHINKING NEW YORK

Do we even *want* to recreate the industrial mix that New York had in the fifties? In the fifties, nearly three out of ten jobs in manufacturing were in the needle trades. Do we want to turn a quarter of a million New Yorkers into cutters and sewers?

It begs the question to argue that this is impossible. It may not be. As Asian wages continue to rise steeply, and New York's fall, these industries could well come back. This datum, is, as they say "merely anecdotal", but as I was sitting on the subway recently, shuffling my Chinese flashcards, an older gentleman next to me introduced himself as a former worker from Hong Kong. He explained that he had decided to take retirement in New York because the cost of living was lower. Per capita income in Hong Kong is equal to per capita income in New York outside Manhattan and Queens. As New York City wages continue to fall, relative to East Asia, it's plausible that manufacturing capital could be redeployed here to exploit our "cheap labor."

Something like this is happening in L.A. During the eighties the number of garment workers nearly doubled on the basis of wages about equal to those in New York, albeit much lower benefits. Question is, do we want to rebuild the New York that was?

Here's where the question of criterion comes in. Post-industrialists always warn us against "nostalgia." Their notion of "nostalgia" however is any effort to use the past as a check to see how much progress we've really made. But what is nostalgia? A sentimentalism about the past. Filtering out all the pain and limitations and concentrating on the happy moments, the achievements. By all means, let's have a proper accounting of what was healthy and what wasn't in New York City's past.

But is it nostalgia to want to regain the achievements of which you were capable? If you've lost your honor, is it nostalgia to want to recoup it? If an athlete has lost the use of a limb, is it nostalgia to want to recover it? If a city has lost the productive capacities that made it pre-eminent, is it nostalgia to want to regain them?

To avoid the sentimentalism of nostalgia, we need an inventory of the valuable things we've lost, as well as an account of those features of the past which we are well rid of. In the last generation, New York City has lost not only jobs but lost functions, not only wealth but the capacity to produce wealth. Our economy has lost the capacity to work intelligent ways. We've lost the structures that facilitated this type of working.

*New York City had flexible production.*   Nobody had named it that. Most experts were embarrassed by it, but it turns out now that you either produce flexibly or you don't produce. The Fordist era is over. What's required are small firms that produce in batches, design-driven, non-standardized products. New York City's chance to become competitive, as opposed to post-modern, was destroyed by its own policy makers.

*Economic diversity.*   A more balanced economic structure combined the three basic economic functions of production, circulation and accumulation. Having the national casino located in lower Manhattan subjected the city to inherent economic peaks and valleys as this "industry" hired and layed off sales people, and the peaks were almost as painful as the valleys. But a better distribution of industry cushioned the shocks.

*Our manufacturing was ecologically compatible with urban life.*   People sewing and cutting fabrics, putting print on paper, weren't dangerous and didn't create any major effluent.

*The city produced a high volume of exports.*   We led the U.S. in industrial exports, in value added by manufacturing. The individual goods weren't particularly high in value added, but there was a great magnitude of them.

*The city was capable of producing housing for more than a small stratum of rich people.*   A lot of theories have been invented to justify lack of housing production – e.g., "filtering theory," we don't need new housing because poor people will occupy rich people's houses as the rich move out. "Post-shelter" society-housing is no longer a consumer good, but a form of capital, and everybody can't be a capitalist. But the fact is that a city which can't generate new housing as the old units decay is a decaying city.

*The city had a CBD which served as an incubator for industrial novelty.*   New York's manufacturing incubator served the entire region, because as some successful firms outgrew loft space, they moved to the boroughs or to New Jersey.

*An infrastructure that served manufacturing.*  As New York adapted to flexible production, its industries relied less on imported raw materials. But the food industry required raw materials, and having a rail network decreased our dependence on trucks.

I can't see how we're better off having lost these economic functions and structures. Our goal then should not be simply to "rebuild New York" but to re-acquire the functions and capacities that made expanded reproduction possible, that created the kind of diverse economy that survived a whole generation, from the twenties to the sixties when the rest of the north-eastern cities were declining.

But, at the same time, as long as we're being selective, we need to acknowledge the features of the structure which were harmful and destructive. A criterion for what needs to be regained and what needs to be reformed is this: does it lead to the material well-being and conscious organization of the city's working people – the vast majority? Does it raise their wages, promote their health? Improve their skills? Give them a greater share of the wealth they produce?

*Discrimination.*  There is a famous picture from the early thirties depicting the construction of Rockefeller Center: a bunch of iron workers are having lunch on an iron beam extended far out above the city which lies dozens of stories below. It's a striking picture, but what you can't help noticing today is that all the workers are white. There is an almost equally famous photo from the fifties of the completion of the frame of the Chase Manhattan bank. All the hundreds of construction workers who built it are gathered together inside the shell for a group photo. Scan it carefully. It's hard to see any non-white faces here either.

*Inequality.*  New York City has become more unequal in its income distribution since de-industrialization,[12] but in the fifties, although the rate of dependence was far lower, the income extremes were still appallingly great. It was those great inequalities which made possible the urban renewal programs that further immiserated the poor, shattered their neighborhoods and drove these families into even more desperate conditions. For it was the very poorest neighborhoods that had the hardest time resisting urban renewal.

*Low Wages.*  It's been claimed that at one time, wages in the garment industry were the equal of wages in the auto industry. Perhaps. But not as long as the Bureau of Labor Statistics has been keeping track. New

York City wages, including those in the garment industry have gotten lower, relative to manufacturing wages in the rest of the country, but the likelihood is that the composition of industry – weighted towards spheres where capital investment was low and skills were low and labor was plentiful – tended towards a relatively low wage structure.

*Job Insecurity.* Built into New York's "creative destruction" process and its industrial flexibility was a high toll on workers in the form of seasonality and job insecurity. The garment industry could be flexible, shut down and start up, because it was easy to off-load workers. The CBD was an incubator of jobs, ideas, and new innovations, but it also saw a high rate of failures.

*No economic democracy.* In the 1950s Saul D. Alinsky wrote,

New York . . . has the least citizen participation, the least effective local democracy, and the individual has the least degree of individual self-determination that is to be found in any major city in the United States.[13]

Lack of political democracy can be understood in part by the structure of the city's industries which made industrial unionism of the UAW-type difficult to develop. Construction, food, trucking, garment, longshore industries have proved quite vulnerable to control by organized crime. Working people have not been able to influence the institutions which in theory are theirs to control, much less the larger city. The New York City's high union density has rarely meant union democracy, mass movements of working people, or urban reform.[14]

*Fiscal instability.* There have been at least four times in this century when the city has been threatened by bankruptcy: 1907, 1914, 1933, and 1975. Instability derives not from "the political city" – which is operated on a short lease from the "economic city" – but from the economic city itself which has historically been too dependent on speculative industries – real estate and finance.

*Urban mercantilism.* Relations between communities in the New York metropolitan region have long resembled trading relations between nations in the 1930s, the old "beggar-my-neighbor" system. It is urban mercantilism – a competitive system based on exporting the poor and importing the rich; expelling factories and attracting office buildings.[15] So that the way we experience our neighbors is not through co-operation or mutual aid but as threats to our livelihood and communities. New

Jersey is seeking our tax base; trying to swipe our jobs and office buildings. And vice versa.

What's clear is that the strengths of the old New York were tied inseparably to its failings. New York City had a flexible production system – and in all flexible production systems, the potential exists for despotism and exploitation as well as economic democracy and workers' control. Without a strong workers' movement, without an equally strong movement for urban reform, New York could wind up re-acquiring a mode of manufacturing that combined the standards of living of the Bronx with the intensity of labor of South China.

Evidently, we don't want to "rebuild" the influence of organized crime in the unions, pervasive discrimination, low manufacturing wages, regional rivalries, income inequality, etc. What we do want is to restore New York's lost capacities and to put them in the service of goals working people can agree on and aim at. If we can target the goals, the methods will come into clearer focus.

## GOALS: MO', BETTER, FAIRER

New York City's chief problem is that: (a) there aren't enough jobs, (b) jobs we have aren't shared fairly, and (c) most of them don't pay enough.

Just to identify the problem however implies breaking with the official Democratic Party doctrine which insists that we must bring people to the jobs ("mobility") rather than bring jobs to people ("anchoring"). None of the outside forces the doctrine points to as being decisive can bring about a more just or prosperous city. Only New Yorkers can do that.

We must:

*Raise the labor force participation of our young people to the national average* New York is not the murder capital of the country, but we ought to draw no satisfaction from being the nation's mugging capital. Our survival instincts ought to tell us that New York cannot maintain itself as a community unless there are jobs for our youth – especially working-class and poor children from the outer boroughs. Over the long run, there is nothing that will contribute more to bringing down crime, dependency, and raise the quality and character of life in the city.

*Raise the city's employment/population ratio to the national average for cities by concentrating on development in the outer boroughs.* The present jobs strategy is adjunct to the city's real estate strategy: save tenants in office buildings. It adapts to the ever-increasing rise in rents and the dwindling number of non-elite jobs by arguing that New York City must prepare youth for jobs in Manhattan's FIRE and business services. This is simply a prescription for failure. In direct opposition to official "people to jobs strategy" articulated by the national Democratic Party, the City must establish a jobs-to-people strategy.[16]

*Focus job growth in the productive sector.* Most of New York's young people, especially in the outer boroughs, are not going to be lawyers or bankers. We must concentrate the increase in jobs in the productive sector of New York's economy: including manufacturing, infrastructure, and housing construction. Jobs which add wealth to the city; jobs which build up the region at the same time they employ the city's workers.

*Make retention of New York's existing manufacturing industries and industrial land a top priority.* A basic de-industrial strategy of New York City's elite planners relies on the simplest maneuver imaginable: they illegalize manufacturing by up-zoning the land. When manufacturing closes down or leaves for lack of space, they point to declining job totals to justify another re-zoning which illegalizes more manufacturing. This strategy must be stopped with a counter-strategy of retention and expansion of manufacturing areas.

*Prepare for New York's industry for a high technology, high-value added future.* There is no true shortage of highly skilled labor in New York. Skills are low. But the vast bulk of jobs being offered today are quite undemanding. Basic literacy and numeracy will suffice for these jobs. The city must aim at a higher standard both for jobs and skills. What's required here is a comprehensive *urban industrial policy* – which coordinates capital and skill needs. The present exclusive focus on skills deficiency simply lets capital off the hook: allowing capital to invest its surplus primarily in local FIRE and other advanced industrialized countries.

*Raise the wages of New York City industrial workers to the national average.* The emerging strategy of New York manufacturing interests, abetted by corrupt and ineffective trade unions, is to compete with the rest of the world through the super-exploitation of the members – chiefly women and minorities – i.e., a low-wage strategy. As unconscionable as this is from the standpoint of trade union principles, it is from a long-run perspective probably self-defeating. Haiti will defeat Harlem. Guangdong will win out over Chinatown. Such a strategy may survive the pension horizon of certain superannuated trade union bosses, but it leaves the city totally stripped of manufacturing.

New York ought not to try to compete with third-world countries by offering third-world wages. If workers in third-world countries can't survive on them, how can ours? What we have is a fast-sinking low-wage economy. What we want is a viable high-wage economy.

Everyone has an interest in raising New Yorkers' wages, whatever they might think at first. High wages are good for merchants, for restaurants, for banks – even for landlords.

Most important of all when high-wage, high value-added industries thrive, workers thrive, their organizations thrive and the city takes on a whole new progressive dimension.

*End "urban monoculture": the over-reliance on speculative office building development. Diversify the economy.* An economy based on a wide array of products people need, organized around the principles of tax justice, will be much less prone to fiscal crisis. The public sector should be able once again to provide workers and the city with employment continuity. Not an endless round of lay-offs, cut backs, early retirements, spelled by sharp escalations of unsustainable growth.

*Promote equal access to skilled jobs.* The focus of affirmative action must be broadened. Asians, Latinos, African Americans and women must be allowed to participate in the construction trades, in the public utility and transportation sectors. This no longer needs to be argued. It has to be done.

## PROGRAM

When you talk to politicians, even friendly ones, who see that post-industrial New York doesn't work, they ask, "Well what industries should I push?" It's essential to resist what might be called "The Graduate" temptation: to answer, "plastics".

Maybe New York, unlike Dustin Hoffman, does have a future in plastics. But the point of a program is not to identify particular 3 digit SIC code industries New York should acquire or develop. In a world of flexible production, what is important is less this or that particular industry, than the skills and capacities to produce what people need. Small-scale, inter-dependent production means niche manufacturing

"Industries" are constantly changing. The point of a program is not to try to impose a new industrial structure on the city, it's rather to indicate how to acquire new structures and capacities; how to identify the obstacles that have to be transformed into avenues.


## TAX "FICTITIOUS CAPITAL" TO CREATE REAL CAPITAL

New York City has the highest per capita taxes in the country. Taxes here are too high. But the method of reducing taxes favored by our elites will continue to produce the opposite effect – by destroying real capital, they will increase joblessness and poverty and thus raise the need for revenues to warehouse the poor.

More fundamentally, the problem with New York's tax structure isn't simply that the taxes are too high, it's that we tax the wrong people. Bronx workers are taxed at a rate ten times higher than Fairfield County commuters who average four times as much yearly income.

New York also taxes the wrong industries. We tax manufacturing and exempt land speculators. Any city which has land values as high as Gotham's is going to have high *per capita* taxes. The point is to use the tax system to bring down the artificially high land values, and thus redistribute workers from unproductive to productive industries, e.g, from speculating in land to building houses.

In order to accomplish this transformation, New York needs to reverse its fiscal policy. Presently, the city spends billions abating taxes to reward speculators; it levies no stock exchange tax; no business services tax. Foreign banks pay no taxes whatever. The strategy of a new fiscal policy must be:

tax the existing unproductive structure to create the basis for a new productive economy that provides good jobs, and generates enough wealth for the services that make urban life tolerable.

We should tax air rights, development rights, tax the speculative gains which pile up when property transfers hands.


## MUNICIPALIZE NEW YORK CITY LAND

In 1817, New York government made what most historians regard as its best decision ever: to build the Erie canal. Just about the same time, however, the city commissioners made what may have been its worst: the decision to get rid of the government's considerable holdings of Manhattan land. A trickle of sales grew into a flood. The transfer of government land to private speculators created a class of parasites who lived off the industry of others and contributed nothing. The Astors, Roosevelts, Van Cortlandts, Rockefellers, Goelets, Pines, augmented by the twentieth century newcomers and institutional supporters, became, by far, the dominant political force in the city. And by means of regulation and planning, private landownership gradually choked off all land uses that didn't promote the appreciation of land values. To diversify land use and restore productive enterprise, the city must take back the land.

But, it will be pointed out, this is communism. Not for nothing did Marx and Engels make government ownership of the land point one of their Communist Manifesto. But New Yorkers should decide to take back their land on the merits, not on the basis of what Marx and Engels said.

Certainly no city government has even been more anti-communist than the colonial government of Hong Kong. Moreover, its capitalist class was made up chiefly of refugees from Shanghai. Yet the British crown there promoted a policy of nearly complete government land ownership – about 95 percent of the land is government owned.

When free enterprise conservative economists point out how low the personal and corporate income taxes are in Hong Kong, they somehow ignore the reason – the government owns the land and leases it to business for its use. More than a third of all government revenue is earned this way.[17] It also puts up inexpensive public housing for the majority of workers reducing the cost of living. Had the authorities not done this, it is highly likely that development would have been quickly choked off – Hong Kong is a small island after all and the dangers of monopoly are obvious. Singapore, a more resolutely socialist city-state has obviated these dangers the same way.

## BRING NEW YORK'S ELITE NON-PROFITS
## UNDER CITY CONTROL

The total budget of the city's non-profit sector in 1989 – $32 billion – well exceeded the city budget.[18] The non-profits, chiefly foundations, universities, voluntary hospitals, churches own about 6 percent of the city's $400 billion property roll – yet they pay no taxes. Foundations, in particular, exercise enormous influence through their contributions to government agencies; their subventions to conforming intellectuals; their grants to community organizations which have transformed the promising movements of the sixties into semi-governmental agencies, blocking rather than promoting desperately needed redistribution of local wealth and power.

The Ford and Rockefeller Brothers' Foundations, the Empire Blue Crosses, the "voluntary" hospitals, and the private universities have become what John D. Rockefeller III hoped: a veritable "third sector" of society – but the least democratic, the least accountable. Thus, they can work for the aims of those who control them without having to compete either for votes or for dollars in the market place. The $14,133 Empire Blue Cross spent on silver punch bowls and ladles for its directors at Christmas while pleading poverty in Albany is redolent of the whole elite non-profit culture.[19] With these advantages, it is no wonder that they constitute the fastest growing sector of the economy: the most self-serving, and the least accountable.

Why have laws regulating political contributions at all, if by means of foundations, they can be easily evaded – just by calling them "philanthropy"? Why, for example, should the Rockefellers, through the Rockefeller Brothers' Fund be able to give unlimited amounts of money to city government and community organizations to promote their real estate interests? But even more broadly, what does "non-profit" mean when the average non-profit executive director's salary in New York is upwards of $175,000?[20] These are hardly volunteers.

At a minimum, there should be a stiff wage tax on non-profit executives who make more than the mayor. In addition, the elite non-profits, i.e., non-governmental non-profits, with a budget of over five million dollars a year, must pay something to the city proportionate to their income and their use of city facilities. The income thus received could be "dedicated."

The Ford Foundation has created through the Fund for the City of New York what amounts essentially to a bank for fellow non-profits. Why not use the revenue obtained by taxing elite non-profits to capitalize banks for the rest of us? These banks could help start small firms and provide working capital for existing firms – like those in the garment industry – that have seasonal cash flow irregularities.

## FOUND "THE NEW YORK BANK FOR JOBS
## AND COMMUNITY DEVELOPMENT"

Despite its status as the money capital of the world, ordinary New Yorkers know better than to try to get a loan from a local bank. In the seventies, our banks only lent to places like Argentina and Bolivia. In the eighties, their priorities were LBOs and office buildings. Now, in the nineties they have learned their lesson: New York City banks simply don't lend at all. They take deposits and put them in government bonds. The credit demand is there, but the banks have better things to do with deposits than lend them to the community.[21]

It's not just some neighborhoods that are red-lined, it's everywhere in New York where small business tries to manufacture, or trade something besides securities. But why not New York? By careful analysis of target projects, the World Bank (IBRD) makes soft loans to the poorest economies in the world. If the IBRD can make money lending to Bangladesh and Ethiopia, why not to entrepreneurs, manufacturers and co-operative development companies here in New York?

Where would the capital come from? IBRD's capital is subscribed by member nations and private banks. Similarly, New York City should look to capital contributions from elite non-profits, governmental units like the Port Authority and the Metropolitan Transit Authority (MTA) as well as its resident commercial banks and investment banks. Contributions of capital should be made a requirement for all those institutions which wish to serve as depositories for city cash; or participate in city bond syndicates; or manage city pension funds.

## FUND AND FINANCE PRODUCER CO-OPS,
## SMALL AND MINORITY OWNED BUSINESS

Orthodox Marxists could have as hard a time with this one as orthodox bankers. Marx wrote dozens of eloquent and insightful pages in the *Grundrisse* explaining why state aid to worker-owned co-operatives wouldn't work,[22] why it is the nature of capitalism and money for them to fail. He convinced me. But Italian communists in the red belt apparently didn't read the *Grundrisse*. They funded workers' co-ops; they financed small business, and the region not only survived, but thrived. It became the most prosperous in Europe.

For a long time, radicals have believed that trend of economic development ran only one way. Towards greater and greater accumulation, concentration and centralization of capital. Problems of small business were self-dissolving: as these units either died or became absorbed in larger business. Evidently, in the U.S. at least that's not happening. The Fortune 500 sinking fast as a percentage of total employees – down to less than 10 percent in 1990.

In New York, any tendency towards concentration is barely detectable. Manufacturing has maintained an average of about 30 employees per establishment for the last three censuses. Establishment size has shrunk in retail. Service employment is concentrating, but the city's 53,000 service establishments still only have about 12 workers each.

Instead of regarding small business as something transitional, waiting until it dies or gets gobbled up by big business, traditional leftist attitudes have to change. It's not a matter of romanticizing petty capitalism, or small business tyrants, but recognizing that small business *is* the institutional framework of modern urban capitalism.

Certainly Marx was right to denounce Proudhonian credit gratuit illusions. But liberal credit to small and co-operative business to save jobs seems like something a serious left would support. What's the alternative: New York in the nineties, where garment companies crash, and lay-offs mount because of LBO-driven retail failures. And also because there is no commercial bank that deigns to deal with the lowly schmata-makers.

Surely, the left can be more liberal than the Chase.


## STOP THE LOSS OF INDUSTRIAL LAND AND BUILDINGS. TREAT OUR INDUSTRIAL LAND LIKE PARK LAND; TREAT INDUSTRIAL BUILDINGS LIKE NEW YORK CITY LANDMARKS.

As the City Planning Commission says, "zoning shapes the city."[23] Through zoning, our planning apparatus determines how land is to be used. By transforming industrial land into residential and commercial land, through re-zoning, the city has closed the ring on industry.

The claim of those who support conversion, as might be expected of course, is that with less industry, we need less industrial land. But we have seen the extent to which New York City has disproportionately few manufacturing jobs: only two-thirds as many as those available in the top ten U.S. cities.

Meanwhile, the upzoning of industrial locations proceeds to the point that any wholesale re-industrialization strategy is placed in jeopardy. The Dinkins Administration, following in the wake of the Koch Administration's "New York Ascendent" is calling for the transformation of the waterfront. Its waterfront plan targets 46 industrial neighborhoods for upzoning. Big sections of industrial Long Island City has been upzoned through the actions of the Urban Development Corporations. And in the outer boroughs, industrial land has been lost through the development of Metrotech, Lutheran Hospital and Pratt Institute.

Even when the land adjoining industrial parcels is purchased, it creates a disability for commercial and industrial enterprise: the prospect of redevelopment makes it difficult to get credit; landlords, seeing which way the real estate winds are blowing, seek to end their leases.

To make re-industrialization possible, and to retain the industrial jobs we have, the city must set up a revised zoning procedure. It must be as difficult to re-zone manufacturing land as to de-map parkland. It should be just as hard to tear down a manufacturing loft as it is to tear down a building that is architecturally distinguished. Industrial preservationists must be as tenacious as historical preservationists.

## ROLL BACK SUBSIDIES FOR LUXURY DEVELOPMENT

Like our public development agencies which received a mandate for industrial development and then used it for real estate development, the "industry" in the Industrial and Commercial Incentives Program (ICIP) has been a diminishing magnitude. Meanwhile hundreds of millions are being doled out to real estate developers for office buildings which never should have been built: structures which now stand empty.

Members of the Real Estate Board of New York, who insist that they are the most appropriate target of city subsidy, mislead the public by making it appear that the boroughs or small business are really the largest recipients of the funds. As Appendix 11 shows, although the largest numerical recipients of ICIP are small businesses in the outer boroughs, the largest amounts of subsidy go to the biggest midtown developers.

ICIP, however, is only the largest of the real estate subsidy programs which include 421a, 421b, and J-51; and the whole alphabet soup of benefit programs for the rich. And the tax expenditure programs are far outstripping, in the rate of increase, social service programs. (See Appendix 12.)

While the Citizen's Budget Commission has called for an *end* to ICIP, this is not enough. In the present fiscal crisis and with the growing employment crisis, we need an administration that can sit down with developers, just as they do with trade unionists, and discuss givebacks. The extra revenue made available from these negotiations can be used to provide the founding capital for the "Bank for Jobs and Economic Development."

## ABOLISH THE PUBLIC DEVELOPMENT AUTHORITIES; PRIVATIZE THE WORLD TRADE CENTER

Under the heading, "Building a Record of Accomplishment," a recent Economic Development Corporation (née Public Development Corporation) report intones:

Through PDC initiatives, many of the city's major financial service firms have found ways to keep their businesses growing here. And the evidence is everywhere. On the booming west side of Lower Manhattan, Drexel Burnham Lambert will build a new headquarters . . .[24]

Flip to the section, "On the Waterfront", the text reads,

At the southern tip of Manhattan, the city's skyline will soon be enhanced by South Ferry Plaza. This $400 million mixed-use complex will be developed. . . . Further north, Julian J. Studley plans to construct the $636 million Hudson River Center, which will combine a hotel with recreational facilities, creating more than 1,500 jobs for the city."[25]

None of these projects will be built in this millennium. The developers and tenants are bankrupt. And the labor and expenditures lavished on them must be written off. These are only a few of the busted and fatally delayed projects PDC – now EDC – has produced for us. The Fulton Landing project has been stalled for the better part of a decade–with devastating impact on adjacent industrial and warehouse jobs. Other bungled jobs included Bridgemarket – which closed its construction loan ten years after Board of Estimate approval. The Brooklyn Atlantic Terminal which never found a private tenant, etc., etc.

Just how much capital EDC actually sunk into any of these projects cannot be determined because the powerful officials[26] who run EDC without public hearings – need not even issue reports that reveal relevant financial information. Not even the Council knows.

It is EDC, not any public officials, which determines economic priorities, environmental concerns, neighborhood impact, etc. Clearly, EDC like so many other authorities has slipped its traces. Just like UDC and the Port Authority, EDC was given its mandate to promote industrial development, but now chooses to focus the majority of its time and resources on real estate development which it does badly. If there were no EDC, the city would survive. We must insist that EDC stick to its original mandate or suffer swift closure.

While we're dealing with agencies that have lost their mission, there's the Port Authority's World Trade Center. Most real estate men opposed its creation, arguing that it would permanently depress the market. They were right. Now it's time to sell it off, all eleven million square feet plus, for whatever it will bring. Not that the city will derive much in income from the sale – it doesn't belong to the city – but once it is privatized, the new owners will start paying taxes. At present, the WTC doesn't, but if it did, the city would have received about $100 million in revenue. That's more money then the city spends on the New York public, Queens public and Brooklyn public libraries.[27]

CREATE A MULTI-CENTERED URBAN SPATIAL STRUCTURE . . .

A great strength of New York is its centripetal power. Thanks to the robber barons like Russell Sage, and J.P. Morgan, who built the transit system, we can stuff two million people a day into eleven square miles of urban land between 59th Street and the Battery. This has made possible a complex division of labor capable of producing, inventing, and flogging an astonishing variety of products, but the toll in congestion, monopoly rents, high housing costs, needs to be reckoned too.

Density is a prerequisite for civilization, for cultivated tastes, for refined needs, but a civilization that is maintained on the basis of the IRT has a shaky foundation.

. . . Build a new trolley loop.

New York City not only needs to break out of economic monoculture, it has to escape from its monocentral structure. And it has to do so in a way that permits more dignity, safety and comfort than the present dispensation. The one is the prerequisite to the other. Presently, all the lines, except the GG, constitute feeder lines into the Manhattan CBD. Generally speaking, it's not that hard to get from the outer boroughs to Manhattan, but it's exceedingly difficult to get from one borough to another. If you live in the Bronx, you can't get to Queens, unless you go through Manhattan. If you live in Brooklyn, you can't get to Bronx, except via Manhattan. Queens and Brooklyn are joined very tenuously, by the GG. This is no accident.

New York City never grew up organically, it was never truly a planned city like D.C. It was soldered together around the turn of the century to facilitate real estate expansion in the outer boroughs: so that the costs of infrastructural expansion would be spread over a wider tax base. The first subway lines were designed to create density, revenue and a new structure of real estate values for their promoters, but the result doesn't work as a city. Either New York becomes one city – with real opportunity for people in what are now the Kishniev's of the realm – or it will begin to fragment, as the boroughs start to go the way of Staten Island.

New York needs a transit system structured like Vienna's *Ringstrasse* or Tokyo's Yamanoto Line. When you have a ring, you no longer have outer and inner.

Such a revised transit structure could be the basis for establishing manufacturing as well as revived commercial centers in the periphery. A transit-led industrial restructuring is very different from the present efforts to get industry out of Manhattan and into the boroughs. Industry finds that once it's out of the CBD it's out of the place where it can find adequate workers, services, etc., but by redistributing density, it would make possible a multi-centered city.

## BUILD A NEW PORT – RESTORE THE CITY'S RAIL FREIGHT LINKAGE TO THE U.S.

There is probably no single statistic more telling about the poverty of post-industrial life in New York than that the largest single export that's now shipped out through our port is waste paper – more than the next ten commodities combined.[28] The rest of the world sends us cars, bananas, cocoa, electronic goods, all manner of ingeniously made and rare commodities. We ship back waste paper. This is what our economic metabolism with the rest of the world has come down to.

No single set of policies did more to throttle productive enterprise in New York than the gradual strangulation of the city's port. The port and the railroad facilities stood in the way of Lower Manhattan redevelopment. That's why they were attacked. Not because they weren't modern. They weren't modern enough because they were always being attacked. The Citizen's Budget Commission has never attacked real estate subsidies to board members as wasteful. It never found expenses for urban renewal imprudent, but a bond issue for something productive like development of the port was something it consistently refused to abide.

The effort to shift the port has been underway since the creation of the Port Authority more than 70 years ago. The goal of getting the port out of the city was articulated editorially by the *New York Times* in 1922.[29] It was a major aim of the First Regional Plan in 1929, which called for its removal to New Jersey; or even Jamaica Bay – anything being better, it seems, than wasting those great views on longshoremen.[30] Port removal was a goal of the World Trade Center Corporation established in 1947 by David and Nelson Rockefellers' uncle, Winthrop Aldrich, then head of the Chase.[31] It was re-articulated by the Second Regional Plan.[32] During the fiscal crisis, the city's lack of funds became the pretext for turning over all port development to New Jersey.[33] And the struggle continues today with the DCP's plan to install a sludge removal plant in the middle of the Brooklyn port.[34]

All questions about New York's lack of space, its technological obsolescence, the recalcitrance of its longshoremen, turn into mere pretexts when you realize how long ago the effort began to shift the port; who was involved and why.

The question is, however, not should the port have been shifted, but what good would it do to bring it back now? How many jobs would it create? Why have a port in New York when there's already one now in Newark? In other words, what's done is done, why refight old battles?

The short answers to very serious questions are that first of all, the city needs a port and rail infrastructure if it wants to regain manufacturing capacity. Even if the city just wants to cut down on the disproportionate number of trucks pounding its streets, and fouling its air, it needs a new transportation infrastructure. But some segments of the garment industry could also benefit, and a new port would make possible the revival of the food and beverage industry. Congressmen Jerry Nadler points out how beer brewing could start up if the city could transport hops from the west coast. It was, he argues, the severing of the lighter system that forced the Brooklyn breweries to shut down. If the city could import hops, it would be cheaper to make beer here than in eastern Pennsylvania.

Estimates of how many jobs the port created in New York City in the fifties range from the Port Authority's estimate of 400,000 total including about 125,000 in manufacturing[35] to a much lower figure of 90,000 by the RPA just in manufacturing.[36] Modern ports require fewer longshoremen and overseas markets have been lost, so even at the height of a port revival, the total figure would probably be closer to the RPA's than the Port Authority's. But even if only 50,000 jobs were created, that would be worth fighting for in a city with over 400,000 unemployed.

However, what about the existence of the New Jersey port? Isn't this just another example of urban mercantilism? Fighting with another state to get a bigger share of jobs? If it turns out that the New Jersey port is really capable of carrying out the multi-billion dollar dredging program and overcoming the environmental problems involved in accommodating deep-draft ships, then plans to build a competitive Brooklyn port should be reconsidered. But if the obstacles are as great as they seem, then the region's port should be built where it is geographically most advantageous – in New York – which is why the city is here in the first place.

## REVIVE NEW YORK'S HOUSING INDUSTRY: START BUILDING 50,000 UNITS A YEAR AGAIN

In the 1990s, production of housing in New York city has returned to the levels of output more characteristic of eighteenth century colonial New York, than a modern metropolis with 7.3 million people. Output fell beneath 10,000 units last year.

On the face of it, what seems startling about our terrible performance is that it was achieved during an economic boom. Yet during the entire decade of the 1980s we produced only 110,000 units. This is unacceptably few. (See Appendix 13.)

Consider the total number of units in the city: approximately

2,840,000.[37] If we assume that the average housing unit lasts fifty years, that would mean a yearly need for more than 50,000 units.

During the entire decade of the 1980s, the New York City housing industry produced only about 113,000 units. Of course the Federal Government didn't do its share. It cut housing subsidies, Section 8, etc., and the mayor played little role in housing production until just before the campaign in his final term. But the problem is not just subsidies. Even the upper middle class is house poor in New York. It is excessive costs and low incomes that make subsidies necessary.

In the 1950s when far less subsidy was available from the federal and local government, the industry was producing at twice the rate of the 1960s – the high watermark for housing subsidy.

So, with housing output falling, together with wage stagnation, New Yorkers found that they were paying a record percent of their income for housing. According to the most recent Housing Vacancy Survey the average New Yorker is paying an all-time high of nearly 30 percent, and for those New Yorkers in the bottom 30 percent of the income pyramid, more than half pay 50 percent or more of their income in rent.

But just as devastating as the effect of stagnation in the housing industry has been the effect on the producer. Our construction labor force is a fraction of what it should be. U.S. residential construction workers constitute over half the labor force in the construction industry. It is by far the most labor-intensive segment of the construction industry.

But only one city of the nation's top ten cities has a lower share of its work force in construction industry than New York. (See Appendix 14.)

These figures actually understate the number of jobs in the construction industry for New York *residents*. If we look at the series for resident employment, what we see is that the share of workers in construction is only 1.9 percent – the lowest of any city in the series. Just consider if New York had the same number of construction workers as a percentage of its work force as Houston.

We would have an extra 114,000 construction workers.

What if, further, the city were to intervene in the industry so that the jobs were shared fairly and New Yorkers were able to compete for the jobs on the basis of merit.

Consider the impact that this extra increment of the high-paid labor force would mean to poor communities in this city. Neighborhoods like

Central Brooklyn, Washington Heights, East Harlem would begin to form around a solid working-class, and middle-class core. Kids could count on their parents being able to afford to send them to college. African American carpenters and Latino electricians would get their kids apprenticeships in the trades just as trades people in Long Island and New Jersey do now. Increased political power would accrue to those communities as workers rose through the trades and became journeymen, foremen and managers. New York would be a different place.

It could happen here. But not with our present emphasis on pushing up land prices; subsidizing upper-class housing with J-51 subsidies; and frightening off working and middle class people from publicly owned housing by restricting residence to welfare recipients. These policies must be reversed, and the city must begin to take responsibility for the housing needs of working and middle-class residents as well as the poor.

Our private sector in housing has demonstrated that it is not up to the job of meeting the average New Yorkers' basic housing needs. It is capable only of overproducing and then warehousing "luxury" housing for the rich. The argument that if the free market can't supply the need, people should simply do without, is unacceptable with a basic human need like housing. The city has proven, in the case of Battery Park City, that it can spend billions to subsidize luxury housing on expensive landfill for the rich. It ought to be able to devote at least an equal amount for working and middle-class housing on the thousands of acres of cheap, city-owned land standing idle.

To finance construction, a new housing development authority could be established along the lines of the Municipal Assistance Corporation, but instead of using the existing sales tax as a revenue base, the funds could come strictly from a 4½ percent tax on business services used by the FIRE sector.

## SAVE JOBS: EXTEND RENT REGULATION TO COMMERCIAL AND INDUSTRIAL ENTERPRISE

New York presents to the world the image of the retail emporium of America. "If there's anything you want in the world, you can buy it in New York – at any time of the night or day," the saying goes. The problem is there are relatively few jobs in those stores.

Retail employment is lower here as a fraction of total employment than in any other U.S. city in the top ten. Only 17 percent of total employment is in retail. This is less than 70 percent percent of the total in sun-belt cities; only about three-quarters of the average for the top ten U.S. cities as a whole. (See Appendix 15.)

If you care about jobs, this is cause for concern because while retail jobs tend to pay less than manufacturing jobs, they don't require advanced degrees or years of apprenticeship. They are just the kind of entry jobs that ought to be available to New Yorkers.

The two most important factors in keeping New York's totals down are the underlying poverty of its population – especially in its outer borough neighborhoods – and the extortionate cost of rent. In the long run, the overall effect of the jobs program can be expected to impact on poverty. In the short run, the city must undertake a vigorous effort to keep commercial rents down. Not just to support small retailers, convenience consumers, and to keep consumer prices down, but to maintain employment.

The problem is not only the size of rent; but steep and unpredictable increases. When leases expire, landlords often behave irrationally, charging several multiples of the existing rent. The same shops will often go vacant for months and even years. Then the rent is lowered to what the previous tenant was willing to pay.

Commercial rent control would mean not only more jobs; more people spending money; it would mean the price all of us pay for consumer items would be less. All New Yorkers, consumers, workers, as well as small business owners have an interest in fair rents.

"Fair" is not whatever the market will bear. A fair rent is determined by the audited costs of the owner plus a normal rate of profit – whatever the prime rate is plus two percent. Since land is always a monopoly and since land use is a necessity, it should be treated like public utility.

The city should set up a Commercial and Industrial Rent Regulation Commission. The Commission would operate like a public utility commission. It would guarantee a fair profit to landlords, hear hardship cases, etc.

## FORM A TRIPARTITE COMMISSION TO
## REFORM APPRENTICESHIP AND HIRING HALL
## PRACTICES IN THE TRADES

Representatives from the trades, the city, and third parties agreed upon by both, must form a public commission to reform entry and hiring into the city's skilled occupations. Construction work sites now resemble battle fields with ethnic armies of "coalitions" clashing among each other and with white workers on the sites for jobs. Each year workers are murdered just because they are trying to get a job.

Asian workers, for example, are largely restricted to low-wage garment and restaurant industries: and excluded from relatively high-wage construction work. An Asian man is thirty-two times more likely to be working as a waiter in a restaurant than as a laborer on a construction site.[38] Anyone who has observed their protests against exclusion from the trades, knows this ratio expresses systematic discrimination, not a desire on the part of Chinese-Americans to live off tips left by Chinatown tourists.


## PROMOTE ECONOMIC DEMOCRACY

Traditional left economic thinking has divided as follows: there were the social democrats who ultimately believed in corporate ownership of the means of production, i.e., capitalism, as modified by improved welfare benefits, higher wages, longer vacations, etc., plus government ownership where needed; then there were the communists who believed in a party-run state which would operate the economy according to a central plan devised by the party. Whether communism or social democracy or both were superior to predatory capitalism is not the point. The point is that neither of these two supposed alternatives inspire much conviction any more.

Practically speaking, neither of the two socialist models has allowed much scope for participatory democracy. By "participatory democracy" I mean direct democracy as opposed to representative democracy. Workers themselves deciding how to run things at the shop floor; how much to pay themselves; the extent of authority for technical managers.

This is what "socialism" used to mean, in the days of Proudhon, and Fourier, Orestes Brownson and the American "workies", as members of New York's Workingmen's party were called.[39] Their ideas would later be termed "utopian" – because the workers believed naively, it was decided, in small, self-managed units as the foundation of society.

They were utopian because they tried to impose their "own subjective values" on history, and of course history *was* running against them in the direction of bigger and bigger units – which would render small-scale decision making, however democratically arrived at – irrelevant.

For more than a century, the main drift has been towards communities and regions more and more disassociated from each other by globalism, bigger and bigger units of production; longer assembly lines; more concentration of capital. The consequence has been increased centralization and greater monopoly of knowledge, power and wealth at the top.

But the main drift is not just ebbing now; it is shuddering to a halt. The giant corporations are all down-sizing, and it is not just a cyclical trend. Instead of integrating more and more functions they are disintegrating them. Contracting out. And struggling to survive against smaller rivals. Who would have thought five years ago that IBM would be close to bankruptcy as its new Chairman recently acknowledged?

As modern capitalism turns away from mass production and more towards flexible production methods, it finds it can't compete without tapping workers skills – without drawing on their knowledge and enthusiasm. It's not enough to be, or own, robots. But why should workers participate in management at the technical level but have the boardroom door slammed in their faces when it comes to allocating shares of wealth? Because they have no alternative. But why not create one?

At every level, in unions, in business, in city contracting, the city should promote social ownership and worker participation. Just as the city now favors minority business, it should also promote democratically controlled and owned business. In contracts. In loans from city-run banks.

## DEVELOP A CITY-LED INDUSTRIAL POLICY

City-led? New York's kleptocratic regimes figure prominently in America's urban history as the last people on earth you'd choose to lead anything. *Books* are written about New York City's economic development scandals and fiascos – from the Tweed Court House to Manhattantown to the Parking Violation Bureau and Wedtech. This is the city that couldn't get water to freeze at Wolman Skating Rink and had to turn to Donald Trump to find the secret. Under New York City leadership the construction of the Second Avenue subway has been underway since the 1920s!

On the other hand, consider the kleptocrats' eternal rivals, the plutocrats. Has there ever been a more abject failure in urban history than FIRE's development of New York City's downtown? Shut down the port. Cut off the railways. Pave over the rivers. Bulldoze the food markets. Sweep out the electrical district. Use Title I to knockout 250 acres of businesses. Spend billions in subsidies and forgone revenues. All to nurture office buildings. And now what's the plan? To knock down the office buildings and build a plaza.

Evidently, neither kleptocratic nor plutocratic traditions can serve as the inspiration for a new economic development regime. New Yorkers need to create new communities of interest; new identities that form out of common struggles against common adversaries. Only a movement coming out of such efforts can develop the self-under-standing needed to break with the karmic cycles of corruption and austerity promoted by our political and business elites.

But there is simply no alternative to a city-based, city-led economic development policy. The notion that the Feds will take care of us, or the claim that global forces are somehow working inexorably to expand New York's intellectual capital are simply pillows to rest on. The New York of today is the Detroit of ten years ago. Without a movement for economic justice, today's Detroit is our twenty-first century future.

## TOWARDS AN ECONOMY OF DIVERSITY

Rational analysis of the problem is worth about 5 percent. A plausible program is probably worth 5 percent more. The other 90 percent will have to come from passion – the passion for social justice. Even Hegel, perhaps the most rational person who ever lived, who believed that "ultimately" reason ruled the world, was also wise enough to point out that nothing great was ever accomplished without passion. "Abstract analysis couldn't get a cat to jump off a hot stove," he observed.

Nor is analysis, however compelling and cogent, going to bring the city's establishment to shift its priorities. They simply lack all motivation. How could a system that provides them with such large amounts of income and prestige be fundamentally flawed?

Our establishment reasons like Brecht's German communists. When East Berliners rioted, it was time, the government thought, to dissolve the people and elect a new one. Here in New York, when it becomes clear that the city's means of production are insufficient to employ all the people, the answer is not to increase the means of production, it's to decrease the number of people.

This is the capitalist way. You don't shrink the return to capital. You shrink the number of people until they equal the number who can be profitably exploited by capital.

Treating the city as landed capital, its main industry as creating fictitious capital and dealing with the people as human capital has now been tried. The effort was bound to fail anyway: because for whatever its failings, the energies and landscapes of New York are too prodigious to be treated as something inert, inorganic, dead.

Ultimately New York represents a hope that transcends even the people who live here. With all its antagonisms and bias, with all the segregation and discrimination, and the sentimentalization of our diversity, you can't help but be struck by the range of races, religions, dress, customs you encounter just by taking the 7 train to Shea Stadium. The faces across the isle have all the variation and richness of the figures in a Diego Rivera mural.

New York will probably never resemble a World War II movie in which all the ethnic groups decide to make up and storm Mt. Surabachi. But a century of immigration has made impossible a culture based simply on score settling; on the sleepwalking memories of ancient crimes committed against defunct ancestors. Our ancestors came here to escape those nightmares.

With its filthy streets, and beggars on nearly every corner. With welfare rolls rising to over one million recipients and murder victims totaling over 2,000 victims a year, and with an economy whose private sector payroll hasn't grown in thirty years, its easy to forget the dimensions of New York City's former greatness and the secrets of its prosperity.

New York was never a one-product town like Detroit or Akron. It was not about Fords or tires. Block-long River Rouge-type assembly lines were impossible here but gritty ingenuity, cast-iron construction and vertical lifts made possible the world's biggest manufacturing city.

New York was never a capitol city like D.C. or even Albany. It never relied on lawmakers or justices who could force people to be here because of the legislature or the courts. But people came anyway because New York provided more opportunity than any place else in a country of opportunity.

New York was never a tourist city like San Francisco or Miami. Its climate couldn't compare to California or Hawaii, and outside of

Greenwich Village there has never been anything quaint or cute about its streets. But New York still attracted more tourists than any other city.

What New York had more of than anywhere was economic diversity. If it took big amounts of steel or coal, New York couldn't produce it. But the first stage of practically any product could be created here, and New York led America in patents, in innovation, in product design and creativity.

New York had more industries than anywhere else – true they were small and dependent on each other, but the diverse mix worked and worked well. Jane Jacobs tried to argue twenty years ago that our emphasis on small-scale manufacturing and economic diversity was the genius of the city.[40] It turns out, as a recent article in *Scientific American* pointed out, she was right: economically diverse cities do best.[41] But there was nothing in her diagnosis that suggested how more office buildings could be built, or more apartments converted into condos. So her analysis was ignored among top policy makers.

For more than a century, New York played many roles in America's economy. It offered space for the national casino and the Fifth Avenue shopping mall. But the city has also served (i) as the incubator of industrial innovation; (ii) the center of world trade; (iii) manufacturing leader; (iv) railroad center of the region; and (v) as the country's greatest port.

These roles stimulated the kind of energies that made the city home to Walt Whitman and Melville to Langston Hughes and Garcia Lorca. What they celebrated was not just diversity of ethnicity but diversity of work, of worlds, of potentials. This is why New York seemed to be a model not just for poets but for the world.

When all the analysis is done, you have to ask yourself, "What is the meaning of the lady in the harbor?" Why is she lifting her lamp? Is it just so she can read the visitors' business cards?

Vast as they are, the canyons along Wall Street and Madison Avenue are not big enough to contain the dreams of those who aim for these shores. Nor will they fit the aspirations of those waiting in the outer boroughs to live out the full meaning of the dream. New York needs to re-industrialize to regain its capacity to respond to these aspirations. The challenge of New York is to play out for the twenty-first century – as it did in the nineteenth and the twentieth – the full meaning of diversity. That is not nostalgia; it's destiny.

# NOTES

1. See A. Leo Openheim. *Ancient Mesopotamia* (Chicago: University of Chicago Press, 1977), pp. 74–143.
2. Ibid., p. 84.
3. Ibid., p. 74.
4. See David's statement in Rockefeller Brothers' Fund Annual Report for 1987, p. 12.
5. Laurie McGinley, "HUD's Cisneros Has Big Plans, Fiery Charisma Clinton's Ear And Few New Sources of Funds," *Wall Street Journal*, April 20, 1993, A22.
6. David Osborne and Ted Gaebler, *Reinventing Government* (Reading, Massachusetts: Addison-Wesley Publishing Company, Inc., 1992).
7. Hugh O'Neill and Mitchell Moss, "Reinventing New York: Competing in the Next Century's Global Economy," Urban Research Center, Robert F. Wagner Graduate School of Public Service, November 1991.
8. Reich in turn relies on the growth of the "human capital" theory.
9. Alfred Marshall, *Principles*, Book V, ch. 8, sect. 4 cited in Mark Blaug *Economic Theory in Retrospect* (Cambridge, 1983), p. 437.
10. Alfred Marshall, *Principles of Economics*, 8th Edition. (London: Macmillan Press Ltd.), p. 207.
11. *Scientific America*, March 1993.
12. New York State Department of Taxation and Finance, Bureau of Tax Data – Office of Tax Policy Analysis "New York Personal Income and Tax Liability for Income Year 1987 By County of Residence," RS-431 (November 90), p. 13.
13. Cited in Joel Schwartz, *The New York Approach* (Columbus, Ohio: Ohio University Press, 1993), p. 295.
14. See, for example, Mark H. Maier, *City Unions. Managing Discontent in New York City* (New Brunswick, New Jersey: Rutgers University Press, 1987), passim.
15. I owe this term to Professor Eliott Sklar.
16. See for example the prescription contained in the President's Commission for a National Agenda for the 'Eighties, *A National Agenda for the Eighties* (New York: New American Library, 1980), ch. 4.
17. Jeffrey Henderson, *The Globalization of High Technology Production* (London: Routledge, 1989), p. 106. See especially ch.5, "Hong Kong: The Making of a Regional Core."
18. Nonprofit Coordinating Committee of New York, the Fund for the City of New York, and the City of New York. The Nonprofit Sector in New York City, May 1992, iv.
19. Jane Fritsch, "At Empire, The Glow of Greed," *New York Times*, July 11, 1993, p. 20E.
20. See The Chronicle of Philanthropy, July 16, September 10, and November 5, 1991. Obviously, it is possible to get a lower figure if you include daycare centers and other community social service organizations with budgets under $100,000. This is the methodology of Ford-run Nonprofit Coordinating Committee of New York. See NCC of NY, Fund for the City of New York and the City of New York, The Nonprofit Sector in New York City, May 1992, pp. 70–1.
21. The "spread" between deposit rates and loan rates is at an all time high. Whereas in 1980 they were below 2 percent; today they exceed 10 percent. "If the weak credit growth was entirely demand drive," note two researchers at the New York Fed,"we would expect to see these rate spreads narrow as banks cut loan rates relative to funding costs to attract new business." Richard Cantor and John Wenninger, "Perspective on the Credit Slowdown," Federal Reserve Bank of New York, Quarterly Review, Spring 1993, p. 11.
22. Karl Marx, *Grundrisse* (Harmondsworth: Penguin, 1973). See the chapter on Money, pp. 115–238.
23. New York Department of City Planning, "Zoning Handbook: A Guide to New York City's Zoning Resolution," NYC DCP 90-37 (New York City, July 1990), p. 1.
24. New York City Public Development Corporation, brochure (New York City: n.d.), p. 2.
25. Ibid., p. 8.

26. Roger Altman, head of PDC at the time the report in question was issued, was appointed Deputy Treasury Secretary in the Clinton administration, i.e., Deputy Secretary for Real Estate Tax Breaks.

27. The City of New York, Executive Budget Fiscal Year 1993, Message of the Mayor, p. 219.

28. Port of New York and New Jersey, Oceanborne Foreign Trade Handbook 1991. Issued: September 1992, pp. 38–9. The number one import is Alcoholic Beverages, see p. 37.

29. *New York Times,* January 3, 1922 (clipping file, Municipal Research Library).

30. Regional Survey, vol. IV.

31. *New York Times,* March 4, 1947, p. 16, col. 4.

32. See Regional Plan Association, The Lower Hudson, December 1966. The plan turns on the elimination of the freight yard and port facilities on both sides of the river. See the maps on pp. 16–17. See also p. 20. "The area from 14th Street south to Battery Park," the plan suggests, "except for the new pier 40, might be completely transformed."

33. *New York Times,* March 4, 1976, p. 33.

34. See statements by council member Stephen DiBrienza, City Council Hearing Economic Development Committee, February 8, 1993. DiBrienza, along with congressman Jerry Nadler are among a handful of local representatives who have fought to preserve the city's industrial base.

35. The Port of New York Authority, "The Port and the Community," 1958, p. 5

36. Benjamin Chinitz, *Freight and the Metropolis* (Cambridge, Massachusetts: Harvard University Press, 1960), p. 96.

37. Department of Housing Preservation and Development, Housing and Vacancy Report (New York City, 1987), p. 30.

38. See Roger Waldinger, "Race and Ethnicity," in *Setting Municipal Priorities* (New York: New York University Press, 1989), p. 65, table 2.7, derived from the 1980 Census of Population. Waldinger's table shows that Asians are more than four times more likely to work in a restaurant. And about eight times less likely to have a construction job.

39. Daniel De Leon writes of the "Workies" that they "viewed themselves as representatives of the 'producing classes' – a category taking in farmers and self-employed manufacturers as well as wage workers. They saw a sharp cleavage in society between producers and accumulators of wealth; the latter class consisted mostly, in their scheme, of merchants and bankers. The workies tried to make American party lines conform to that cleavage." David Herreshoff, *Origins of American Marxism* (New York: Pathfinder Press, 1967), pp. 32–33.

40. Jane Jacobs, *The Economy of Cities* (New York: Random House, 1969), see especially ch. 6.

41. Elizabeth Corcoran and Paul Walich, "The Rise and Fall of Cities," *Scientific American,* August, 1991.

# APPENDIX 1

# NEW YORK'S TWO BIG BUSTS COMPARED

| | Job Loss | |
|---|---|---|
| | *1969–76* *(in thousands[%])* | *12/89–1/93* *(in thousands[%])* |
| Total | 587 (15.4) | 439 (12.0) |
| Construction | 39 (36.8) | 46 (37.4) |
| Manufacturing | 285 (34.5) | 72 (20.6) |
| Transportation/Public Utilities | 60 (18.5) | 31 (13.4) |
| Trade | 64 (14.5) | 112 (17.3) |
| FIRE | 42 (9.2) | 58 (11.0) |
| Services | 11 (1.4) | +11 (+1) |
| Government | 22 (4.5) | 31 (5.1) |

*Source*: New York State Department of Labor, unpublished figures.

# APPENDIX 2

# COMPONENTS OF GROSS CITY PRODUCT*

| | *mfg* | *const.* | *t/u*** | *FIRE* | *govt* | *svc.* | *trade* |
|---|---|---|---|---|---|---|---|
| 1960 | 15.4 | 6.1 | 7.9 | 26.6 | 14.1 | 17.4 | 12.4 |
| 1992 | 9.3 | 2.6 | 8.3 | 32.1 | 13.8 | 24.4 | 9.5 |

*As percentage of total Gross Product.
**Transportation/public utilities.

*Source*: Office of the State Comptroller, Office of the State Deputy Comptroller for the City of New York, Analysis of the New York City Economy, October 29, 1992; Technical Memorandum, February 93.

# APPENDIX 3
## STRUCTURE OF EMPLOYMENT IN 10 LARGEST U.S. CITIES*

| City | const. | mfg | t/u** | trade | FIRE | svc. | govt |
|------|--------|-----|-------|-------|------|------|------|
| New York | 3.2 | 9.5 | 6.3 | 17.0 | 14.5 | 32.6 | 17.0 |
| Los Angeles | 5.5 | 20.0 | 5.2 | 22.6 | 6.8 | 29.0 | 12.5 |
| Chicago | 4.0 | 17.5 | 6.5 | 23.7 | 8.4 | 27.9 | 11.8 |
| Philadelphia | 2.1 | 11.0 | 5.4 | 18.2 | 8.7 | 35.6 | 19.1 |
| Detroit | 3.3 | 22.9 | 4.6 | 24.4 | 5.8 | 26.9 | 12.1 |
| Dallas | 3.4 | 16.1 | 6.0 | 25.7 | 9.2 | 26.7 | 11.6 |
| Houston | 4.9 | 10.9 | 6.9 | 23.4 | 6.4 | 28.4 | 12.9 |
| San Diego | 6.3 | 13.8 | 3.7 | 24.0 | 6.8 | 27.8 | 17.8 |
| Phoenix | 5.6 | 14.0 | 5.9 | 25.2 | 7.7 | 28.0 | 13.5 |
| San Antonio | 5.6 | 8.6 | 4.2 | 25.0 | 7.7 | 27.0 | 23.1 |

*as percent of total employment; mining omitted.
**transportation/utilities

*Source*: Department of Labor, BLS, "Employment and Earnings," May, 1991.

# APPENDIX 4
# RATIO OF MANUFACTURING
# EMPLOYMENT TO FIRE EMPLOYMENT:
# 10 LARGEST U.S. CITIES

| City | mfg/FIRE |
|------|----------|
| New York | 1.00:1.53 |
| Los Angeles | 2.94:1.00 |
| Chicago | 2.08:1.00 |
| Philadelphia | 1.21:1.00 |
| Detroit | 1.75:1.00 |
| Dallas | 2.02:1.00 |
| Houston | 1.81:1.00 |
| San Diego | 2.02:1.00 |
| Phoenix | 1.81:1.00 |
| San Antonio | 1.16:1.00 |

# APPENDIX 5 INCOME BY BOROUGHS*

| Income Class | Bronx No. | Bronx Total Income | Brooklyn No. | Brooklyn Total Income | Richmond No. | Richmond Total Income | Queens No. | Queens Total Income | Manhattan No. | Manhattan Total Income |
|---|---|---|---|---|---|---|---|---|---|---|
| Under 5,000 | 51,563 | 140,237 | 115,313 | 308,642 | 22,813 | 56,176 | 107,345 | 283,398 | 83,308 | 214,634 |
| 5–5,999 | 12,457 | 68,421 | 27,734 | 152,443 | 4,013 | 22,045 | 824,513 | 134,756 | 19,374 | 106,454 |
| 6–7,999 | 25,519 | 178,892 | 56,465 | 395,607 | 7,131 | 49,668 | 48,193 | 337,173 | 39,369 | 275,880 |
| 8–9,999 | 24,734 | 222,290 | 53,891 | 484,479 | 6,132 | 54,987 | 44,596 | 400,462 | 36,297 | 325,933 |
| 10–14,999 | 57,318 | 713,633 | 122,663 | 1,526,853 | 13,793 | 171,944 | 98,771 | 1,230,260 | 81,193 | 1,008,749 |
| 15–19,999 | 58,716 | 1,029,109 | 115,099 | 2,011,422 | 14,585 | 255,604 | 95,536 | 1,670,998 | 75,837 | 1,326,747 |
| 20–24,999 | 46,639 | 1,040,341 | 88,960 | 1,987,013 | 13,440 | 301,298 | 82,305 | 1,842,259 | 64,473 | 1,443,138 |
| 25–49,999 | 90,235 | 3,092,229 | 189,307 | 6,526,510 | 46,392 | 1,682,688 | 211,379 | 7,405,419 | 154,578 | 5,387,747 |
| 50–99,999 | 19,509 | 1,222,430 | 50,106 | 3,212,334 | 24,063 | 1,558,050 | 69,658 | 4,472,876 | 67,822 | 4,646,715 |
| 100+ | 1,965 | 417,062 | 8,719 | 1,935,025 | 3,385 | 667,107 | 9,309 | 1,839,695 | 45,584 | 15,642,140 |
| Total | 388,655 | 8,124,643 | 828,257 | 18,540,329 | 155,747 | 4,819,567 | 719,605 | 19,617,296 | 667,835 | 30,378,137 |

*Dollar amounts in thousands.

Source: New York State Department of Taxation and Finance, Bureau of Tax Data-Office of Tax Policy Analysis "New York Personal Income and Tax Liability for Income Year 1987 By County of Residence," RS-431 (November 90), p.13.

## COMPARATIVE INCOME BY BOROUGHS

| Place of Residence | Average Income (1987) ($) |
|---|---|
| Bronx | 20,905 |
| Brooklyn | 22,385 |
| Queens | 24,712 |
| Richmond | 30,945 |
| Manhattan | 45,487 |
| New York City | 28,770 |
| New York State | 29,021 |
| New York suburbs | |
| Westchester | 44,060 |
| Nassau | 40,449 |
| Suffolk | 31,979 |
| Rockland | 35,214 |
| Putnam | 34,055 |
| Non-resident workers* | |
| Nassau | 52,760 |
| Westchester | 70,729 |
| Suffolk | 42,680 |
| Connecticut suburbs | 90,260 |
| New Jersey suburbs | 46,970 |
| U.S. | 25,986 |

*Data do not include approximately 600 millionaire returns.

*Sources*: New York State Department of Taxation and Finance, Bureau of Tax Data-Office of Tax Policy Analysis, "New York Personal Income and Tax Liability for Income Year 1987"; U.S. Bureau of Census, "Money Income of Households, Families and Persons in the United States: 1987." cited in Kevin Phillips, 1990: Appendix C, New York City Office of Management and Budget, "Preliminary New York City Non-Resident Earnings Tax Paid by Taxpayers Residing in Places Surrounding N.Y.C. and Other Selected Areas." 1988.

# APPENDIX 6

## COMPARATIVE INCOME NEW YORK CITY
## AND NEW YORK STATE (1963 – 1987)*

| Year | New York State | New York City (%) |
|------|----------------|-------------------|
| 1963 | 39.871 | 18.757 (47.0) |
| 1967 | 50.989 | 22.459 (44.0) |
| 1972 | 68.927 | 28.080 (40.7) |
| 1977 | 93.473 | 34.818 (37.2) |
| 1982 | 141.889 | 52.880 (37.2) |
| 1987 | 208.125 | 77.711 (37.3) |

*In billions of dollars.

*Source*: Bureau of Tax Data-Office of Tax Policy Analysis, New York State Department of Taxation and Finance, "New York Personal Income and Tax Liability for Income Year(s) 1963, 1967, 1972, 1982, 1987."

# APPENDIX 7

## COMPARATIVE JOB LOSS*

|  | January 89 | December 92 | total | loss (%) | NYC (%) |
|------|------------|-------------|-------|----------|---------|
| U.S. | 117.3 | 116.1 | −1.2 | 1 | 41.6 |
| N.Y.S. | 8.1 | 7.8 | −0.3 | 7 | 166 |
| N.Y.C. | 3.7 | 3.2 | −0.5 | 13.5 | n/a |
| N.J. | 3.9 | 3.7 | −0.2 | 6.3 | n/a |

*In millions.

*Sources*: NYS Department of Labor (unpublished data); U.S. Department of Labor, BLS USDL 93–78, "The Employment Situation: February, 1993. U.S. Department of Labor. Bureau of Labor Statistics. Middle Atlantic Region, New Jersey Unemployment Rate 7.8 percent in February," March 5, 1993.

# APPENDIX 8
# MANUFACTURING JOB LOSS/GAIN IN
# NEW YORK CITY AND THE U.S.*

|      | New York | change | U.S.   | change |
|------|----------|--------|--------|--------|
| 1958 | 954.2    |        | 15,954 |        |
| 1959 | 962.9    | +8.7   | 16,675 | +721   |
| 1960 | 946.8    | –16.1  | 16,796 | +21    |
| 1961 | 914.0    | –32.8  | 16,326 | +470   |
| 1962 | 911.7    | –02.3  | 16,853 | +241   |
| 1963 | 878.7    | –33.0  | 16,995 | +142   |
| 1964 | 865.5    | –13.2  | 17,274 | +279   |
| 1965 | 865.1    | –00.4  | 18,026 | +752   |
| 1966 | 863.7    | –01.4  | 19,214 | +1188  |
| 1967 | 846.7    | –17.0  | 19,447 | +233   |
| 1968 | 840.0    | –06.7  | 19,781 | +334   |
| 1969 | 825.8    | –14.2  | 20,167 | +386   |
| 1970 | 766.0    | –59.8  | 19,367 | –800   |
| 1971 | 702.2    | –63.8  | 18,623 | –744   |
| 1972 | 675.8    | –27.4  | 19,151 | +528   |
| 1973 | 652.8    | –23.0  | 20,154 | +1003  |
| 1974 | 602.1    | –50.7  | 20,077 | –77    |
| 1975 | 536.9    | –65.2  | 18,323 | –1784  |
| 1976 | 541.1    | +04.2  | 18,997 | +674   |
| 1977 | 538.6    | –02.5  | 19,682 | +685   |
| 1978 | 532.1    | –06.5  | 20,505 | +823   |
| 1979 | 518.5    | –13.6  | 21,040 | +535   |
| 1980 | 495.7    | –23.2  | 20,285 | –755   |
| 1981 | 485.1    | –10.6  | 20,170 | –115   |
| 1982 | 450.8    | –34.3  | 18,781 | –1389  |
| 1983 | 438.2    | –12.6  | 18,434 | –347   |
| 1984 | 429.6    | –08.6  | 19,378 | +944   |
| 1985 | 407.7    | –28.9  | 19,260 | –118   |
| 1986 | 391.5    | –16.2  | 18,965 | +295   |
| 1987 | 379.6    | –11.9  | 19,024 | +59    |
| 1988 | 370.1    | –09.5  | 19,350 | +326   |
| 1989 | 359.5    | –10.6  | 19,442 | +92    |
| 1990 | 337.5    | –22.0  | 19,110 | –332   |
| 1991 | 316.8    | –20.7  | 18,427 | –683   |

*In thousands.

Source: NYS BLS unpublished data; Econ Report of the President, 1992:344.

# APPENDIX 9

# MANHATTAN NEW OFFICE BUILDING
# CONSTRUCTION (1960 – 1992)

| Year | square feet (000s) | Year | square feet (000s) |
|------|------|------|------|
| 1960 | 3,271 | 1977 | 1,900 |
| 1961 | 5,173 | 1978 | 349 |
| 1962 | 3,785 | 1979 | 0 |
| 1963 | 6,738 | 1980 | 250 |
| 1964 | 4,237 | 1981 | 1,649 |
| 1965 | 1,353 | 1982 | 5,593 |
| 1966 | 1,724 | 1983 | 7,248 |
| 1967 | 6,540 | 1984 | 3,480 |
| 1968 | 6,667 | 1985 | 6,606 |
| 1969 | 5,313 | 1986 | 6,203 |
| 1970 | 10,880 | 1987 | 7,492 |
| 1971 | 12,632 | 1988 | 2,700 |
| 1972 | 19,482 | 1989 | 7,852 |
| 1973 | 5,190 | 1990 | 4,804 |
| 1974 | 866 | 1991 | 582 |
| 1975 | 539 | 1992 | 2,292 |
| 1976 | 0 | | |
| 1967–1973 | 66,704 | 1981–1990 | 53,627 |

Source: Real Estate Board of New York, Research Department, Rebuilding Manhattan, A Study of New Office Construction, October 1985; Manhattan New Office Building Construction, Office Building Completions, 1978–1990; New Office Buildings 1991–1992 Completions. Totals from 1947 to 1992 do not include additions, reconstructions or mixed-use buildings.

# APPENDIX 10

## NEW COMPETITIVE OFFICE BUILDING SPACE BY BUILDING PERIODS IN MAJOR DISTRICTS*

| District | 1925–1933 | 1947–1952 | 1954–1964 | 1967–1973 | 1977–1984 |
|---|---|---|---|---|---|
| Financial | 8.4 | – | 6.6 | 16.4 | 4.3 |
| Insurance | 1.8 | 0.14 | 1.67 | 1.9 | 0.55 |
| City Hall | 1.8 | 0.29 | 1.74 | 9.76 | 0.5 |
| Grand Central | 12.0 | 1.6 | 20.3 | 11.1 | 4.8 |
| Plaza | 5.6 | 2.3 | 13.2 | 15.7 | 6.3 |
| W. Midtown | 2.6 | 1.4 | 2.34 | 12.7 | 0.4 |

* In millions.

*Source*: see Appendix 9. Note: Appendix 10 includes formerly non-competitive buildings, building additions, and office space in mixed-use buildings.

# APPENDIX 11

## FIVE LARGEST RECIPIENTS OF ICIP, 1990

| Developer | Project | Tax Exemption ($ million) |
|---|---|---|
| William Zeckendorf | Worldwide Plaza | 100.0 |
| Solomon Equities | 47th and Broadway | 70.0 |
| Bruce Eichner | 46th and Broadway | 63.0 |
| Holiday Inn | 1605 Broadway | 54.5 |
| Rihga Royal | 151 W. 54th St. | 47.7 |

*Source*: Department of Finance, interview 1991.

# APPENDIX 12

# REAL PROPERTY TAX EXEMPTIONS

# AND EXPENDITURES FOR HOMELESS

# FAMILIES (1988 – 1991)

|      | Homeless Families ($ million) | Real Estate ($ million) |
|------|-------------------------------|-------------------------|
| 1988 | 159                           | 1,070                   |
| 1989 | 181                           | 1,125                   |
| 1990 | 160                           | 1,347                   |
| 1991 | 173                           | 1,520                   |

*Source*: Message of the Mayor, 1987–1990.

# APPENDIX 13

# NEW HOUSING UNITS, KOCH ERA

| Year | Units  | Annual Change (%) |
|------|--------|-------------------|
| 1980 | 7,800  | 46.3              |
| 1981 | 11,060 | 41.8              |
| 1982 | 7,649  | 30.8              |
| 1983 | 11,795 | 54.1              |
| 1984 | 11,566 | 1.9               |
| 1985 | 23,368 | 102.0             |
| 1986 | 10,522 | 54.8              |
| 1987 | 13,764 | 30.4              |
| 1988 | 9,897  | 28.1              |
| 1989 | 11,556 | 16.8              |

*Source*: New York State Division of Housing and Community Renewal, Annual Reports.

# APPENDIX 14

## CONSTRUCTION AS SHARE

## OF TOTAL EMPLOYMENT

| City | Share of Employment (%) |
|------|------|
| NYC | 3.2 |
| LA | 3.7 |
| Chicago | 4.0 |
| Philadelphia | 2.1 |
| Detroit | 3.3 |
| Dallas - Ft. Worth | 3.5 |
| Houston | 6.9 |
| San Diego | 6.3 |
| Phoenix | 5.6 |
| San Antonio | 4.2 |

*Source*: BLS, Employment and Earnings, May 1991.

# APPENDIX 15

## EMPLOYMENT IN TRADE

| City | Jobs (000) | Share of total employment |
|------|------|------|
| New York | 605.5 | 17.0 |
| Los Angeles | 972.0 | 22.6 |
| Chicago | 757.8 | 23.7 |
| Philadelphia | 136.5 | 18.2 |
| Detroit | 473.6 | 24.4 |
| Dallas Fort Worth | 503.3 | 25.7 |
| Houston | 373.2 | 23.4 |
| San Diego | 238.1 | 24.0 |
| Phoenix | 248.2 | 25.2 |
| San Antonio | 130.3 | 25.0 |

*Source*: Employment and Earnings, BLS, 5/91. Figures for cities besides New York and Philadelphia are PMSA's. The difference between New York's share of total employment in retail and the PMSA's is less than 1 percent.

# INDEX

# INDEX

Rudin family, 60
Rusk, Dean, 189, 213
Russell Sage Foundation, 60, 61, 66–8, 93
Ryan, Herb, 166

Sage, Margaret Olivia (Mrs Russell), 67, 68
Sassen, Saskia, 180
Schell, Orville, ix
Schiff, Jacob, 61, 63
Schiff, John H., 132
Schwartz, Fritz, 167
Scully, Vincent, 207
Seabury, Samuel (Judge), 202
Seabury-Berle Commission, 200
Second Avenue Subway, 116, 124, 133
self-help, 155–6, 217
Sert, Jose Maria, 195–6
service industries, 176
services, co-ordination, 221
Seventh Avenue, 211
'Shaping the City's Future' (Dinkins), 168–9
Shearson Lehman, 185
Sheinkopf, Hank, 50
Shelp, Ronald, 11–12
Sheraton International Crossroads Hotel, 180–1
Shiffman, Ron, 219
Shmatas, 78–82
Shore, William, 178–9
Silverstein, Larry, 150–1
Singapore, 174
Sixth Avenue, 28, 46–7, 97, 157, 200–2, 211
Sixth Avenue Elevated (El.), 190–1, 198–202
Sixth Avenue IND, xviii, 190, 202–3
60th Street railyard, 118–19
Sloane Coffin family, 93
Slum Clearance, Mayor's Committee on, 132
small businesses, 255, 266
Smith, Desmond, 179
social Darwinism, 62
SoHo, 37, 47
Solomon, Peter, 167, 180
Soros, George, xvi, 7, 241

South Bronx, 37, 161, 215–17, 218, *see also* Bronx
South Bronx Frontier Development Corporation, 216, 217
South Bronx Open Space Task Force, 217
South Bronx Overall Economic Development group, 155
South Ferry Plaza project, 257
South Street Seaport, 29, 150
Standard Oil Trust, 190
Stark, Abe, 100
Starr, Roger, viii, 134–5, 137, 208, 216
Steinbrenner, George, 119
Stern, Leonard, 49
Straight, Willard, 210
Straus, Nathan, 45
Studley, Julian J., 162, 257
Sturz, Herb, 49, 167, 222
Stuyvesant High School, 44, 138
subsidies, for housing, 262; for luxury housing, 138–9, 256, 263; for office building, 123, 150
suburbs, growth of, 96
subways, xviii, 139, 197–200
Sullivan, Barry (Deputy Mayor), 18
Sullivan, Rev. Joe, 167
Sulzberger, Arthur H., 96
Summers, Larry, 170–1
Sumner, William Graham, 61–2
Swope, Gerard, 45

tax, abatements, xiii–xiv, 30, 41, 43; incentives, 221, 223, 225; reforms, 251, 253
Taxi and Limousine Commission, 166
30th Street railyard, 118–19
Thompson, Wilbur, 157–8
Time Life Inc., 207
Time Warner, 152
Times Square development, 152–3, 212, 228
Tisch family, xiii, 152
Tishman, David, 135
Tishman family, 60, 157, 211
Title Guarantee and Trust Co., 63
Title I, 99–100, 101, 134, 136, 141, 143
Todd, John R., 193, 194, 195, 202–3
tourism, 268–9
Townsend, Alair, 45